Unhealthy

PFI in the NHS –
Its real costs and consequences

by John Lister

Commissioned by UNISON Mid Yorkshire Health Branch

Acknowledgements

I have been delighted to have the opportunity to write this book, which brings together much of the work I have done on behalf of London Health Emergency over the past 28 years with what is now the UNISON Mid Yorkshire Health Branch, and its leadership.

I want to thank the Branch for commissioning this, and for all the support they have given over the years to London Health Emergency and more recently Health Campaigns Together.

The book also owes a debt of gratitude to many of the academics and others who have fought for a clear and objective analysis of PFI and helped develop an evidence base for campaigning against it: notable among these are Allyson Pollock and her various collaborators, and Mark Hellowell.

I have also been lucky to be able to draw on a number of detailed studies and campaigning responses to PFI which as director of London Health Emergency I have been commissioned to develop on behalf of trade union bodies and campaigners over the years.

The completion of this book was also materially assisted by the ready sharing of up to date information by Helen Mercer of Greenwich University, whose work with Dexter Whitfield is central to the chapter on what to do about PFI, and by Anna Marriott of Oxfam, with updates for the Postscript on PPPs world wide.

And, not for the first time I want to thank my wife Sue for her forebearance during the long days and weeks of working on this book, and her continued political support.

I can be contacted at *johnlister@healthemergency.org.uk*, and Health Campaigns Together, which is now taking forward the work which was begun 35 years ago by London Health Emergency, is at *www.healthcampaignstogether.com*.

Contents

Contents

Preface

Towards the end of 2015, during a meeting of our branch committee, we were discussing the 'Acute Hospital Reconfiguration' of services from Dewsbury Hospital to Pinderfields. This was to be the final nail in the coffin of Dewsbury as a District Hospital with the centralisation of acute services into the PFI hospital at Pinderfields. We had opposed the AHR as being purely finance driven in order to pay for the PFI.

We had also recently exposed the fact that the Trust had given £15 million to Ernst and Young 'management consultants' between 2012-15 for what was said to be 'cost saving advice'. This, alongside the projected 'Unitary payment' to the PFI company Consort for 2015/16 which was approaching £43 million was another example of how money was haemorrhaging out of the NHS into the coffers of big business. During the discussion over this blatant waste of public money someone said in exasperation "you could write a book about this!"

The idea stuck in our collective minds and following a discussion with John Lister, who over many years has helped the branch with our submissions to the numerous consultations referred to in this book, we decided we should write a book to expose the waste of PFI and corporate profiteering from the NHS.

Our branch has always opposed PFI and warned of the consequences to local services years before the PFI deal was eventually signed. We continue to fight against cuts and privatisation which is the result of a Mid Yorkshire PFI bill of over £45 million a year.

The book is our contribution to the debate on how to end the great PFI rip off and return the £Billions of public assets and staff into democratic public ownership.

We thank John for telling our story and his support over the years.

Yours in solidarity
The Branch Committee
UNISON Mid Yorkshire Health

Introduction

By Adrian O'Malley
Branch Secretary, UNISON Mid Yorkshire Health

I can vividly remember my first day working as a Porter at Pinderfields Hospital in September 1981. I was shown around by the Head Porter of many years Bill Garrett (RIP) who said to me "this won't be here long they're going to build a new hospital." Bill was showing round the old Princess Mary wing at the time, a long corridor with dormitory-style 'Florence Nightingale' wards that were used to treat injured soldiers during the Second World War. Bill couldn't have been more wrong: it would be 29 years before "the huts" were replaced by the new Pinderfields.

This book is the story of the decades building up to and after the completion of the new hospital. It is written from the perspective of those of us who campaigned for a new hospital for the people of Wakefield but watched in horror as it was delivered at the cost of losing equally cherished hospitals in Dewsbury, Pontefract and the rest of the Wakefield District.

It is also a living history of the politics and economics of the NHS both locally and nationally up to the present day. It shows how the Private Finance Initiative concept for financing building and maintaining public infrastructure has had a negative influence on how our public services are delivered. It ties us into rigid contracts that restrict progress and flexibility that the ever changing NHS needs to keep up with developments in healthcare.

Our Mid Yorkshire Health UNISON Branch and its predecessor branches of UNISON, COHSE, NUPE and NALGO consistently argued for public funding of any new hospital in Wakefield. We warned that PFI would come with cuts and closures attached to pay the bill.

Our submissions to the numerous misnamed and undemocratic 'consultations' are open to public scrutiny and have sadly in most cases been proven to be correct.

This book exposes the secrecy and lack of transparency that exists when large amounts of tax payers' money are spent on public infrastructure. Decisions that have serious implications for public health and well-being are often made in secret under the cloak of commercial confidentiality. How hospitals, schools etc. are turned into commodities to be used by big business as high profit, risk free income streams while services and workers terms and conditions are cut.

It explains how politicians of all the main parties Conservative, Labour and LibDem fell for the neo liberal pipe dream of cheaper financed projects with the private sector taking all the risks. As the true cost of the 1000's of PFI schemes comes to light our warnings and opposition are being vindicated. This is no consolation to future generations who will still be paying exorbitant "unitary charges" for today's PFI's in 10, 20, and in some cases 30 years' time.

Working people are often told to leave financial matters, economics and public sector finance to the experts and PFI may not appear to be the most interesting subject for a book but we intend to show that far from being boring, how public money is spent has a direct bearing on our everyday lives. We also intend to show that the so-called experts are not always what they seem.

A book about PFI will inevitably have many statistics in it. I will start with just one. In June 2018 the Mid Yorkshire Trust's monthly Unitary Payment to Consort Healthcare (PFI) was £4,008,793.26p: this was for just the one month, with over 20 more years of payments to come. What could be done to assist a Trust facing a £20 million overspend this financial year with just six months PFI payments? How many extra staff on the wards and departments could that kind of money pay for?

Running through the history of the Mid Yorkshire PFI the first thing that must be said is that it was imposed on the local community against their wishes. The case for public funding was made clear in Wakefield and the local population embraced it. Petitions and referendums all showed overwhelming backing for public funding. Unfortunately PFI was "The only show in town" as far as New Labour politicians, senior civil servants and NHS senior managers were concerned.

Once the PFI was imposed it was the workforce and local community that had to pay for it. This book shows how UNISON, the other Mid Yorks staff side and community groups have fought against the PFI and service centralisation.

From marches and public meetings against the run down of Pontefract in 2005, strike ballots against compulsory redundancy during 'turnaround' in 2006, the Admin & Clerical strike against downbandings in 2012 and fighting off the threat of a Wholly Owned Subsidiary (WOS) this year we have faced many threats from a Trust which is saddled with a permanent PFI debt.

These threats are inevitable as long as the trust is burdened with a £4 million a month PFI rent bill. The rent bill now goes directly via Consort Healthcare (Mid Yorkshire) Limited to HICL Infrastructure Company Limited an offshoot of HSBC bank based in the tax haven of Guernsey. HICL's "principal objective for shareholders is to deliver predictable and sustainable dividends which are derived from the stable, inflation-correlated cashflows from the underlying infrastructure projects." HICL own shares in over 100 "investments" worth £2.8 billion. During July this year, when our members had voted to strike against being transferred over to the WOS, HICL announced its first quarterly dividend payment of 2.01p per share for this financial year. In their annual report they confidently boast that they expect to pay 8.05p per share on all 1,789,556,677 shares. That's just over £144 million in one year. Our hospital, alongside dozens of schools, colleges, libraries, roads and laboratories up and down the country, is just one small cog in a legalised money laundering scheme that transfers £billions of tax payers' money into the accounts big business and city speculators.

Stop Press

This book has told the story of the drastic reduction in hospital beds at both Dewsbury and Pontefract, leading to the centralisation of services on the Pinderfields site in Wakefield.

At every stage of the process UNISON has challenged the flawed statistics that were used to justify the reductions and argued that decisions made were financial rather than clinical decisions. The proposed number of beds in the hospital was challenged from day one.

The events since have proved that the staff were right and the so called 'experts', both clinical and financial, were wrong.

When the new Pinderfields was opened in 2010 much was made of the brand new facilities with 4 bedded bays and single occupancy rooms replacing the Florence Nightingale style dormitory wards at the old Pinderfields.

However this was short-lived. It didn't take long for many of the new 4 bedded rooms to be turned into '5 bedders' to cope with the extra acute patients flowing into the new Pinderfields.

In October 2018, as this book was being finalised, staff were informed that a *sixth* bed was to be placed in many of the so called '4 bedders' to deal with the expected "winter pressures". Within days, and during one of the mildest Octobers on record, the extra beds were full of patients.

Long gone are the days when nurses and support staff had room to work around the patients. 'Cram them in and move them out' is the order of the day. Florence Nightingale wards – smaller and much more cramped for space – have returned to Pinderfields.

If anyone needed any more proof that the Pinderfields and Pontefract PFI has failed, this must be it. Wards and services were slashed at Dewsbury and Pontefract while £millions were spent on a new hospital which cannot cope with the workload without squeezing more capacity into limited space.

This PFI is not fit for purpose. For the benefit of patients and staff it must be renationalised and the money wasted on 'unitary payments' invested in decent facilities across all three Mid Yorkshire hospitals.

The conclusion of this book and the position of our branch is we must end the madness of PFI and invest in our public services. The shareholders of companies based in offshore tax havens have had their days in the sun. It's time to take our hospital back. The fight goes on!

Overview

The high profile collapse early in 2018 of Carillion, the multinational construction and services company deeply involved in Private Finance Initiative projects in the NHS, schools and other infrastructure projects, put the unresolved issue of PFI firmly back on the agenda. Carillion's collapse left two major hospitals unfinished, threw support and maintenance service contracts into chaos, and left thousands of workers unemployed and thousands more contractors and suppliers unpaid.

Carillion's business model seems to have been to prioritise the flow of dividend payments and bonuses to shareholders and directors, even where this meant running up borrowing of £1.3 billion, creating a massive deficit on its pension fund, and paying back out almost all incoming cash as it was received. But as new orders began to dry up and the company hit delays and problems with the construction of Liverpool Royal Hospital, its crisis worsened, and collapse followed.

The whole edifice of Carillion as ostensibly a successful, growing company was based on bluff and self-deception. So, too, is PFI as a concept. It is a system which has made public infrastructure projects dependent on much higher cost private sector borrowing rather than the Treasury, and encouraged gullible – or more likely cynical – public sector managers to argue that quite obviously unaffordable projects might eventually turn out to be affordable after all.

The idea was a simple one: instead of the Treasury borrowing money on behalf of government departments to finance new infrastructure, each project costing in excess of £5m should be put out to tender, inviting bids from the private sector.

However the contracts were not just for private construction firms to build new hospitals for the NHS, as had previously been the case. Under PFI the same companies linked up in consortia, and bid for long-term contracts to 'Design, Build, Finance and Operate' the new facilities over 25-30 year periods, during which they would effectively lease the buildings to the public sector, and provide a variety of support services, in exchange for a "unitary charge payment which would cover the costs of capital, the construction costs, the services, and of course a substantial profit for the consortium. The unitary charge would rise each year by an agreed basic percentage, or by price inflation if this was higher.

This approach was applied to various public sector infrastructure projects, many of which ran into similar problems: this book will focus almost exclusively upon the NHS and the building of hospitals.

While PFI traces its origins back to Tory Chancellor Norman Lamont as long ago as 1992, it only took off in the NHS after the election of Tony Blair's New Labour government in 1997.

The notion of PFI chimed in with the core New Labour assertion that it did not matter whether provision and assets were public or private, and with Blair's "Third Way" notions of making use of competition and market forces in the delivery of publicly-funded services. Embraced in this way, PFI became the preferred method for financing a range of infrastructure projects from prisons through street lighting, schools and government buildings.

Like the "never never" Hire Purchase schemes in the 1960s which became so popular with customers wanting swift access to consumer goods, and less concerned about the inflated long term cost, PFI had an irresistible attraction for New Labour ministers keen to boast of the new hospitals that were being built; from NHS trust bosses snatching at the lure of private funding at a time when public provision of capital investment in the NHS had been deliberately reduced – leaving PFI as "the only game in town". It was also welcomed by local politicians of all parties who would happily bask in the reflected glory of a new hospital – and angrily denounce any campaigners who might challenge the long term cost and impact on local services.

The resulting contracts, crafted by huge, expensive teams of accountants, lawyers and management consultants were enormous, slow to negotiate, complex and eye-wateringly expensive.

The long-running issue of PFI and its increased costs occasionally re-emerged into the headlines from the mid 2000s, when the Conservatives in opposition mounted occasional opportunist attacks on the way New Labour had implemented their party's policy, and pointed to the excess costs or flaws of some especially ridiculous schemes. This did not stop David Cameron's government from continuing to sign off only marginally different schemes from 2010.

However New Labour never learned the lessons of PFI and some old guard Blairites in the Labour Party even now attempt to defend the way they behaved and the contracts they approved.

There was some retreat from defence of PFI from 2010 under the leadership of Ed Miliband, and former Health Secretary Andy Burnham did accept in 2012 that some PFI projects were poor value for money.

However Jeremy Corbyn's team's recent explicit rejection of further PFI projects and criticism of the cost of the 100+ hospital projects signed off under New Labour has now brought a distinct change.

At Labour's 2017 conference Shadow Chancellor John McDonnell declared that no more PFI deals would be signed, and gave a highly-publicised pledge to bring all PFI projects (not just NHS projects) back in house:

> "The scandal of the Private Finance Initiative has resulted in huge long-term costs for taxpayers while providing enormous profits for some companies," he said.
>
> "Over the next few decades, nearly £200 billion is scheduled to be paid out of public sector budgets in PFI deals. In the NHS alone, £831 million in pre-tax profits have been made over the past six years.
>
> "Never again will this waste of taxpayer money be used to subsidise the profits of shareholders, often based in offshore tax havens."

He added:

> "We have already pledged there will be no new PFI deals signed by us in government. But we will go further. It is what you have been calling for. We will bring existing PFI contracts back in-house".[1]

Although this clear statement was swiftly fudged by a subsequent Labour Party statement stating that it meant all PFI contracts would

---

[1] http://www.bbc.co.uk/news/uk-politics-41379849

be "reviewed," McDonnell's stance represented a fundamental break from the position adopted by New Labour over 20 years earlier.

The latest figures show currently 125 PFI contracts with private companies overseen by the Department of Health. The capital value of the assets which have been built is £12.4bn. However, over life of the contracts, the NHS will pay upwards of £80.8bn to PFI companies for the use of these assets.[2]

New Labour ministers such as Alan Milburn enthusiastically embraced PFI, viewing it as a way to enable the building of new hospitals without increasing public sector borrowing, and arrogantly brushing aside the many increasingly urgent questions that were raised by campaigners and trade unions over its long term costs and implications for the NHS.

In the NHS this same flawed approach also led to private, for-profit "Independent Sector Treatment Centres" being established by the Department of Health to deliver uncomplicated elective surgery, with nationally-negotiated 5-year contracts, which gave the companies guaranteed volumes and payment – at higher cost, while diverting revenue from NHS trusts.

And from 2005 onwards the same thinking led to the absurd drive for "World Class Commissioning", through which local Primary Care Trusts would be judged on their success in contracting out increasingly large-scale community health services, primary care services and even the management of NHS hospitals to private companies, and increasingly extensive use of private sector management consultants to shape NHS policies.

Case study: Mid Yorkshire Hospitals

This book, which has been funded by the UNISON branch at Mid Yorkshire Hospitals, is designed to bring together a wide range of information on PFI and serve both as a record of campaigning that has been done and as a resource for future campaigning.

---

[2] CHPI (2018) *PFI: Profiting from infirmaries,* available https://chpi.org.uk/wp-content/uploads/2017/08/CHPI-PFI-ProfitingFromInfirmaries.pdf

The Mid Yorkshire Hospitals Trust provides acute hospital services to more than half a million-people living in the Wakefield and North Kirklees districts of West Yorkshire. It includes hospitals in Wakefield, Dewsbury and Pontefract. Wakefield and Pontefract are PFI-funded hospitals that opened in 2010. The Trust currently has approximately 961 general and acute beds, 60 beds in Maternity and 35 in Critical care beds, and employs around 7,600 whole time equivalent staff including 856 medical staff, 2,226 nursing staff and over 4,500 from many other groups.

The Trust had had total revenue of over £505 million in 2016/17, and a deficit of over £8 million. Trust board papers for May 2018 show the income for 2017/18 was reduced to £498m, and the deficit was £25.8m. This was reduced to £18.4m by £7.4m of 'Sustainability and Transformation Funding' (STF). With the expectation of another slight reduction of income for 2018/19, the net deficit is forecast at £19.7m, which the trust hopes will be reduced to £5.4m by STF funds.

The pattern of year by year deficits is not in itself unusual among NHS trusts, or unique to PFI hospitals: indeed mid Yorkshire is not an extreme on the scale of such deficits among NHS trusts with PFI, so it gives us a working case study that offers many equivalent lessons for elsewhere. One such common feature is the extent to which the available resources in terms of beds, staff and facilities have come under increasing strain as pressures on acute hospitals have increased, while budgets have flatlined in real terms since 2010.

Rigid PFI contracts, with payments increasing each year for at least 20-25 years, offer little scope for savings without cutting patient care.

As with many PFI hospital projects, the new hospitals in Mid Yorkshire were supposed to be part of a new system of health care in which there would be fewer emergencies and hospital admissions, and more patients would be treated by primary care and "in the community. On this basis, it was argued, bed numbers and capacity could be reduced – holding down the cost of the new hospitals.

As UNISON correctly warned for years beforehand, the reality has been very different from the over-optimistic plans. Emergency admissions, which increased by almost 13% between 2001 and 2012, have increased by another 15% since 2012. Emergencies substantially outnumber elective cases: in 2016/17 there were almost 19,000 emergency admissions accounted for 18,777 (34% of caseload), along with 30,000 elective day cases (55%), and just 5,600 (10%) elective inpatient admissions. Winter peaks of demand have become commonplace during the rest of the year as well.

Nonetheless, since 2010 MYHT managers have made repeated efforts to cut back beds and services in Dewsbury hospital (where there is no ongoing PFI liability) in the hopes of generating savings. This is despite the fact that it simply intensifies the pressure on the remaining beds and services at Pinderfields hospital, which has emerged as the main centre for all emergency and specialist care within the trust.

In 2013, plans were published aiming to axe 200 beds and hundreds of jobs through the downgrade of Dewsbury to generate "savings" of £150 million by this year – regardless of the fact that it also meant moving services further away from Dewsbury's deprived population.

Eventually a new management team in the trust recognised that this could not be done, and admitted to staff that Pinderfields was already overrun and stretched to the limit. That issue was highlighted when a delivery of beds taken from closed wards at Dewsbury arrived unexpectedly at Pinderfields, posing the issue of where to put them. Cutbacks in Dewsbury had run alongside efforts in Pinderfields hospital to cram extra beds into what had been proclaimed as "state of the art" 4-bed bays, to ease the pressure on bed numbers – at the expense of patient care, safety and efficiency.

Early in 2017 some managers grudgingly accepted that UNISON's long-running criticism of the trust's plans, and responses showing them to be unrealistic, had been vindicated. According to NHS England "SitRep" reports in the 2016-17 winter, the pressures on front-line beds reached the point in early January where even with 165 temporary "escalation beds" open, the trust had 1043 beds occupied out of a total 1044 – plus people "boarded" – formally admitted but kept waiting for beds until other patients could be discharged to make room for them.

On January 8 2017 Mid Yorkshire had 222 escalation beds open, but still had an occupancy rate of 99.1 per cent. This would have been bad enough if there had been sufficient staff to ensure that patients could be cared for safely and humanely: but this is not always the case. According to NHS figures revealed by the *Health Service Journal,* on some shifts nurse staffing levels in Mid Yorkshire were the worst of any trust in England.

Added costs of PFI

Clearly a factor in this chronic pressure on resources is the inflated cost of the new hospitals built through PFI. The PFI project for new buildings at Pinderfields hospital (Wakefield) and Pontefract General Infirmary has a capital value recorded as £326m: however the PFI deal is set to cost £1.6 billion by 2043. By UNISON's calculations it had already cost the trust £275m by January of 2018, with payments set to increase inexorably from an initial £33m in 2011 to £71m in 2042.

The 35-year contract includes management of support services, although the contract is one that ensures support staff remain as NHS employees (Retention of Employment). The management company has however changed more than once since the original deal was signed with Balfour Beatty, as the shares in the PFI have been sold on to offshore speculators. Support staff in "soft" facilities (non-clinical services other than maintenance) are currently managed by a company going by the name of Engie.

The current trust board is painfully aware of the additional overhead costs arising from the PFI contract: it is a chronic problem, causing them to seek desperate remedies. In May 2018 the Outline Business Case proposing the establishment of a "wholly owned subsidiary" company to deliver a range of support services to the trust, and generating "savings" by undermining the terms and conditions and pensions of staff who would be transferred out of the NHS into the new company, made clear that:

> "The Trust has a persistent underlying deficit of approximately £20m, largely due to the PFI costs for Pinderfields and Pontefract Hospitals. In the past six years, the Trust has not been able to make inroads into this position but unlike some other trusts with PFI pressures the position has not deteriorated any further." (OBC page 19).

The Trust's proposal to make 'savings' at the expense of already low-paid and exploited NHS staff has been strongly resisted in Mid Yorkshire, in line with in many other trusts where similar proposals have been floated since the middle of 2017. The unions in Wrightington Wigan and Leigh Foundation Trust staged repeated strike action in the first half of 2018, before eventually securing an agreement, underwritten by a cash payment to the Trust from Wigan council, to drop the proposals to launch a "wholly owned" subsidiary, which they had misleadingly named "WWL Solutions".

Just prior to this climbdown by trust management in Wigan, Mid Yorkshire Hospitals management had secured a suspension of threatened strike action by reluctantly agreeing to investigate keeping the staff in the NHS pension scheme and employment, and suspending a committee looking at inferior terms and conditions and a potential two-tier workforce. However it took a renewed threat of a 3-day strike by UNISON to force the trust to sign an agreement that lifted the threat. The Trust's original plan had been to transfer over 700 whole time equivalent MYHT staff into the WOS under TUPE rules.

TUPE agreements are no substitute for staff being NHS employees. The agreements can be, and have in the past been ended early by employers claiming an 'economic, technical or organisational reason': they only cover staff in their existing jobs, they do not cover pensions, and they do not cover newly-recruited staff, resulting in a 2-tier workforce.

Having seen the way that other such schemes were set to work in other trusts, UNISON and other MYHT unions fighting to keep staff "100% NHS" were not convinced by the promise in the OBC that:

> "Staff will TUPE to the WOS under their existing terms and conditions. These terms and conditions will be maintained for the duration of the contract between the WOS and the Trust for all transferring staff." (OBC p12)

They fought on and eventually prevented the scheme from going ahead. As the chapters will show this type of repeated conflict between management and unions is driven by the underlying financial pressure on the trust flowing from years of under-funding, which in Mid Yorkshire has been compounded since 2010 by the additional costs of PFI, which have resulted in constant efforts to impose a series of unproven and often wildly impractical plans for "efficiency savings".

The stabilisation of NHS funding at level sufficient to ensure safe services that can meet growing local needs, the scrapping of the competitive market in the NHS, with its constant processes of tendering, privatisation and costly reliance on private management consultants, and an end to the haemorrhage of cash to off-shore finance houses through PFI are the only sure fire way to ensure that a more productive and satisfactory relationship is created between management and staff in Mid Yorkshire Hospitals and many similar trusts.

Three ways of looking at PFI

This book divides up these very wide-ranging but interlinked issues into 3 related sections. It begins by looking at the ideas and assumptions of PFI (**Part 1, the theory**), going back to its origins in the post-Thatcher Conservative government from 1992, and tracing its development and the arguments put forward to defend it under New Labour from 1997-2010. The story is followed through from the establishment of the ConDem coalition government from 2010, its immediate unveiling of previously-concealed plans for reorganisation of the NHS, and the revived interest in and commitment to PFI among Tory ministers.

However since PFI is far from being a theoretical issue, we go on in **Part 2** to look in more detail at a specific example of that theory being tested out in practice – the historical process that resulted in new hospitals being built with PFI funding in Wakefield and Pontefract in what has become the Mid Yorkshire Hospitals Trust.

Several chapters analyse the various management plans that culminated in the PFI deal being signed in 2007, look at the impact on the hospital's workforce, and follow the responses over the years Mid Yorkshire health branch of the largest union representing them, UNISON.

Part 3 widens out to discuss thorny question of what can be done now to minimise the cost and damage that has been done by a flawed policy and ill-judged decisions that potentially have consequences lasting into the 2040s. As we go to press new publications are also identifying and analysing various options, their strengths and weaknesses, and their achievability or otherwise in the political conditions that lie ahead.

This history is by no means consigned to the past: it is very much with us. The irresponsible – and sometimes impossible – contracts signed by trust boards 20 years ago are still causing major problems for the delivery of health care today, while more recent errors threaten more chaos into the mid-2040s.

A **Postscript** on the global spread of PFI and its costs and implications in other OECD and also in poorer developing countries is a stark reminder that the policy is still being adopted by governments, many of whom are themselves now learning the hard way of the perils of PFI and PPPs as means to finance new hospitals and other infrastructure.

In Britain the mistakes will live far longer than many of the ministers, civil servants and hospital directors who made them. The challenge for campaigners is how to stem the flow of profits to a shameless private sector that has cashed in so extravagantly so far, and is looking forward to almost three decades more of profits at the expense of taxpayers and the NHS.

Hammond statement

However just as this volume was about to go to press, there has been a dramatic postscript to the postscript. In his November Budget in 2018, British Chancellor of the Exchequer Philip Hammond announced, as had been widely expected, that he and the Conservative government would not be signing any further new PFI contracts and that the projects awaiting closure would need to seek alternative funding.

This decision was no doubt strongly influenced by the failure to find alternative private contractors to take over Carillion's role in the failed hospital contracts in Birmingham and Liverpool, which had left the government having to pick up a bill that could well exceed £200 million for completion of these hospitals with public funding, and taking over the "risk" that had theoretically been expensively handed over to the private sector.

Whatever the deciding factors behind Hammond's statement, it means that the party that first proposed PFI in Britain has now followed the lead of Labour, the party that has most energetically implemented it, and pulled away from PFI. However unlike Labour, Hammond has so far said nothing about measures to address the increasing flow of cash each year to cover the inflated cost of "unitary charge" payments of more than £2.1bn for hospitals alone in 2018-19, rising to a peak of almost £2.8bn in 2029-30.

Hammond's further statement that he still endorses the principles of Public Private Partnerships theoretically leaves wiggle room for a later rebranded version of PFI to be wheeled out at some time in the future: but it won't be easy to persuade the many critics of PFI that anything containing the same basic principles and flaws will be anything other than a re-run of the same failed experience.

No doubt there will be more twists and turns to come. The fight against PFI has lasted more than 25 years so far: and this book covers that whole period. The fight will go on until the policy has been firmly buried and action has been taken to stem the damage it has done.

Part 1: the theory

Chapter 1

How it all started

In November 1992, some time after the enforced departure of Margaret Thatcher, and just months after John Major stunned the country by winning a surprise Tory election victory over the Labour Party led by Neil Kinnock, and as a recession hit the economy, Chancellor Norman Lamont delivered an Autumn Statement which unveiled what became the Private Finance Initiative (PFI). He said:

> "The Government have taken seriously their pledge to do what they can for capital spending, but there is yet more that can be done. I said in my Mansion House speech that I was examining ways to increase the scope for private financing of capital projects. Obviously, the interests of the taxpayer have to be protected, but I also want to ensure that sensible investment decisions are taken whenever the opportunity arises. [...]
>
> "...the Government have too often in the past treated proposed projects as either wholly private or wholly public. In future, the Government will actively encourage joint ventures with the private sector, where these involve a sensible transfer of risk to the private sector."[3]

This was a distinct change of policy from a Tory government that since 1979 had shown little interest in investment in public sector infrastructure, and focused instead upon controlling "public spending in general and capital spending in particular"[4]. This had generated a cumulative effect of under-investment, with numerous pressing cases for new buildings and equipment to replace clapped out and

---

[3] Commons *Hansard , 12 November 1992, column 998,*
https://publications.parliament.uk/pa/cm199293/cmhansrd/1992-11-12/Debate-1.html
[4] Lightfoot W (2012) The History and Horror of PFI, Searching Finance, available http://www.searchingfinance.com/news-and-views/the-history-and-horror-of-the-pfi.html

crumbling facilities – and private sector pressure for profitable contracts to be opened up.

Indeed PFI was an attempt to break free from the management of the economy by the Treasury in the style known as "Treasury Orthodoxy", often labelled as "the dead hand of the Treasury". Even prior to Thatcher's arrival, under Labour Governments of the sixties and seventies, successive Labour Chancellors had dutifully followed the advice of the Treasury, and saw it as their role to strictly control public spending, capital investment and the public sector borrowing requirement (PSBR).

This resulted in the nationalised industries being starved of funds and the in-house pressure for their privatisation, in order to escape the financial straightjacket. In the NHS it resulted in a very limited capital programme, which failed to keep up with backlog maintenance as well as the requirement for replacement of very old and dilapidated premises. The Treasury would always find ways of saying no.

The Thatcher government tried to escape from this impasse by privatising the nationalised industries – but had baulked at privatisation of the NHS. Instead the NHS faced a squeeze on its budgets that was unprecedented at the time, and has only since been surpassed by the squeeze imposed from 2010 under George Osborne and Philip Hammond.

In terms of political history PFI fits into the category of 'third way' solutions posed between the strict capitalist or socialist solutions for public services. It appears to offer a way to keep public control of the services supplied in public facilities while giving a role to the private sector to provide funding, to take on the construction risk and to manage the facilities over the life of the asset according to a contract agreed in advance … and to generate very lucrative returns for shareholders as a result.

Prior to PFI the stock Tory solution to such problems had been privatisation, but attractive options for this had been pretty much exhausted by 1992. PFI offered many of the benefits of privatisation to the construction and banking sector, while technically leaving the services themselves (and responsibility for paying for the new buildings) in the public sector, and thus guaranteeing the flow of funds to cover the rising bills. It was to provide a rich vein of profits for the consortia that have taken it on.

The move to embrace PFI as a policy brought with it a break from the now little-known "Ryrie Rules" (established in 1981 and named after Treasury bureaucrat Sir William Ryrie)[5]. These rules were originally intended by the Thatcher government to control the use of public and private sector investment in nationalised industries (and were specifically designed to guard against public sector bodies embarking upon schemes which might prove too expensive and undermine tight controls on public spending).

The Ryrie rules required private finance to be used only if:
- there were no favourable risk terms, such as a government guarantee;
- projects yielded benefits in terms of improved efficiency and profit commensurate with the cost of raising risk capital; and
- use of private finance could not be additional to public finance. In other words, public expenditure would be reduced, pound for pound, in consequence of the use of private finance[6]

By 1992 these rules and controls were seen as an obstacle to potential profitable investment of private money in public projects, since they meant any private sector investment had to be a substitute for (and therefore mean a reduction in) public spending[7]. It also opened up new streams of revenue from public sector budgets to boost the profits of private companies.

However while it breached these 11-year-old rules, PFI was clearly in keeping with the post 1980 ideological frameworks of neoliberalism (with its obsession with maximum private sector role,

---

[5] Heald, D. (1997) Privately Financed Capital in Public Services, *The Manchester School*, Volume 65, Issue 5 Pages 568–598, http://onlinelibrary.wiley.com/doi/10.1111/1467-9957.00082/full
[6] http://onlinelibrary.wiley.com/doi/10.1111/1467-9957.00082/full
[7] Broadbent, J., Gill, J., Laughlin, R. (2004) *The private Finance Initiative in the National Health Service*, Chartered Institute of Management Accountants (CIMA), available https://www.cimaglobal.com/Documents/ImportedDocuments/tech_resrep_t he_private_finance_initiative_in_the_national_health_service_2004.pdf

free markets and minimum public/state involvement[8]) and of "new public management" which centres on a maximum level of contracting out services and tasks to the private sector, and "steering, not rowing".[9] Lamont was soon to be replaced as Chancellor by Kenneth Clarke, who was an even more enthusiastic promoter of PFI, which he famously summed up in a 1993 speech to the CBI as:

> "Privatising the process of capital investment in our key public services."[10]

The policy was eventually branded as the Private Finance Initiative – PFI – although the acronym was soon to be parodied in many ways, from the ubiquitous "Profits For Industry", through to the NHS variant "Profiting From Illness," and the dismissive general summary: "Pure Financial Idiocy".

Although the mainstream press shied away from much serious analysis or discussion of PFI, often arguing that it was "too complicated" for news audiences, the concept, as we have said, was a relatively simple one.

Given the shaky state of the British economy and the resultant reluctance of the Chancellor of the Exchequer to furnish public sector capital to fund investment in new buildings and infrastructure on the scale of previous years, PFI required projects above a certain minimum scale (in the NHS this was initially above £5m) to be opened up for bids from the private sector to finance the scheme, with repayments over a prolonged period of 25-30 years or more.

Rather than owning hospital buildings, the NHS Hospital Trusts, (many still newly established, or just emerging after the controversial "internal market" reforms in the Thatcher-inspired 'NHS and Community Act' 1990) would become lease-holders, required to

---

[8] Monbiot, G. (2016) The Zombie Doctrine, available
http://www.monbiot.com/2016/04/15/the-zombie-doctrine/
[9] Osborne, D., and Gaebler,T. (1992) *Reinventing Government: How the Entrepreneurial Spirit Is Transforming the Public Sector*. Reading, Massachusetts: Addison-Wesley
[10] These words were quoted by Alastair Darling in the Commons Hansard 19 April 1994
https://publications.parliament.uk/pa/cm199394/cmhansrd/1994-04-19/Debate-14.html

make annual, index-linked payments for the use of the building and support services provided by contractors for the lifetime of the contract, which could be anything up to 60 years. Hospitals built on this basis would no longer be public assets, but long-term public liabilities incurring increasing payments for a generation or more ahead.

These capital schemes were not investments, but new forms of public sector debt. NHS trust management would be left in control only of clinical care, while other support services including maintenance of the hospital buildings was to be done by profit-seeking private companies.

Another aspect of the 1990 Act was that it established a new system of "capital charges" under which NHS Trusts had to pay a 6% charge on their net assets each year to the NHS Executive. This brought additional administrative costs, while contributing no extra resources in return.[11] The rationale for this was to in effect charge a rent equating to a percentage of the capital employed, to mirror commercial pressures to make a return on assets employed in a business. In this way NHS Trusts would appear to be competing with the private sector on a similar basis.

Its effect was to normalise the idea of NHS hospitals paying out from their core income to cover the costs of buildings and equipment: but there was a difference. While the NHS capital charges effectively recirculated within the NHS itself, the payments for PFI hospitals would flow *out* of the public sector and into the coffers of private companies, of which a sizeable share would be scooped out as profit or dividends.

More flesh was added to the bones of the original proposal, in November 1994, when Kenneth Clarke went further, and, while the government discussed imposition of a massive £5 billion reduction in public spending, he told the CBI conference that in future the

---

[11] Broadbent, J., Gill, J., Laughlin, R. (2004) The private Finance Initiative in the National Health Service, Chartered Institute of Management Accountants (CIMA), available
https://www.cimaglobal.com/Documents/ImportedDocuments/tech_resrep_t he_private_finance_initiative_in_the_national_health_service_2004.pdf - p17

Treasury would only provide capital for projects as a last resort – "after private finance has been explored."

He was determined to push his private finance initiative "right across the public sector," and "maximise the scope for, and use of private finance." By contrast "finite" public capital would only be available for projects where, for whatever reason, private finance was not available. Clarke added:

> "The Treasury is not frightened of the private sector making money out of the initiative. We cannot expect the private sector to assume new risks without the prospect of new levels of reward."[12]

Despite this gung-ho message, the progress across the board on PFI contracts was slow. By July 1996 angry and frustrated CBI leaders who had seen the scheme fall far short of target levels while government capital spending had steadily fallen since 1992, warned Clarke that PFI could fail without more decisive action. Top bosses were angry at the bureaucratic delays and costs which were holding up key infrastructure projects – and limiting the lucrative possibilities they had scented when it was first announced.[13]

Tory legislation in 1996 was expected to free the logjam by giving a commitment that the government would effectively act as guarantor for any debts to PFI consortiums if one or more Trusts went bankrupt, as health ministers had warned was now possible in their new, competitive, internal market in which some trusts were likely to be "winners" – but only if others were losers. Tory ministers believed their short Bill that was passed gave the banking consortiums that intended to help finance the PFI the assurances they wanted. At first it seemed to have sorted the problem – but they were soon proved wrong:

> "one of the banks involved in the Dartford Hospital project raised certain doubts. [...] those involved in other projects also wanted the safety of belt and braces".[14]

So all the negotiations and considerable expenditure on legal and

---

[12] Elliott, L. (1994) *The Guardian* November 9, p18.

[13] Ryle, S. (1996) Industry seeks PFI shake-up, *The Guardian* July 12, p17

[14] John MacGregor MP, Commons Hansard 14 July 1997, Column 105

accountancy advice had been in vain, and despite efforts through legislation in 1996 to reassure nervous private investors that the debts of trusts would effectively be underwritten by the Secretary of State, no hospital PFI schemes were signed under John Major's government which had invented PFI.

Indeed some concerns were raised by prominent Tories that PFI, which despite early and naïve hopes that it might prove cheaper was in fact a more expensive way of borrowing capital than the government doing so directly, might in fact prove not to be such a great idea after all. In 1996 Sir George Young, Secretary of State for Transport, which was signing early PFI deals, wrote to Chief Secretary of the Treasury William Waldegrave, to raise his doubts over the extent to which risks were in fact being transferred by PFI to the private sector:

> "The 'theory' is that all is well if risk transfers to the private sector. It is difficult to see how this happens in the case of services which are free at the point of delivery, and where ultimately the Government has a statutory duty or political imperative to pick up the pieces if there is a default." [15]

Norman Lamont, who had first launched the PFI programme, also later had doubts. In 1999 he might have been predicting the problems that were soon to befall hospital PFI projects when he wrote in his memoirs:

> "The PFI is not a 'free lunch'. For private finance to work properly it has to provide greater value and efficiency to make it worthwhile. The government itself can always borrow money more cheaply than any private sector borrower, so the efficiency test of a private finance project has to be real.
>
> [...]
>
> "Lastly there is the risk that the private sector may provide finance up front but that the long-term consequences will be the silting-up of public expenditure with a stream of never-

---

[15] Parker, D. (2012) The Private Finance Initiative and Intergenerational Equity, Intergenerational foundation, available http://www.if.org.uk/wp-content/uploads/2012/02/PFIs-and-Intergenerational-Equity.pdf - p10

ending rental payments.

"I suspect that in the long run some of these projects will go wrong and appear again on the Government's balance sheet, adding to public spending. We shall see."[16]

Labour's response – from denunciation to promotion

Tony Blair won the 1997 election with a massive majority, raising high popular expectations of radical change. However, to the delight of a few and the dismay of many, Blair's New Labour government appointed ministers even more attentive and eager than the Tories had been to satisfy the demands of the banks.

To break the impasse in signing off PFI schemes, most notably for the building of new hospitals, the new government's only legislation on the NHS in 1997 was another short Bill to facilitate PFI, which in July was passed as The National Health Service (Private Finance) Act. It was pushed through with just one amendment allowed, and with one aim in mind. In the words of Baroness Cumberlege, a former Tory minister, the new Bill was needed to "remove any element of doubt" among the bankers that – despite all the tough-sounding rhetoric insisting that PFI contracts transferred risk to the private sector – there was no real risk at all, and their money was safe.

The New Labour health minister who pushed the new Bill through parliament, Alan Milburn, echoed the words of the Tory peer: the Bill was intended first and foremost to give the bankers just what they wanted:

"[It's] about removing doubt, providing certainty, and above all getting new hospitals built".

A Labour peer, Baroness Jay made it even clearer who was pulling the strings and effectively dictating the legislation:

"the banks concerned have seen and agreed the wording of the Bill and have made clear that it satisfies all their concerns."[17]

Labour had completely changed its position on PFI, from a sceptical rejection in 1993, to embrace the policy enthusiastically and nurture it as their own in 1997. New Labour ministers now insisted

---

[16] Lamont, N. (1999) *In Office*, Little, Brown and Company, London; 309.
[17] Broadbent, J., Gill, J., Laughlin, R. (2004): pp 19-20.

that for the "overwhelming majority of new hospitals" limited availability of public capital meant it was now "PFI or bust". [18]

Four years earlier, in July 1993, Harriet Harman, then Shadow Chief Secretary to the Treasury, speaking in the Commons did not dismiss any form of partnership with the private sector, but did take a different tone from that subsequently adopted by New Labour. She strongly questioned whether PFI was a genuine partnership, as had been claimed:

> "The Government boasted about the public-private finance initiative, yet the record since then has been one of ignominious failure. The CBI has said, politely, that progress has been painfully slow. Even the Chancellor had to admit that the flow of projects had been "disappointingly small".
>
> "This is not some unfortunate accident, as the Government would have us believe. It is a direct result of the Government's prejudice against any kind of public sector investment, even when it involves private investment working together with it.
>
> [...]
>
> "It is clear that that initiative is not about partnership. It is about the Government abandoning their responsibility to modernise our economy and our infrastructure and it is about them passing the buck to the private sector."[19]

Margaret Beckett, as shadow health secretary, toughened up the line in 1995, summing up what had become Labour's critical response, when she told the *Health Service Journal*:

> "As far as I am concerned PFI is totally unacceptable. It is the thin end of the wedge of privatisation."[20]

It was not until the summer of 1996 that Shadow Treasury minister Mike O'Brien announced a change – in fact a reversal – of New Labour's policy:

---

[18] *Health Service Journal* (*HSJ*) July 10 1997.

[19] Commons Hansard 12 July 1993
https://publications.parliament.uk/pa/cm199394/cmhansrd/1993-12-07/Debate-8.html

[20] *HSJ* June 1 1995

"This idea must not be allowed to fail. Labour has a clear programme to rescue PFI" [21]

The "rescue of PFI" was duly included in New Labour's 1997 manifesto, sitting strangely alongside promises to scrap the NHS internal market. The pledge to scrap the market rather predictably proved to be an empty one: but the promises to implement PFI were sincere enough. By the spring of 1998, PFI was declared to be:

"A key part of the [New Labour] Government's 10 year modernisation programme for the health service." [22]

New Labour's then Paymaster General Geoffrey Robinson claimed that his party had managed to free up PFI after years of Tory failure:

"The Initiative had been floundering, the system was gunged up with innumerable hopeless projects and bureaucracy was seemingly unable even to communicate among itself." [23]

While Kenneth Clarke had openly boasted that PFI would generate new profits for the private sector, New Labour, forgetting the criticisms Harman and Beckett had made, begun emphasising that using private investment to modernise public services was a "partnership," an example of the 'Third Way' as argued by Tony Blair, finding common ground between neoliberalism and social democracy.

Health minister Alan Milburn, one of the leading New Labour converts to and advocates of PFI, went further still and gave a gung-ho report on the policy and its ability to deliver actual savings as well as value for money to the Commons Select Committee on Health on July 22 1998, stating:

"… any scheme that is given the go-ahead has to prove it is cheaper, better, better value for money and better for patients than the public sector option, and I am convinced from all of the work that I have seen from officials that all of these

[21] *HSJ* August 22 1996

[22] Department of Health Press Release April 7 1998

[23] Treasury News Release 27 April 1998, (cited in Froud, J. and Shaoul, J. (2001) Appraising and Evaluating PFI for NHS Hospitals, *Financial Accountability & Management* 17 (3) August 2001 pp247-270)

schemes we have given the go-ahead to and all the schemes that we will give the go-ahead to in the future will prove, if they are built through the PFI, better value for money".[24]

In the years that have followed there have been few politicians unguarded enough to echo Milburn's transparently false claim that PFI schemes are cheaper than publicly-financed schemes.

Indeed the scepticism was growing in parallel with New Labour's fanatical conversion to PFI as a method of funding. While Blair's party had shifted in one direction, opinion elsewhere had hardened up against PFI. According to *Guardian* financial columnist Larry Elliott in the same year, PFI was simply "a scam":

> "Of all the scams pulled by the Conservatives in 18 years of power -and there were plenty -the Private Finance Initiative was perhaps the most blatant. ... If ever a piece of ideological baggage cried out to be dumped on day one of a Labour government it was PFI."[25]

Despite its popularity with New Labour ministers (most notably with the Treasury team) PFI soon began to incur the increasingly vociferous opposition of the BMA, the Royal College of Nursing, UNISON and almost all trade unions, local campaigners in affected towns and cities, and a growing body of academics. This was because PFI came to be associated with contracting out of support services and to "efficiency savings" which swiftly would be a burden on local services and staff – while also funnelling profits to the private sector.

As soon as the 1997 Act went through Parliament the first wave of PFI contracts were signed, and after a prolonged period of standstill on any new hospital building the go-ahead was suddenly given to 15 hospital projects in 1997: since this was before devolution the first lists of schemes agreed included one in Wales (Baglan Moor, Neath) and three in Scotland (Law and Hairmyres in Lanarkshire and the Royal Infirmary, Edinburgh)[26].

---

[24] https://publications.parliament.uk/pa/cm199798/cmselect/cmhealth/98 8/8072208.htm - paragraph 122

[25] *The Guardian*, October 26 1998

[26] A list of major schemes is given in Sussex, J. *The Private Finance*

Although several of these contracts were to prove extremely expensive, even unaffordable to the trusts concerned, one of the most remarkable features of these early projects, looking back, is the comparatively low capital costs of new PFI hospitals, until specifications were changed and later plans mushroomed in cost. 17 of the first 22 PFI hospitals were costed at below £100m[27]. Even with the more expensive schemes[28] the first wave averaged less than £100m each.

Most of these first wave PFI hospitals – each of which embodied at best a standstill in bed numbers, but in most cases sharp reductions ranging from 20%-40%[29] – have struggled both financially and clinically as a result of flawed schemes.

The bed reductions appear to flow from a combination of strenuous efforts to hold down the cost of the scheme by restricting the scale of the new buildings on the one hand, and the involvement of management consultants committed to the introduction of "innovative methods" with hugely over-optimistic assumptions on the increase in throughput of patients per bed that could be achieved through the move to a new building, and consequent sharp reduction of average length of stay. In Worcestershire, for example, the PFI scheme, shaped by management consultants SECTA and the propositions put forward by the King's Fund, sought to reduce bed numbers by 35%, and cut beds per 1,000 patients by 40%. This meant hoping for a truly massive increase in throughput per bed by reducing average length of stay – without any actual evidence that

---

Initiative, p32, available
https://www.ohe.org/system/files/private/publications/273%20-%202001_Economics_of_Private_Finance_Init_Sussex.pdf?download=1

[27] English examples included Amersham/South Buckinghamshire £38m; Wellhouse (Barnet General) £40m; Bishop Auckland £52m; Hereford £63m; Carlisle £63m; Calderdale £77m; South Manchester £89m; Dartford £94m Worcester £96m; North Durham £96m; Greenwich £96m.

[28] South Tees £122m; Edinburgh £180m; Bromley £118m, Norwich £158m, UCLH £422m.

[29] Dunnigan, M.G., Pollock, A.M. (1998) The shrinking Acute Hospital. *The British Journal of General Practice*. 48(429):1197-1212.

this could be achieved[30].

Most first wave PFI hospital trusts have subsequently found it difficult to maintain safe and adequate services for a rising number of patients with inadequate numbers of beds and insufficient supporting services in the community and primary care: several of these same schemes are still in severe difficulties now, 18 years after the first of the PFI hospitals opened.

However all this remained at an abstract level when the proposals were first revealed, since no new hospital projects had begun since 1993. To make matters worse it was difficult to get any detailed or serious public discussion or political critique of specific issues by local MPs, since the media remained largely oblivious to the whole question of PFI, and pro-PFI enthusiasts were keen to brush aside and ridicule any critics of the scheme, dismissing them as negative opponents of building a new hospital.

Such was the pent-up level of expectation of good results that when in 1997 another 23 schemes were postponed to future rounds, it was described by *Financial Times* health correspondent Nick Timmins as the biggest-ever "hospital cancellation programme".[31]

However experience over the following 20 years has confirmed many of the warnings of the critics who warned that buildings would be too small, often in the wrong location, and bring excess costs – in some cases so substantial that other much-needed local service developments became increasingly unaffordable. In one South East London trust, Queen Elizabeth Hospital, Woolwich, which opened in 2002, the scale of the financial problem reached the level of 'technical bankruptcy' just 3 years later, with the trust paying out 14.5% of its income on the "unitary charge" for use of the building and support services, according to a 2005 Audit Commission report[32]. Seven years later, after the Trust had been forcibly merged

---

[30] Lister, J. (1998) *Casting Care Aside*, response researched for Wyre Forest District Council, available
https://healthemergency.org.uk/pdf/WORCS%20Kidderminster.pdf

[31] *Financial Times* July 17 1997.

[32] Carvel J (2005) Flagship PFI hospital 'technically insolvent', *The Guardian*, December 16, available
http://www.guardian.co.uk/uk/2005/dec/16/publicservices.topstories3

with another near-bankrupt PFI Hospital in Bromley (Princess Royal University Hospital), and with the struggling Queen Mary's Hospital, Sidcup in the disastrous South London Hospitals Trust, the whole, merged Trust submerged into bankruptcy.

In 2012 it was subjected to the attentions of a Trust Special Administrator, who partly blamed, but tried to divert attention from the inflated costs of the PFI schemes as a key factor in the crisis that had developed[33]. However the impasse of the trusts saddled with the extra costs of PFI had previously been explained by the King's Fund's Keith Palmer:

> "Two of the DGHs (Queen Elizabeth, Woolwich, and Bromley Hospitals NHS Trust) are whole-hospital private finance initiative (PFI) sites. The annual payments to the PFI service providers are fixed in real terms (and rise in line with inflation) throughout the duration of the contracts. There is almost no scope to change the service specification or to reduce the annual payments for more than 20 years.
>
> "These annual payments exceed, by a large amount, the Market Forces Factor (MFF)-adjusted funding provided in tariffs to pay for them.
>
> "Even if these trusts were more efficient than the average trust, because of this underfunding they would still incur significant recurrent deficits, and legacy debt would continue to increase.
>
> "The corollary is that, were they to cut controllable costs to the level necessary to restore financial balance, then their spending on patient care (to fund staff costs and drugs) would be significantly lower than that of other hospital trusts. Patient care would suffer as a result."[34]

Many staff working in the new hospitals, especially the first wave PFI hospitals, have been profoundly unimpressed by the quality and

---

[33] See Lister, J. (2012) *Saving the Cancer, Sacrificing the Patient*, available https://healthemergency.org.uk/pdf/SavingtheCancerDec2012.pdf

[34] Palmer, K. (2011) *Reconfiguring Hospital Services – Lessons from South East London,* King's Fund. https://www.kingsfund.org.uk/sites/default/files/Reconfiguring-hospital-services-lessons-South-East-London-Kings-Fund-March-2011.pdf

design of the buildings, criticising predictable practical problems, the limited or non-existent engagement with staff in drawing up the plans, and the failure to learn lessons from the first hospitals before completing others with similar problems.[35]

On the financial front, it is grimly amusing to note in retrospect, for example, that among the trusts aggrieved at missing out on the first wave, but subsequently given the go-ahead in the same year as Mid Yorkshire Hospitals, was Peterborough and Stamford Hospitals: its plan was presumably what its chief executive Malcolm Lowe-Lauri meant when he spoke to the *Health Service Journal*, complaining that:

> "There are some really good PFI schemes around. ... We need new guidance on PFI and how to get those good schemes included in the next round." [36]

In the event, far from being a "really good" scheme, the Peterborough City Hospital PFI which later went ahead, proved to be one of the most unaffordable and crisis-ridden PFI developments. A scathing National Audit Office report at the end of 2012 castigated the Trust Board for signing off the contract, the regulator Monitor for allowing it through, and the Department of Health for rubber stamping it. Noting the trust's deficit in 2011/12 of £46m (22% of the trust's turnover) and an even larger deficit expected the following year, Amyas Morse of the NAO stated:

> "The trust board's poor financial management and procurement of an unaffordable PFI scheme have left it in a critical financial position
>
> "The board developed and enthusiastically supported an unrealistic business case built on over-optimistic financial projections. The regulatory and approval processes did not work in this case and did not ensure affordability.
>
> "Irrespective of how far the PFI scheme contributed to the current deficit, the latter is now too great for the trust to balance its finances by managing its own resources. The

---

[35] Lister, J. (2003) *The PFI Experience: voices from the front line*, UNISON, London, available https://healthemergency.org.uk/pdf/PFI_experience.pdf
[36] *HSJ* August 28 1997.

trust, the department, commissioners and Monitor need to work together and take urgent action to help the trust get back on its feet."[37, 38]

Further waves of PFI schemes were rubber stamped or urged forward in the years after 1997. Some of the significant problems with the design of the first wave of new buildings – in which circulation space, office space, storage space and, most contentiously, bed numbers had been tightly constrained to restrict the 'footprint' size of site required and thus minimise costs, were addressed – but at a very substantial extra cost.

Bigger – and less affordable

New planning guidelines from 2000 meant that many of the hospital schemes signed off were required to be at least "bed neutral". New architectural guidance required greater space between beds[39], wider corridors in patient areas, and more generous space in public access areas: but all this came with a significantly higher price tag.

Whereas the highest capital cost of a PFI hospital in England prior to 2000 had been £158m for the 900-bed Norfolk & Norwich hospital, a revised and greatly expanded plan for University College Hospital London, with fewer (721) inpatient beds, came in at almost three times as much – £422m, (£292m of which was raised through PFI, and the remainder through land sales).[40]

A number of much larger and more extravagant projects followed UCLH: in 2002 came the £379m University Hospital Coventry & Warwickshire; the following year a £312m new hospital in Derby; in 2004 three major projects, in Romford (Barking Havering & Redbridge), Leeds (St James) and Central Manchester were signed

---

[37] http://www.buildingbetterhealthcare.co.uk/news/article_page/Poor_financial_management_and_unaffordable_PFI_hospital_cripple_NHS_trust/82349
[38] https://www.nao.org.uk/wp-content/uploads/2012/11/1213658.pdf
[39] "Bed spacing is being increased to 2.7m between each bed centre, a significant increase against most current configurations; in high dependency areas the bed spacing is more generous, reaching 3.3m in Critical Care." http://www.hospitalmanagement.net/projects/uclh/
[40] Ibid.

off, at £266m, £265m and £512m; in 2005 came a £299m Newcastle project, plus the £326m Sherwood Forest Hospital in King's Mill, Nottinghamshire; in 2006 three monster projects were also finalised – the biggest PFI of all (Barts Health at £1,149m) was followed by St Helens & Knowsley at £338m and Birmingham's new Queen Elizabeth Hospital (£695m).

2007, the year in which the Mid Yorkshire Hospitals PFI was signed off, at £311m, also saw the University Hospital North Staffordshire in Stoke on Trent at £415m and the Peterborough City Hospital project signed off at £336m. It's interesting to note by contrast that when what became the Mid Yorkshire Hospitals project was first agreed by ministers to go forward with the PFI process, the estimated cost for the "Pinderfields Hospital" scheme was just £164m – including the development of primary care services in the area. Alan Milburn replied to a question in the Commons in February 2001:

> "I am grateful to my hon. Friend for his kind comments. The Wakefield development involves £164 million of investment. As he knows, it is long overdue in the area and will bring benefits to the local health service. However, there will not only be a new hospital at Pinderfields general; I can confirm that the development will also involve additional primary and intermediate care facilities in the north Kirklees area. That is good overall news for the local health service."[41]

The rapid inflation of costs came with a narrowing of scope of the PFI schemes to focus almost exclusively on acute hospitals, which represented defined property assets for the private sector. This was preferred to projects in mental health or community health services which sought to invest in the development of wider services with less obvious financial value.

In the same way the relatively small number of PFI schemes which centred on mental health tended to focus narrowly on the construction of hospital buildings, and if anything the demands of

---

[41] http://hansard.millbanksystems.com/commons/2001/feb/15/nhs-hospital-building

servicing these schemes drew funding away from community health and other services outside hospital, even as it squeezed down the numbers of beds provided and the size and scope of the new buildings.

In all, in the ten years from 2000 to the 2010 general election, 17 major schemes costing in excess of £200 million were signed off, at a total capital cost of £6.9 billion (£6,883m) and incurring cumulative 'unitary charge' payments over periods ranging from 30 to 43 years, and estimated by Treasury figures to add up to £43.6 billion (£43,646m).[42]

The most recent PFI details published by the Treasury show 124 schemes, totalling £12.4 billion, with repayments up to 2049 adding up to £78.7bn[43]: this does not include the (still incomplete, and at time of writing, still inactive) £300m Midland Metropolitan Hospital, or take account of inflationary increases in unitary charge payments.

A wider view of PFI

By 2011, after the change of government, the Treasury Committee report cited analysis by the new Office of Budget Responsibility (OBR) looking not just at hospital projects but all PFI contracts across the public sector – transport, schools, prisons, local government – which estimated the total value of all 800 PFI projects at more than £35 billion, and argued that the combination of schemes on and off balance sheet at the equivalent of 2.9% of GDP.[44]

Of course advocates of PFI are swift to argue that the total payable under the "unitary charge" also includes contracts for a combination of non-clinical support services, including maintenance ("Hard FM" – Facilities Management) and various combinations of

---

[42]https://www.gov.uk/government/uploads/system/uploads/attachment_data/file/503954/current_projects_as_at_31_March_2015.xlsx , accessed February 16 2018.

[43] The DHSC in its 2017/18 Annual Accounts (pp166-7) estimate the 'present value' of future payments [i.e. discounting future payments to represent the declining value of money], to be much lower, at around £32bn, but declines to say what the undiscounted figure might be.

[44] Smith, D. (2012) *The Private Finance Initiative and Intergenerational Equity*: p39

other "soft FM" services:

> "As its name suggests a Unitary Charge is one payment (made monthly) that encompasses the costs of building the asset, financing it, and operating it for the whole length of the contract. Think of it as a mortgage for your house, maintenance costs, insurance and housekeeping all rolled into one payment. If the lighting doesn't work in your kitchen or your dining room is unavailable because of lack of maintenance then you don't need to pay for that portion of your house.

> "Often in the press you see references to a £100m hospital which will cost many times more than £100m over the life of the contract. Embarrassingly often, the press neglects to tell their readers that the fee also includes the maintenance, cleaning, catering, portering and other services for more than 20 years."[45]

The FM service element of the unitary charge paid by hospital trusts in the early PFI schemes (but largely eliminated in subsequent PFI and PF2 schemes) averages out at around 40% of the total payment each year, according to analysis by Mark Hellowell and Allyson Pollock[46]. The private provision of these services, with long term contracts and costs rising each year by inflation or 2.5% whichever is the higher, is part of the income stream of the PFI consortium.

However the inflated cost of the capital borrowing, as reflected in the "availability" component of the unitary charge, also pushes the trusts' overhead costs above the average for non-PFI hospitals trusts, which means that even after receiving subsidy payments, 33 of the 40 trusts analysed by Hellowell and Pollock were paying out more in

---

[45] P2G *(2013) What is a PFI and how does it work?* http://www.p-2-g.co.uk/blog/what-is-a-pfi-and-how-does-it-work

[46] Hellowell, M. Pollock, A.M. (2009) The Private Financing of NHS Hospitals: politics, policy and practice. *Economic Affairs,* March 2009, available https://www.allysonpollock.com/wp-content/uploads/2013/04/EconomicAffairs_2009_Hellowell_PrivateFinancingNHS.pdf

capital costs than they were being funded for, and effectively building in an underlying financial shortfall.

If the 60:40 split between the availability charge element and support services is applied to £78.7bn total payments due for NHS PFI deals agreed by 2015, it means the NHS is due to pay out £47bn for the buildings themselves – almost four times their capital value . This is a far higher amount than would have been payable even on a conventional mortgage, let alone through much cheaper direct government borrowing. This is a long-running income stream flowing out of the NHS into private sector shareholders' pockets and off-shore accounts, and a long-term liability for the taxpayer: repayments on NHS PFI schemes in England run at over £2 billion each year to 2038, and do not fall below £1 billion per year until 2043.

Treasury data also show that even though the number of PFI deals has fallen back since 2010, and despite the negative findings of a Commons Treasury Committee report on PFI in 2011, more deals (albeit very few) have since been signed. The weight of evidence highlighted by the Treasury Committee report makes this an astonishing commitment to pursue policies not only in the absence of compelling evidence but in defiance of blatantly obvious warning signs that the policy had up to then failed to deliver any of its claimed positive benefits.

Looking back at over a decade of PFI projects, the Committee notes:

> "6. *The use of PFI has the effect of increasing the cost of finance for public investments* relative to what would be available to the government if it borrowed on its own account.
>
> "17. […] there has been, and continues to be, at least a small incentive to use PFI in preference to other procurement options, as it results in lower headline government borrowing and debt figures in comparison to other forms of capital investment.
>
> "22. […] In the long term, the PFI arrangement will build up big commitments against future years' current budgets that have not even yet been allocated or agreed. *We are*

concerned that this may have encouraged, and may continue to encourage, poor investment decisions. PFI continues to allow organisations and government the possibility of procuring capital assets without due consideration for their long-term budgetary obligations.

"51. The fixed nature of PFI contracts means they are likely to provide more certainty regarding price and time. *However there is no convincing evidence to suggest that PFI projects are delivered more quickly and at a lower out-turn cost than projects using conventional procurement methods.* On the contrary, the lengthy procurement process makes it likely that a PFI building will take longer to deliver, if the length of the whole process is considered. Proposing that post-contractual price certainty can be taken as a good measure of overall cost efficiency is to use a comparison already likely to favour PFI. This is because the PFI contract price is set at a much more advanced stage in the process. It is evident that a project delivered "to time and to budget" (in post-contractual terms) may nonetheless represent poor value for money if the price paid for the risk transfer was too high.

"71. *The price of finance is significantly higher with a PFI.* The financial cost of repaying the capital investment of PFI investors is therefore considerably greater than the equivalent repayment of direct government investment. *We have not seen evidence to suggest that this inefficient method of financing has been offset by the perceived benefits of PFI from increased risk transfer. On the contrary there is evidence of the opposite.* Organisations which have the option of other funding routes have increasingly opted against using PFI and have even brought PFIs back in-house."[47] [emphasis added]

The following year (2012), Health Secretary Andrew Lansley set

---

[47] Treasury Committee (2011) Seventeenth Report: The Private Finance Initiative, available
https://publications.parliament.uk/pa/cm201012/cmselect/cmtreasy/1146/114608.htm

up a £1.5 billion bail-out fund to offer long term financial support to seven trusts struggling to meet the unaffordable costs of ill-advised PFI contracts[48]. The fund offered payment subject to conditions over 25 years, but is expected to prove insufficient given the larger number of trusts that will require financial support to cover these inflated bills[49]. In the autumn of that same year, with the first NHS Trust declared bankrupt and being broken up under the NHS "failure regime" largely as a result of PFI costs, the Commons Public Accounts Committee warned that 22 hospital trusts were at risk because of the costs of "botched" PFI deals.[50]

Nonetheless there has been no clear break from PFI, nor has there been any systematic review of the costs and consequences of the PFI schemes that have already been signed, many of which are now operational.

The more recent major PFI hospital projects have been conducted under a revised, so called PF2 arrangement, in which a substantial payment of government money is advanced in the NHS as Public Dividend Capital. This, together with an increase in the proportion of money raised through equity, helps to reduce the total to be funded (more expensively) through borrowing by the private sector, and appears to reduce the cost. However a closer examination reveals that the use of Public Dividend Capital itself carries a long-term financial cost, with interest payable indefinitely, and the cost of equity investment is much higher than the use of bank finance. As a result PF2 is still substantially more expensive than the government borrowing the money in its own name and providing the capital

---

[48] Kirby, J. (2012) £1.5 billion bailout for seven NHS trusts, *Independent*, February 3, available
http://www.independent.co.uk/news/uk/politics/15bn-bailout-for-seven-nhs-trusts-6357078.html
[49] Whitfield, D. (2013) Fingers in the PFI, *Red Pepper*, April 11, 2013
https://www.redpepper.org.uk/fingers-in-the-pfi/
[50] Daily Mail Reporter *(2012) Hospitals 'may go bust because of botched Labour PFI deals'*
October 30 http://www.dailymail.co.uk/news/article-2225087/NHS-Trusts-bust-botched-Labour-PFI-deals.html#ixzz57SkboIQI

required.[51]

To make matters worse, early in 2018 both of the major hospital projects being built under PF2 – Royal Liverpool and Broadgreen University Hospital and the Midland Metropolitan Hospital in Smethwick – fell foul of the financial collapse of their lead construction contractor, Carillion.

We will return to this aspect of PFI, and the consequences of high-cost schemes for trust finances and surrounding services, in later chapters.

---

[51] Lister, J. (2016) *The right hospital and the right size?* Report for Keep Our NHS Public Birmingham, available
https://healthcampaignstogether.com/pdf/Final%20update%20The%20Right%20Hospital%20--%20and%20the%20right%20size.pdf

Chapter 2

How PFI is supposed to work

Under PFI large-scale building projects, which would previously have been publicly funded by the Treasury, were to be put out to tender, inviting consortia of private banks, building firms, developers and service providers not just to put up the investment, but to "Design, Build, Finance and Operate" the new hospital or facility, and lease the finished building back to the NHS - generally with additional non-clinical support services (maintenance, portering, cleaning, catering, laundry, etc.).

The claimed advantages of this were (from the standpoint of the NHS):

• Speeding up the possible programme of investment in new hospitals and facilities, while access to public funding remained tightly restricted.

• Maintaining value for money by requiring competitive bids for PFI contracts and comparing each PFI scheme with a "Public Sector Comparator".

• "Encouraging the allocation of risks to those most able to manage them." By effectively transferring risk to the private sector the NHS purchased a degree of longer term certainty over costs.

• "Encouraging innovation and good design", and increased productivity and quality in delivery.

• Delivery on time and on budget. "The private sector is not paid until the asset has been delivered which encourages timely delivery. PFI construction contracts are fixed price contracts with financial consequences for contractors if delivered late."

• Encouraging ongoing maintenance – by building in maintenance costs and long term "Hard FM" maintenance contracts into PFI schemes and "constructing assets with more efficient and transparent whole-life costs." [52]

---

[52] Quotations are from the longer but rather repetitive and not entirely relevant list compiled in the Treasury Committee report 2011 referred to above.

These claims each raise further questions, and have in many cases already been shown to be less than accurate. They will be examined below in this chapter.

Other claims have also been made for the advantages of PFI. Among them, according to Prowle[53]:

- "Better management – a belief that the private sector will bring improved approaches and talent to the management of health services

- "Reduction of restrictive practices – a belief that professional and trade union restrictive practices which exist in the NHS will be broken down in the private sector

- "Flexibility and responsiveness – a belief that the private sector is more flexible and will respond to changing circumstances more quickly than the public sector;

- "Greater innovation […]

- "Capital funding – a belief that the private sector will be able to access private sources of capital funding."

Prowle himself fails to follow up on many of these claims, but does examine and effectively dismiss a few false assumptions, pointing out the widespread view that that the so-called 'efficiency improvements' resulting from improved management "are not real improvements, but mechanisms for the private sector to reduce the wages of already low paid public sector workers" (p5).

He also dismisses the final point about new sources of finance, pointing out that:

> "This is not the case … Under a PFI arrangement, although the costs of new facilities are initially financed by the private sector, the costs of building and operating the new facilities still come from the public purse eventually." (p6)

The "professional restrictive practices" which are referred to by Prowle appear to relate to the delivery of clinical services, which are

---

https://publications.parliament.uk/pa/cm201012/cmselect/cmtreasy/1146/114608.htm

[53] Prowle, M. (2006) *The role of the Private Finance Initiative in the delivery of health services in the UK*. Technical approach paper. London: HLSP Institute.

specifically excluded from the scope of PFI contracts, so there is little chance PFI could reduce them, while there is no elaboration on what might be meant by the vague reference to trade union "restrictive practices".

Other analysts have shot down any notion that PFI delivers innovation. In a report based on interviews with people working in eight various sized PFI hospitals, Barlow and Köberle-Gaiser come to the opposite conclusion – arguing that PFI, from its bidding process right through to the delivery of services "stifles innovation"[54]. They specifically note that:

> "Collaboration and open discussion of new ideas was constrained by commercial sensitivities and the fear of consortia that they might lose the project ..." (p10)
> "Trusts were highly price sensitive and unwilling to pay for innovation that often involved additional short-term costs." (p110)

The same researchers find equally little substance to claims that PFI results in improved flexibility and responsiveness:

> "In fact it was suggested that there is a disincentive to plan for adaptability because the SPV [PFI company] could achieve additional income through alterations needed in the future." (p10)

So what of the longer list of claimed advantages of PFI set out by the Treasury Committee?

Speeding up investment

New Labour ministers argued that their policy of seeking to build hospitals using PFI enabled them to embark upon the "biggest ever programme of hospital building in the NHS". To test out this bold claim we need to look back in time to the last major building programme in the NHS.

---

[54] Barlow, J. Köberle-Gaiser, M (2008) Delivering Innovation in Hospital Construction: contracts and collaboration in the UK's Private Finance Initiative hospitals program, *California Management Review*, vol 51; No. 2, Winter 2008, pp1-18, available https://spiral.imperial.ac.uk/bitstream/10044/1/1455/1/Barlow%20CMR%20wi09%20JB%20changes.pdf

New Labour's NHS Plan (2000) called for a total of 100 new hospitals by 2010: but the claim was only partly accurate. This is because the difference between PFI and conventional hospital building is that before PFI all of the hospitals and facilities that were built were owned and paid for by the public sector, and became *public assets*. By contrast PFI hospitals are leased for decades from the private sector, throughout which time they become *liabilities*, draining precious revenue from NHS trusts and GP practices.

The sums of money involved in the PFI investment programme obviously appear larger than the only previous major programme of hospital modernisation, the 1962 Hospital Plan for England and Wales, 35 years before PFI, when the value of money was rather dramatically different. But so too was the thinking of government: 1962 predated the lurch to neoliberalism that changed the political and ideological climate from the 1980s.

The 1962 Hospital Plan was eventually approved by the then Conservative government on the urgings of then Health Minister Enoch Powell, and was hugely ambitious for its time. It included proposals for 90 new hospitals and another 134 major redevelopment programmes. The 280-page Plan also listed a further 356 smaller schemes "which represent a large volume of modernisation and upgrading"[55].

The Hospital Plan was initially costed at £707 million – the equivalent of £2.85 billion in 2002, and £14.3 billion in 2017: it was equivalent to almost three quarters of the entire NHS budget of 1962 (£971m): a similar proportional share of spending today would amount to an £80 billion investment in new buildings. £500m was to be to be spent between 1962 and 1971 – an average of £50m a year, more than double the going rate at the time. It was the amount called for by Labour in opposition[56].

The Hospital Plan recognised that such a massive leap in public investment would represent a major change of policy, after years in

[55] Ministry of Health (1962) *A Hospital Plan for England and Wales* (Cmnd 1604), HMSO London.
[56] Webster, C. (1996) *The Health Services since the war*. London, Stationery Office, Vol. 2: 99

which NHS capital to modernise the aged building stock nationalised in 1948 had been in desperately short supply. In 1962 the government was spending a much smaller share of national wealth on the NHS, just 3.4% of GDP – compared with 5.3% in 1997[57] when Tony Blair took office [the international system of calculation changed in 2010, making direct comparisons of current levels of spending with earlier figures impossible] .

Within this limited pot of cash, NHS capital budgets in turn consistently accounted for less than 3% each year (though allocations had increased slightly, peaking at £24m in 1960-61). As a result, there was not enough capital to enable any substantial modernisation or even systematic repairs to buildings which were often unsuitable for modern medicine: 70% of hospitals when taken over by the NHS in 1948 had fewer than 100 beds, and in 1962 20% of the building stock was found to be over 100 years old.

The situation called for a major change of policy: but perhaps surprisingly, given Enoch Powell's subsequently notorious right wing leanings and the dominance of a Conservative government just 16 years after the party had voted repeatedly to block the nationalisation of hospitals to form the NHS, the whole 1962 investment programme was to be funded by the government from general taxation. As a result the completed hospitals would also be assets wholly owned by the NHS – assets which various capitalist interests have been trying to get their hands on at least since the 1980s.

The debate was framed by the prevailing consensus around the NHS as a key component of welfarism. There was no serious discussion of seeking the finance from elsewhere: the only debate within the Tory cabinet was over how much or how little should be invested in the modernisation of the NHS.

The Hospital Plan also looked forward to the likely patterns of population and health needs in 1975, and pioneered the concept of the District General Hospital of 600-800 beds covering a catchment population of around 150,000 as the key building block for acute

---

[57] Harker, R (2012) *NHS funding and expenditure*, House of Commons Library, http://www.nhshistory.net/parlymoney.pdf

(short stay) hospital services – the very pattern of provision that has been called into question since the early 1990s by academics and NHS managers calling for further "reconfiguration" and "centralisation" of services, and – more significantly – by the growing financial pressures on the NHS.

The 1962 Hospital Plan involved a 6% reduction in numbers of acute hospital beds, but (reflecting the medical model of the time) a 35% *increase* in numbers of maternity beds. 1,250 hospitals – most of them small or very small – would close in the process. But in mental health the Hospital Plan also commenced the shift from institutional to community-based care, proposing a drastic cut in hospital bed numbers. It also took an important step towards setting up a nation-wide plan and a coherent policy.

Unlike PFI schemes 35 years later, the 1962 Hospital Plan laid down 'norms' for minimum levels of bed provision per head of population[58], and addressed the issue of staffing levels, both within the NHS as it then was, and within the Local Authority Health and Welfare Services (many of which are now council social services). The plan undoubtedly had weaknesses and flaws, but it was nevertheless an important step along the road to more equal allocation of resources according to population, breaking from the previous pattern of huge inequalities.

The Hospital Plan recognised that the schemes would take time to get up and running, and "assumed" spending of £200m in the first five years, rising to £300m in the following five years. It accepted that "the sums which will eventually become available may be somewhat more or less, dependent on the state of the economy". In fact the costs were much higher than expected: but the policy change had been made.

Only six new hospitals had been built between 1955 and 1965: but between 1966 and 1975 another 71 were started – and some completed, changing the shape of health care for a generation. Even though the full Hospital Plan was never completed, by 1968 large

---

[58] The new norm was 3.3 beds per 1,000 people (Mohan 2002: p112). However as Mohan points out, this figure was not based on needs or on any substantial evidence base.

schemes (carrying out building work costing over £1m a year) accounted for more than half of the NHS capital programme: there were 66 of these schemes – 6 of which were projects planned to cost over £10m [£165m in 2017 money]. Capital expenditure that year was almost 10 percent of current NHS spending, and it continued to rise to a peak of 12.8% in 1973-4, before being cut back again to 9.9% in 1974-5. Cost estimates were distorted by high levels of inflation in the increasingly turbulent economic situation: but the new Royal Free Hospital with its tower block was completed in 1973 at what today seems an incredibly modest cost of £20m [indeed still modest at £229m in 2017 money, compared to equivalent PFI projects].

The 1970s saw a change in the economic climate, and a retreat by successive governments from investment, not only in the NHS, but throughout the public sector. Government net capital spending plunged from a peak of £28.8 billion in 1974-5 to just £12.5 billion in 1979-80, and fell again to a nadir of just £1.9 billion in 1988-89. In only one year during the 1980s (1983-84) did public sector capital investment reach £10 billion.

Moreover though it rose again briefly to double figures (with a peak of £14.2 billion in 1992-93), it fell back again sharply in the second half of the 1990s. (Figures are all at 1999-2000 prices)[59].

All this serves to confirm that far from speeding up investment, PFI was brought in from 1992 alongside an accelerated *reduction* in government capital allocations. The 1995 budget from John Major's government projected successive *cuts* in NHS capital spending – reducing by 17% in 1996-97, another 5% cut in 1997-98, and 6.5% the following year: at the same time PFI investment was supposed to increase year by year, from £47m in 1995-96 to £300m in 1998-99.[60]

Capital charges

However PFI – and NHS land sales, which had become a regular feature of the Tory government's asset-stripping approach to the NHS – were not the only ways in which governments found ways to

[59] HM Treasury (2001) *Budget*, Chapter C, Table C24. London, Treasury
[60] Department of Health (1995) NHS's 1.6 per cent budget boost, Press Release, 28 November

masquerade as investing generously in the NHS, while injecting comparatively little new capital.

During the mid-1990s the establishment of NHS Trusts within the Tory "internal market" reforms brought the introduction of *capital charges,* which were to be levied on each Trust's land and property assets. This meant that a growing percentage of the NHS budget each year was generated *internally* from these "capital refunds"[61]. Beginning at 1.2% of NHS total spending in 1993-94, these capital refunds steadily increased in scale as new Trusts were formed and more began paying charges on a greater share of their assets. By 1998-99 capital refunds amounted to a hefty 8% of the NHS budget[62].

So despite the appearance of allocating large sums for investment in new hospitals and other NHS facilities, and despite the apparent upturn in allocations after Labour took office in 1997[63], in practice the New Labour government began by injecting even less public capital for major hospital projects in real terms than the miserly amounts available in 1961. Indeed in the two years 1997-98 and 1998-9, the injection of Treasury capital for Hospital and Community Health Services (HCHS) was more than outweighed by the cash generated from land sales and the refund to the government of capital charges paid by NHS Trusts on their assets.

Far from pumping in desperately-needed capital, the government effectively pocketed a *surplus* from existing NHS assets in these two years – of £139m in 1997-8 and £348m in 1998-9[64].

After PFI got going the real figures were also disguised by the

---

[61] Gaffney, D., Pollock, A.M., Price, D. and Shaoul, J. (1999) NHS capital expenditure and the Private Finance Initiative – expansion or contraction? *BMJ* 319, 48-51 (3 July).

[62] Department of Health (1998) The Government's expenditure plans 1998-1999. Fig 2.7, available at http://www.archive.official-documents.co.uk/document/cm39/3912/3912.htm, accessed 15 December 2007.

[63] Denham, J. (2000) Commons written answer, *Hansard*, February 2.

[64] Gaffney, D. Pollock, A.m., Price, D. and Shaoul, J (1999) NHS Capital expenditure and the Private Finance Initiative – expansion or contraction? *BMJ,* 319; 48-51 (3 July).

inclusion of PFI money under the general heading of "health capital investment" – of which the PFI share swiftly rose to around a quarter of the claimed total[65].

However the extent to which PFI could legitimately be seen as "NHS investment" at all is not clear, given that the assets to be constructed did not belong to the NHS, and could not do so for around 30 years or more. Instead the (inflated) cost of paying for the hospital projects financed through PFI was to be met from NHS revenue budgets over the next 25-30 years.

Despite claims by the DoH that PFI is simply "one of the weapons in our armoury of procurement tools", the pool of NHS capital has remained too small to offer Trusts a real choice of whether or not to seek private finance.

This squeeze, tighter than ever from 1992, meant that PFI was openly described by New Labour health ministers such as Alan Milburn –and seen by NHS managers – as "the only game in town"[66].

By January 2009, then Health Secretary Alan Johnson (soon to be replaced by Andy Burnham) declared: "PFIs have always been the NHS's 'Plan A' for building new hospitals ... There never was a 'Plan B'."[67]

Only six major NHS-funded schemes, totalling less than £300m, were given the go-ahead in the five years from 1997. This followed a long lean spell for NHS investment under the Tories: from 1980 to 1997, only seven publicly-funded schemes costing more than £25m had been completed.[8]

---

[65]https://publications.parliament.uk/pa/cm199798/cmselect/cmhealth/988/8072206.htm table 7.2

[66] Parliament, 'Health - Minutes of Evidence' (2002). House of Commons Select Committee on Health, 1 May. At:
http://www.publications.parliament.uk/pa/cm200102/cmselect/cmhealth/308/2010907.htm [accessed 21 November 2012]

[67] Monbiot, G (2009) The Biggest, Weirdest Rip-Off Yet,
http://www.monbiot.com/2009/04/07/the-biggest-weirdest-rip-off-yet , citing Rebecca Omonira-Oyekanmi, 4th February 2009. Root of the Problem. PPP Bulletin. http://www.pppbulletin.com/features/view/791.

Value for money or skewed evaluation? The Public Sector Comparator

Every PFI scheme is supposed to prove that it represents value for money, by contrasting the privately financed plan with what is described as a "Public Sector Comparator". But it is clear from the outset of such an exercise that the comparison is not between like and like: the investment of energy and commitment into selling the PFI scheme to attract the only likely source of funding was understandably never matched by the ritualistic development of a hypothetical and unloved alternative, which there is no intention to promote or build, and whose main virtue is to appear less attractive.

Government guidance spells out that the public sector scheme is not as a real plan for a real hospital but just a fig leaf to hide the blushes of the PFI plan:

"The purpose of the PSC is to provide a benchmark against which to form a judgement on the value for money of PFI bids"[68]

One of the manipulative techniques that works consistently to the advantage of a PFI deal in comparison with the PSC has been the calculation of the "net present costs". This assumes that money spent now is worth more than money spent in five, ten or twenty years – and that the full costs of a hospital development will be paid in the first few years of a publicly-funded scheme (when the value is highest) while the costs of a PFI deal can be defrayed over the whole life of the contract. This unbalanced comparison also ignores the inclusion in every PFI scheme of an escalator clause that increases the unitary charge payments each year by inflation of a minimum amount (often 2.5%) whichever is the higher. This means there is little real-terms depreciation in the value of PFI payments. The calculations and comparisons were for several years made surreal by selecting an arbitrary, and high, level of 6% per year – well above current and projected levels of inflation – as the basis for discounting the value of future payments.

As the NAO's deputy controller and auditor general Jeremy Colman pointed out, speaking to the Financial Times, much of the

---

[68] Public Accounts Committee (2000) *The PFI contract for the new Dartford and Gravesham Hospital*, Twelfth Report, March.

financial analysis comparing PFI projects against so-called public sector comparators has from the outset ranged from the "spurious" through "pseudo-scientific mumbo-jumbo" to "utter rubbish". He pointed out the painful reality leading to the many distortions of reality being passed off as comparisons:

"People have to prove proper value for money to get a PFI (or PPP) deal. If the answer comes out wrong, you don't get your project. So the answer doesn't come out wrong very often." [69]

As with the examples of **Worcestershire** and **North Durham**, the subsidies may be implicit, in the assumption that a large – but completely separate – increase in spending on community hospitals and community health services will create a new system of care which the PFI planners hoped would be forthcoming, and allow the new hospital to deliver its target of much more rapid throughput. In practice the extra costs of many PFI schemes soak up such a large share of any available local funding that far from being accompanied by extension of out of hospital services, they make such schemes unaffordable. Local services then face the double blow of an inadequately-sized hospital and equally inadequate services in the community.

In **Worcestershire**, for example, the management consultants drawing up the scheme pointed out – without any evidence to support their assertion, other than other PFI schemes – that "many acute service reviews and proposed hospital business cases have assumed that future targets of between 8-10 beds per 1,000 in-patient episodes are feasible". These assumptions amounted to a 40 percent increase in throughput for each bed in the new Worcester Royal Infirmary. It was on this same fragile basis that health chiefs decided they could close down 229 acute beds at Kidderminster Hospital and reduce bed numbers by 112 in Worcester, even though their own advisors warned that achieving these bed capacity targets across the county "would be a major challenge"[70]. Throughout the NHS bed

---

[69] Timmins, N. (2002) Warning of spurious figures on value of PFI, *Financial Times* 5 June.
[70] Lister, J. (1998) Casting Care Aside, a response for Wyre Forest District Council to plans by Worcestershire Health Authority, available

throughput had largely levelled off at around 56-57 patients per bed per year. The PFI plans for **Edinburgh** Royal Infirmary aimed to increase this to a massive 88: but the Worcestershire plans aimed at almost doubling the national average, to over 100 patients per bed per year. The driving force in this was PFI, and in particular the rigid financial envelope within which the project had to fit if the Treasury was to give its approval.[71]

Such a big increase in throughput per acute bed in **Worcestershire** or elsewhere could only be achieved by discharging more patients to less intensive, "intermediate" or "step-down" beds. But this calls for additional investment in community health services and an expansion of these beds. As we have seen, this investment was less likely to be forthcoming because of the increased costs of renting and running the PFI hospital.

Nevertheless similar unrealistic assumptions on increased levels of throughput per bed encouraged PFI planners in many other areas to propose other massive reductions in bed numbers. And because the assumptions were unrealistic many of them, including **Dartford, North Durham** and **Carlisle,** also struggled from the outset to cope with pressures on the depleted numbers of beds remaining.

Subsidies – overt and covert

To further stir the pot of obfuscation on the genuine comparative costs between a privately-funded hospital and a publicly funded project, a variety of subsidies for the PFI option can be openly or covertly slipped in.

Other subsidies in the early days of PFI took the form of "smoothing" payments from a special slush fund held by the NHS Executive, effectively providing a direct subsidy for the introduction of the PFI scheme where it is clear that there is insufficient cash in the local kitty to pay the increased costs. However as PFI hospital Trusts such as **Dartford**, and the two South East London PFI hospitals [**Queen Elizabeth**, Woolwich and **Princess Royal**,

https://healthemergency.org.uk/pdf/WORCS%20Kidderminster.pdf

[71] Price, D. (1997) Profiting from closure, the private finance initiative and the NHS. *BMJ.* 1997 Dec 6;315(7121):1479-80

Orpington] that were merged into the doomed **South London Hospitals Trust** later revealed, these smoothing payments were always intended to taper off, and can be ended by government as easily as they are put in place, leaving the Trusts to pick up the remaining, unaffordable bill.

More recently unaffordably expensive PFI schemes such as **Peterborough** have been routinely subsidised behind the scenes by NHS England. The Trust's Annual Report showed that the first full year's "unitary charge" payment in 2011-12 was £41.3m – almost 20% of its total £211m income, far higher than the already high projection of 15% when the deal was signed. In the final quarter of 2011/12 the Trust was again bailed out with another "temporary advance" of £41.2m from the Department of Health with no specified repayment date. In 2016, as it outlined plans to merge with the cash-strapped Hinchingbrooke Hospital 25 miles away, which was recovering from the chaos caused by a period of privatised management under private hospital chain Circle, the trust admitted it would need subsidies adding up to a massive £650m – more than twice the capital value of the hospital – by the end of the PFI contract[72]. The Outline Business Case made clear that the subsidies the Peterborough Trust have been receiving would need to increase:

> "The Department of Health *will need to commit to giving the trust long-term financial support* at a level that provides stability for the trust.
>
> "The National Audit Office (2012)[73], the Contingency Planning Team (2013)[74] and PriceWaterhouseCooper (2015)

---

[72] http://www.hsj.co.uk/hsj-local/providers/peterborough-and-stamford-hospitals-nhs-foundation-trust/merger-trust-predicts-it-needs-650m-bailout/7009513.article

[73] National Audit Office (2012) Peterborough and Stamford Hospitals NHS Foundation Trust, Report by the Comptroller and Auditor General HC 658 Session 2012-13, 29 November, https://www.nao.org.uk/wp-content/uploads/2012/11/1213658.pdf

[74] PWC (2013) *Peterborough and Stamford Hospitals NHS Foundation Trust Assessment of sustainability*, Contingency Planning Team (7 June) noted (p5): "The Trust is not financially sustainable. Even if it achieved cost improvement plans (CIPs) and delivered best in class efficiency it would

all identified the need for £25m additional ongoing tariff subsidy to meet the additional costs of the PFI. The trust currently receives £10m support in the form of a subsidy, *and an additional £15m is required in future.*"[75]

Contrary to fears in some circles, however, with the sole exception of the now dismembered South London Hospitals Trust, bail-outs and reconfiguration cutting back on non-PFI hospital services have ensured that the increased costs of PFI have not forced trusts into bankruptcy and closure. The explanation is simple: closure would not only cause a major embarrassment for whichever government was in charge at the time, but closing the services would also not bring an end to the contractual requirement to pay the unitary charge to the end of the contract – forking out tens of millions of public money on an empty building, while neighbouring hospitals would inevitably struggle to cope with the excess demand for services for displaced patients..

The financial imperatives of PFI mean that there is relatively little saving to be made by closing beds, wards and services at a struggling PFI hospital, let alone closing the whole building. The "payment by results" system also means that any reduction in staffing costs from closing beds is accompanied by a loss of clinical income and possibly also a severe reduction in quality of care – while the underlying overhead cost of the unitary charge continues to increase each year.

So the immediate risk from a worsening financial situation is not so much to the deficit-ridden PFI hospital trust and its services, but much more to surrounding hospitals and trusts which are not tied in to large PFI contracts.

---

have a sizeable deficit each year for the next five years."
https://assets.publishing.service.gov.uk/government/uploads/system/uploads/attachment_data/file/283595/Final_PSHFT_sustainability_report_7_June_2013.pdf.
[75] *Merger of Hinchingbrooke Health Care NHS Trust and Peterborough and Stamford Hospitals NHS Foundation Trust. Outline Business Case, v2.0 Final,* 16 May 2016, p7, available via
https://www.nwangliaft.nhs.uk/_resources/assets/attachment/full/0/1593.pdf

This was illustrated clearly in the dismemberment of **South London Hospitals Trust** from 2012, with the closure of the non-PFI hospital in the trust, **Queen Mary's Sidcup**. It is also shown in the continuing threat to **King George's Hospital**, Ilford, as collateral damage from the financial crisis of the same (Barking Havering and Redbridge University Hospital) trust resulting from the costs of the PFI-funded **Queen's Hospital in Romford**. There are many similar cases still unresolved, including the run-down of services at Dewsbury Hospital to centralise services in the PFI hospital in Wakefield.

Even where changing local plans and priorities have subsequently meant PFI hospitals have quite obviously been built in the wrong place, long-term, tightly-written contracts tie trusts to decades of payments regardless of how little of the finished building is used for its intended purpose. One example of this is the small general hospital built in Bishop Auckland to serve Tony Blair's constituency, which had only just opened and still had 27 years of unitary charges to pay when it was found to be surplus to requirements[76]

But while contracts tie in trusts rigidly to paying for buildings even if the services within them are cut back, some PFI deals also explicitly require payment by the trust of increased unitary charge payments if higher than expected use is made of facilities. Far from being any genuine "partnership" with the private sector, PFI is a relationship in which all of the shots are called by the private sector, and all of the financial risks devolve back to the public sector.

This is why successive governments have been so determined to avoid bankruptcy of PFI hospitals at all costs. This was underlined in 2012, when Tory Health Secretary Andrew Lansley set aside a massive £1.5 billion bail-out fund was put in place, so that unaffordably expensive PFI schemes signed under New Labour (such as Peterborough) could be routinely subsidised behind the scenes, with the trusts further propped up by NHS England and the

---

[76] Lawrence, F. (2002) PFI 'white elephant' hospital faces merger, *Guardian* February 8,
https://www.theguardian.com/society/2002/feb/08/hospitals.privatefinance

Independent Trust Financing Facility (ITFF)[77, 78].

"Risk transfer"

To stack the odds even further in favour of the PFI option, the costs of the Public Sector Comparator (PSC) are commonly loaded to compensate for "risks" allegedly transferred to the private sector consortium under the PFI deal. Each "risk" transferred is given a notional cash value, which is then added to the costs of the Public Sector Comparator, since in theory a publicly funded scheme would have to take on these risks.

It is often only after this and other statistical sleight of hand that the PFI option can be shown as even marginally better value than a publicly-funded scheme.

Numerous studies since the work of Allyson Pollock and colleagues in the 1990s have shown how this mechanism has been used to skew the apparent balance sheet in favour of PFI. In 2003 Broadbent, Gill and Laughlin analysed eight PFI cases, and noted the pressure brought to bear on the Trust by the private sector "partners" and the various advisory teams:

> "In all the cases we examined this whole process was fraught, with extensive involvement by financial and legal advisers for both parties to the contract. [...]
>
> "In each case the ex-risk net present cost of the PSC was smaller than the PFI alternative.
>
> "However when the transferred net present cost of the risk was added to the net present costs of the PSC, the PFI alternative was cheaper than the PSC."[79]

[77] Kirby, J. (2012) £1.5bn bailout for seven NHS trusts, *Independent* February 3, https://www.independent.co.uk/news/uk/politics/15bn-bailout-for-seven-nhs-trusts-6357078.html

[78] https://www.gov.uk/government/groups/independent-trust-financing-facility

[79] Broadbent, J. Gill, J., Laughlin, R. (2004) *The Private Finance Initiative in the National Health Service*, Nature, Emergence and the Role of Management Accounting in Decision Making and Post-Decision Project Evaluation, CIMA, available https://www.cimaglobal.com/Documents/ImportedDocuments/tech_resrep_t

The central risk in the construction phase is that of cost over-runs. But while the average over-run of eventual building costs in NHS projects had been between 6% and 8.5% for the previous 10 years, PFI business cases arbitrarily assumed much higher levels of 12.5% – or up to 34% in the **Norfolk & Norwich Hospital**[80].

Other "risks" which are given a notional cash value and added to the cost of the public sector comparator are either similarly inflated or fictional – such as the £5m added to the Carlisle PSC to compensate for the "risk" that clinical cost savings would not be made, despite the fact that the consortium was under no obligation to compensate the Trust if this happened.

Among the risks which were enthusiastically itemised by the proponents of the eight PFI schemes studied by Broadbent and colleagues were:

• Construction taking longer than planned – and delaying access to the hospital.

• Failure to deliver a building that meets specification – although the decision on whether the building is satisfactory remains with the contractor

• Construction costing more than expected

• Changes to the terms of planning permission.

• The contractor providing support services failing to meet performance standards: the trust may reduce payments to the contractor, although if the contract is terminated the trust might have to pay compensation.

• Areas of the hospital not made available for use by support services: the trust may reduce payments to the contractor, although if the contract is terminated the trust might have to pay compensation.

• The hospital's condition not being properly maintained; if not, the trust may reduce payments to the contractor.

• Maintenance costs increasing above the rate of inflation: the

he private finance initiative in the national health service 2004.pdf: p33.
[80] Mercer, H. Whitfield, D. (2018) *Nationalising Special Purpose Vehicles to end PFI: a discussion of the costs and benefits*. PSIRU, available:
https://gala.gre.ac.uk/20016/1/20016%20MERCER_Nationalising_Special_Purpose_Vehicles_to_End_PFI%20_2018.pdf

contractors would cover any excess cost above the Retail Price Index.

- Revenue from alternative sources (car parking, concessions etc.) less than planned: the contractor's fee would not increase.
- Sale of surplus land raises less than expected: the contractor takes the risk of any potential shortfall.

More modern public sector contracting through smart procurement has established ways of dealing with such problems, making it highly questionable whether – for all their additional cost – PFI deals in practice take on any tangible risk that would otherwise carry a cost for the trust.

Or, as referred to in the Norfolk & Norwich case, the estimated level of risk is hugely exaggerated.

In reality the trust, as the body whose income from patient care depends upon the availability of adequate safe, properly clean and serviceable hospital premises, always carries the major risk of any new building project, with only the most marginal prospect of financial compensation in the event of late completion, poor quality buildings, and poor support services.

Penalty clauses have often been hard or almost impossible to invoke where PFI consortia have fallen short of required standards, and NHS management time required to carry through such procedures can often be better spent addressing issues in front line services.

The final "risk" in the above list is almost laughable: in reality there is no risk. Far from losing out on the sales of surplus land, some of these aspects of PFI have proved the most lucrative income stream for the private sector.

In the case of Edinburgh's Royal Infirmary, the eventual proceeds from the sale of the city centre land and buildings released by the new hospital were so large they could have averted the requirement for any PFI borrowing at all, but in the event the money lined the pockets of the contractors, leaving the trust with three decades of payments.[81]

---

[81] Lister, J. (2003) *The PFI Experience: voices from the front line*, UNISON, London, available https://healthemergency.org.uk/pdf/PFI_experience.pdf

"Encouraging innovation and good design"

As referred to above, case studies in eight assorted PFI projects concluded quite decisively that this assumed advantage is largely imaginary. In reality:

> "The project director from an SPV summarised the position thus: 'PFI stifles innovative solutions. Investors and financiers are not interested in innovation. They do not want to take risk'."[82]

> Nor does PFI allow any role for the trust in driving innovation: in fact the trust appears to be largely sidelined by the PFI relationship, in which from the PFI contractors' point of view "The client is the bank; the trust is just a tenant".

> "Interviewees often pointed out that since the hospital trust is not the owner of the facility, it only had a limited role in overall project delivery. One interviewee compared the SPV to "a king in a castle" who had to agree to any changes the hospital wished to make …. The project director for another hospital trust even felt that it was 'not seen as the client but rather as an impediment'." (p12)

Delivery on time and on budget.

The Treasury Committee sums up the way in which this claimed advantage seems to operate:

> "The private sector is not paid until the asset has been delivered which encourages timely delivery. PFI construction contracts are fixed price contracts with financial consequences for contractors if delivered late."[83]

However the same Treasury Committee report also points out that in practice the performance is not so impressive, since the PFI contract builds in extra costs to cover these risks:

> "The NAO, in a report for the Lords Economic Affairs Committee, noted that: "Most private finance projects are

---

[82] Barlow and Köberle-Gaiser (2008): p10

[83] Treasury Committee report 2011, https://publications.parliament.uk/pa/cm201012/cmselect/cmtreasy/1146/114607.htm

built close to the agreed time, price and specification." However they noted that **of their sample of PFI projects over 31% had been completed late and 35% had not been delivered for the contracted price. They explained that "using PFI is not a panacea for solving construction problems."**

The Committee report goes on to note that the public sector pays the PFI consortia very handsomely for accepting the 'risk' of late delivery or budget over-run:

"Any improved performance in terms of time and budget is only an achievement if the benefit outweighs any extra cost involved."

The extra cost could be as much as 30%:

"[...] hospital trusts were paying a 'risk premium'—conservatively estimated at 30% of the total construction costs—to ensure projects are running to time and budget. So while it is true that the private sector absorbs the cost of overruns etc., additional charges are written into the contracts to account for this."

[...]

"If the budget is already 20% higher in a PFI procurement then a budget overrun of less than 20% in a conventional procurement would mean it was still cheaper. It is therefore important to consider how much projects which do not meet their budget exceed it. A National Audit Office report which considered a group of public sector projects that went over budget in 2003 and 2004, reported that the average level of overspend was 4.1%."

(Treasury Committee 2011: paragraphs 48-49)

The Treasury committee also notes the extensive delays built in to negotiating PFI contracts: eventual delivery of an already delayed project "on time" is therefore less of a convincing benefit.

"The UK Contractors group told us that "even now the procurement process for a new hospital project in the UK can take over two years before any construction work is undertaken." The NAO reported in 2007 that on average the overall tendering process took over two years for schools and over three years for hospitals." (Treasury Committee 2011: paragraph 49)

To make matters worse, as the NAO has shown above, a significant number of PFI schemes are in fact even then delivered late. It seems as if these benefits of PFI are also largely illusory.

Hard FM – maintenance – contracts

The Treasury Committee suggests that a further advantage of PFI is that it means "constructing assets with more efficient and transparent whole-life costs." [84]

Although there have certainly been long-standing problems caused by the NHS seeking short-term savings through under-investing in maintenance of its estate, which has run up a backlog maintenance bill recently estimated at £5 billion across England's NHS[85], here too the long term savings on any particular PFI project would need to be very substantial to represent a net benefit from a more costly finance arrangement.

Mark Hellowell, advising the Treasury Committee, gave the example of a 2010 Outline Business Case for the Royal Liverpool Hospital PFI to show that the increased cost of borrowing the money through the PFI mechanism for that project rather than the government directly raising the money would have been £175m. He points out that as a result:

> "Assuming that PFI does not deliver efficiencies in construction, maintenance and/or services then, for the same present value of finance-related payments, the government could have secured 71% more investment by borrowing on its own account." [86]

---

[84] Quotations are from the longer but rather repetitive and not entirely relevant list compiled in the Treasury Committee report 2011 referred to above.
https://publications.parliament.uk/pa/cm201012/cmselect/cmtreasy/1146/114608.htm

[85] Naylor, R (2017) Should we welcome plans to sell off NHS land? *BMJ* https://www.bmj.com/content/358/bmj.j4290

[86] Pollock AM, Price D. (2013) *PFI and the National Health Service in England,* http://www.allysonpollock.com/?page_id=1737

The Hard FM contracts themselves can represent a substantial income for the company which lands them, as in the ill-fated £285m Birmingham Metropolitan Hospital (which was financed under PF2 but has been hard hit by the collapse of Carillion). Just two years ago Carillion was celebrating landing the long term contract worth upwards of £140m for maintenance over 30 years, a relatively high cost given that the actual cost of the building over the same period through the PF2 contract will be £670m.[87,88]

In another article also in 2011, Hellowell raises the general claims of greater efficiency and benefit from PFI schemes, noting that as special adviser for the Treasury Committee:

"Despite reams of written evidence and many long and tiring oral evidence sessions, we saw no evidence of any savings or benefits in the operational tasks performed by PFI contractors (construction, maintenance and services). In other words we found nothing to suggest that private sector involvement through PFI brought efficiencies of any great scale, and certainly not large enough to offset the significantly higher cost of finance ....

"In one oral evidence session the committee chairman, [Conservative MP] Andrew Tyrie asked a selection of the great and the good from the PFI industry if they could cite a single piece of evidence to suggest that such efficiencies existed. He did not receive an answer."[89]

The National Audit Office in 2012 questioned the amount of risk involved in PFI schemes, especially in the NHS, where the government is underwriting costs. The NAO states:

"Equity investors' returns are expected to be high relative to

[87] http://www.morningstar.co.uk/uk/news/AN_1450082382030972000/AllianceNewsPrint.aspx

[88] Lister, J. (2016) *The Right Hospital and the Right size?* Birmingham KONP, available https://healthcampaignstogether.com/pdf/Final%20update%20The%20Right%20Hospital%20-%20and%20the%20right%20size.pdf

[89] Hellowell, M. (2011) Money for Nothing, *Political Insight*, September, pp8-11, available (£) http://onlinelibrary.wiley.com/doi/10.1111/j.2041-9066.2011.00078.x/full

the senior debt lenders because they take on greater risk. There has not, however, been a recent conclusive overall evaluation of whether equity returns are justified by the amount of risk equity investors bear."[90]

Professor Allyson Pollock has also challenged the way in which the assumed cash value of "risk" is used both to distort comparisons and make publicly-funded options appear more expensive, and to inflate the interest rates payable:

"The UK parliament has repeatedly questioned the lack of evidence in support of risk transfer and value for money claims. In July 2010, a National Audit Office paper to a House of Lords committee described value for money as "subjective judgements of risk, which can easily be adjusted to show private finance as cheaper." The chairman of the Public Accounts Committee described PFI as "probably the most secure projects to which the banks could lend."[91]

Back in 2001 – when the use of PFI as the way to fund new hospital projects was first becoming established – Julie Froud and Jean Shaoul investigated the way in which the figures were manipulated and came to the conclusion that the cash pricing of "risk transfer" was the key to the argument for PFI financing:

"The process of risk transfer is ... central to PFI, not least because, as the Health Minister recognised, a privately financed option is unlikely to represent value before risk transfer. Quite how much risk should be transferred is a matter of some ambiguity."[92]

---

[90] National Audit Office (2012) *Equity investment in privately financed projects* (page 15), Report by the Comptroller and Auditor General HC 1792 Session 2010–2012, 10 February 2012, HMSO, London

[91] Pollock AM, Price D. (2013) *PFI and the National Health Service in England*, http://www.allysonpollock.com/?page_id=1737

[92] Froud J & Shaoul J (2001) Appraising and evaluating PFI for NHS hospitals, *Financial Accountability & Management*, 17(3), August 2001, 0267-4424 available (£): http://onlinelibrary.wiley.com/doi/10.1111/1468-0408.00130/epdf

Chapter 3

Obvious disadvantages of PFI

Assessing the cons as well as the alleged pros of PFI in 2011, the Commons Treasury Committee summed up the disadvantages as:

- Higher cost of finance than government borrowing.
- Skewed evaluation of projects (or in the actual words of the Committee: "The prospect of delivering the asset using private finance may discourage a challenging approach to evaluating whether this route is value for money.")
- Reduced contract flexibility - the bank loans used to finance construction require a long payback period. This results in long service contracts which may be difficult to change.
- The public sector pays for the risk transfer inherent in private finance contracts but ultimate risk lies with the public sector.
- Private finance is inherently complicated which can add to timescales and reliance on advisers.
- High termination costs reflecting long service contracts.
- Increased commercial risks due to long contract period and the high monetary values of contracts.[93]

Each of these overlapping issues has been well documented already, to the satisfaction of the Treasury Committee. But we will revisit some of these issues briefly here.

Higher costs of finance

The Treasury Committee in 2011 attempted to put a figure on how much more expensive it was to borrow money via the public sector. It noted:

> "Private finance is invariably more expensive than direct government borrowing and therefore we explored the difference in the availability and cost of private and government debt in our evidence. Balfour Beatty told us in

---

[93] Treasury Committee (2011) Introduction, available:
https://publications.parliament.uk/pa/cm201012/cmselect/cmtreasy/1146/114604.htm

written evidence that the 'financing costs of PFI are typically 3–4% over that of government debt'."[94]

Analysis for the Committee of the specific example of the Royal Liverpool and Broadgreen Hospital PFI by Mark Hellowell showed that using public funding rather than private sector borrowing would generate a massive 42% saving, or enable an extra 71% of investment for the same outlay, or in other words:

"all else being equal, paying off a PFI debt of £1bn may cost the same as paying off government debt of £1.7bn." (page 18)

The National Audit Office in 2018 made a further analysis of the working of PFI and PF2, comparing the initial claims made and the actual performance in practice. It notes that in general:

"HM Treasury discourages public bodies from borrowing privately, as the government can raise finance at a lower cost than the private sector. However, it makes an exception for PFI owing to the potential of PFI to provide efficiency gains in the delivery of a project"[95]

However the "efficiency gains" are generally more theoretical than real, and the same report notes that this is especially the case with NHS PFI schemes:

"Our work on PFI hospitals found no evidence of operational efficiency: the costs of services in the samples we analysed were similar. Some of those data are more than 10 years old. More recent data from the NHS London Procurement Partnership shows that the cost of services, like cleaning, in London hospitals is higher under PFI contracts." (p10)

Skewed evaluation of projects

While Alan Milburn was among the ministers and advocates of PFI who attempted to argue that the process of checking the proposed deals was watertight[96], Jeremy Colman, deputy controller

---

[94] https://publications.parliament.uk/pa/cm201012/cmselect/cmtreasy/11 46/1146.pdf p15

[95] NAO (2018) PFI and PF2, available https://www.nao.org.uk/report/pfi-and-pf2/ - page 8.

[96] https://publications.parliament.uk/pa/cm199798/cmselect/cmhealth/98

and auditor general at the National Accounting Office in the UK, took a very different view. He was especially outspoken in his criticism of the Value For Money process for PFI schemes when he spoke to the *Financial Times* in 2002. He argued that many public sector comparators demonstrate a "spurious precision" while others resort to:

> "pseudo-scientific mumbo-jumbo where the financial modelling takes over from thinking... It becomes so complicated that no one, not even the experts, really understands what is going on."

Mr. Colman did not go so far as to argue that the figures were fictional, but he did go on to make the painfully obvious point, but one carefully sidestepped by many politicians and managers trying to find a positive in PFI:

> "People have to prove value for money to get a PFI deal... If the answer comes out wrong you don't get your project. So the answer doesn't come out wrong very often."[97]

Recent proposals for PFI-funded schemes continue to display the same preference for selecting aspects of the scheme that appear to be most positive, while ensuring that possible cheaper alternatives and any public sector comparator are portrayed as fatally flawed or dismissed out of hand.

The full Business Case outlining plans to close down acute in-patient services and A&E at Huddersfield Royal Infirmary, to relocate on the site of the same trust's PFI hospital, Calderdale Royal, for example rested heavily on (strongly contested) claims that the HRI building was infected with "concrete cancer" and the absence of any "do minimum" option. There was little serious attempt to argue that the plan for new PFI schemes totalling £298m was affordable (the FBC does not even claim financial balance could be achieved for another 8 years), or that the reduced capacity that would be available from the new and existing buildings would be

---

8/8072208.htm - paragraph 122
[97] Timmins, N. (2002) "Warning of 'Spurious' figures on Value of PFI." *Financial Times* 5 June.

adequate to replace the beds and facilities to be closed down.[98]

The FBC was so weak, and the flaws and omissions so serious that the plan was put on hold by then Health Secretary Jeremy Hunt in May 2018 after Calderdale and Kirklees councils had joined forces to object to the proposals and concerns were expressed by the normally pliable Independent Reconfiguration Panel.

Reduced contract flexibility

Examples have already been given of the problems that can arise from signing a 30 or 35-year binding contract to secure funding for a new hospital, especially at a time when new models of care, new technology and "digital roadmaps" are being developed and advocated that could radically alter the role of hospitals.

Heavy investment in acute hospitals means that a fixed or rising share of local health budgets are locked in to a model of service, restricting the resources that could be devoted to developing community-based services, primary care or public health measures.

As we have seen, many of the first wave of PFI hospitals have had to be heavily subsidised by local health authorities in order to make them affordable. The **Worcestershire** scheme meant that an extra £7 million was allocated to acute services to enable the Trust to pay for the new hospital: this had to be found by squeezing cash allocations for mental health, community services and primary care.

Nor is there any obvious escape route established. Despite extensive and expensive efforts by management consultants to find ways to chisel down the costs of PFI schemes, they have had little success in denting the tightly (and expensively) constructed contracts. One small scheme has been bought out, with the assistance of a large loan from a local authority, but since most schemes are many times larger, and local government funds are constantly being cut back it is clear there will be few if any repetitions of this process.

In August 2012, with seven hospitals reportedly at risk of insolvency as a result of PFI debts, the government sent in hit squads

---

[98] Calderdale and Huddersfield Foundation Trust (2017) Reconfiguration of Calderdale and Huddersfield NHS Foundation Trust Hospital, available http://www.cht.nhs.uk/fileadmin/site_setup/contentUploads/Publications/Full_Business_Case_-_FINAL_Approved_by_Board_August_2017.pdf

of lawyers and auditors to the struggling trusts to help the trusts find savings and renegotiate contracts. This produced very little in the way of savings.

In November 2013 a National Audit Office report on the outcome showed that only a small minority of contracts had been squeezed to produce any savings: the Department of Health had performed particularly badly in this exercise, reporting a total saving of just £61 million, a microscopic fraction of what was then a £69.4 billion unitary charge remaining.[99]

The myth of risk transfer

This has been extensively discussed in the preceding pages, and vividly illustrated by the collapse of Carillion at the beginning of 2018. The extent to which the NHS, defence, education, energy, and prisons were all still carrying the risk for PFI contracts which private consortia had been so lavishly paid to shoulder instead was exposed.

Two urgently needed hospitals – the Midland Metropolitan and the Royal Liverpool – remain in limbo, with especially the MMH deteriorating rapidly since roofing remains incomplete, and it's clear the bill for repairing the damage done and completing the job will land firmly back on the NHS; no alternative contractor is willing to step in to complete the contract that Carillion signed up for without extra money on the table – public money.

As an opinion piece from The Conversation summed up:

"The primary justification given for why PFI/PF2 is pursued is that it allows risk to be transferred from the public sector to the private sector and hence demonstrates value for money by being a less costly alternative to public financing. So central is the assumed transfer of risk to PFI schemes that virtually no PFI scheme is seen as less costly than its public counterpart, until the assumed risks involved are costed up and added to the public counterpart.

"… Public agencies might seek to transfer risk through PFI, but they ultimately remain responsible for the delivery of

---

[99] https://www.nao.org.uk/wp-content/uploads/2013/11/Savings-from-operational-PFI-contracts_final.pdf

public services. In failed schemes, it is the taxpayer that ends up picking up the tab for the private sector's mistakes."[100]

Complexity of contracts, and high termination costs

The complexity of the procedures and process of PFI and the negotiations that it involves has brought a new level of delay to schemes which might otherwise have proceeded with public funding.

In **East Kent** NHS Regional bosses warned that the plans for a new PFI hospital to replace four existing hospitals – the projected cost of which had already almost doubled to £102m – could take 4-7 years to complete the complex PFI process: the project was eventually killed off two years later when the cost more than doubled again in 2003.[101]

The first 15 PFI schemes for new hospitals also spent a combined total of £45 million on advisors, with costs varying between 2.8% and 8.7% of the capital cost of the project. These costs are heavily inflated by the need to strike legally-binding deals with private sector firms in what are often very complicated deals.

However the process has been somewhat streamlined since the early days under the Tories, when a contract for **Coventry's Walsgrave** Hospital – long before financial close – came out at a colossal 17,000 pages in 1996 – at which point the two consortia vying for the deal reportedly asked for government cash to pay lawyers to read it all![102]

Then Health Secretary Alan Milburn insisted in 2002 that these

---

[100] Khadaroo, I. and Salifu, E (2018) PFI has been a failure – and Carillion is the tip of the iceberg, the Conversation, January 24, http://theconversation.com/pfi-has-been-a-failure-and-carillion-is-the-tip-of-the-iceberg-90487

[101] *Construction News* (2003) Kent PFI hospitals scheme killed off as costs soar to £250m, 7 August, https://www.constructionnews.co.uk/home/kent-pfi-hospitals-scheme-killed-off-as-costs-soar-to250m/858706.article

[102] House of Commons Health Select Committee (2002) First report The Role of the Private Sector in the NHS (May 15), available https://publications.parliament.uk/pa/cm200102/cmselect/cmhealth/308/30802.htm: para 104 ff. The reference to the lawyers is drawn from *Mail on Sunday*, June 23 1996.

ridiculous costs which applied also for the first wave of signed PFI contracts had become over 40% less ridiculous by the time of the second wave:

> "As far as average legal fees and average financial fees are concerned between the first wave of PFI and the second wave of PFI on legal fees we have seen a 41 per cent improvement, 41 per cent cheaper to the National Health Service, on financial fees a 48 per cent improvement, 48 per cent cheaper to the National Health Service" [93]

These disadvantages all flow from the private sector's need to ensure that the deals are solidly-enough constructed to withstand later challenges from government and NHS bodies in the event of a change of circumstances. Such a change began with the banking crash in 2008, and the situation deteriorated further as a result of the post 2010 coalition government's imposition of rigid austerity policies on the NHS and other public services. PFI schemes that had been irresponsibly signed in the sunnier times of the mid 2000s, when it appeared the NHS would be receiving annual above inflation increases in funding into the future, became increasingly unaffordable. The complexity of the contracts did mean that they took longer to draw up and sign off: but it's clear that the costs of the armies of management consultants, accountants and lawyers involved in the process were simply added in to the total cost of the PFI – and have been carried by the public sector through inflated costs.

High termination costs were clearly seen by these legal teams as an essential barrier to prevent troubled public sector bodies pulling out before the full profit stream had been extracted.

Additional disadvantages of PFI

The Treasury Committee list of disadvantages misses out some very important aspects of PFI, which have not always been well publicised. Some have been touched upon earlier, but the most important ones are identified here in a little more detail.

Increased "headline" costs of schemes

PFI hospital projects have become notorious for the massive level of increase in costs from the point at which they are first proposed to the eventual deal being signed.

In part this is because PFI consortia are keen to make each scheme as big as possible, and also because private firms prefer to buy and then build on greenfield sites and lease buildings back to the NHS rather than refurbish existing NHS hospitals.

Among the more dramatic increases in prices from original plan to PFI deal are:

- **Greenwich (Queen Elizabeth Hospital, Woolwich)**: up from £35m in 1995 to £93m in 1997
- **UCLH**, London: up from £115m to £404m
- **Leicester**: up from £150m in 1999 to £286m in 2001: the scheme continued to rise dramatically in cost until it reached a staggering £760m in 2006, when it was eventually scrapped by health secretary (and then local Leicester MP) Patricia Hewitt.
- **South Tees**: up from £65m to £122m
- **Swindon**: a £45m refurbishment of Princess Margaret Hospital in Swindon turned into a £96m new hospital on a greenfield site out by the M4.
- The **Worcester** Royal Infirmary, a project which was originally estimated at £45m when it was first advertised for PFI tenders in 1995, was eventually given the go-ahead at a total cost of £110m.

The first 14 PFI deals escalated in cost by an average of 72 percent, from a total of £766m to £1,314m by the time they were approved[103]. This inflation has obviously had an impact on the final bill to be paid. The new **Dartford** Hospital was originally projected to be "at worst cost neutral", but it soon emerged that purchasers would have to foot the bill for an extra £4m a year if the Trust were to be enabled to pay the PFI costs.[104]

The costs of PFI also impact on other local services: in South Manchester, a deal through which mental health beds in the PFI-funded Wythenshawe Hospital have been sub-let to Manchester

---

[103] Price, D. (1997) Profiting from closure: the private finance initiative and the NHS, *BMJ* 314;461-2

[104] National Audit Office (1999) *The PFI contract for the new Dartford and Gravesham Hospital*, May, London, NAO.

Community and Mental Health Trust resulted in a hefty hike to £5m annual rent, which soaked up almost ten percent of the Trust's revenue in 2004, effectively "crippling the mental health economy." [105]

Monopoly position for "preferred" bid

One of the main reasons for the consistent pattern of final contracts being signed off at multiples of the initial starting cost is that the limited amount of competition between providers that might keep costs down comes to an abrupt end with the selection of a preferred provider.

From that point onwards no other bids are relevant, and the trust concerned to negotiate the deal has committed to doing a deal with that one consortium, knowing that if the negotiations collapse there will be no new hospital built. It's the other side of the argument that PFI is "the only game in town".

In addition, the relatively few major players in PFI consortia have experience of negotiating a number of deals, and expert panels of advisors, while too often the NHS trusts have been led by managers out of their depth, negotiating for the first time on any contract of equivalent size. Many of the external consultancies they might bring in to advise will also be involved elsewhere in working with PFI consortia on the other side of the negotiating table.

To make matters worse, most of the senior executives and directors of NHS trusts are on short term contracts, well aware that by the time the full consequences of the deal become apparent they could be many miles away from the problems their negotiating failures have created.

Rate of return for private investors

PFI consortia don't build hospitals for the sake of our health. They want profit for their investment – and lots of it. A BMJ article in 1999 pointed out that shareholders in PFI schemes "can expect real returns of 15-25 percent a year", and went on to explain how

---

[105] Manchester Community & Mental Health Trust (2004) *Visioning mental health services for Manchester*, 20 September, Manchester.

little actual risk was involved for the companies in PFI consortia[106]. In **Barnet**, the second phase of the new general hospital, originally tendered at £29m, went ahead at a cost of £54m, with capital borrowed at an eye-watering 13% over 25 years.

Even the PFI companies themselves admit they require a hefty return compared with many other industries: In 2011 David Metter from Innisfree, one of the main financers of PFI, told the Commons Public Accounts Committee that they would not be interested in a project if they could not secure a profit margin of 8-10%, and openly admitted that meant that financing through PFI was upwards of 2% more expensive than a government-funded scheme[107].

Margins for PFI consortium partners

The profits flow to the private sector at every level in PFI.

Building firms, banks, business consultants and other PFI hangers-on eagerly anticipate a generous flow of profits as the first hospital schemes take shape. As we have seen with Carillion, where these margins are squeezed it can force all kinds of risky behaviour by the construction firms to maintain dividends – even at the expense of large scale borrowing.

It's clear that in recent years the biggest returns have not come from the construction of new hospitals, but from financing and other support services once the construction is complete.

That was not always the case. An investigation in the *Health Service Journal* showed building contractors "expecting returns of up to 20 percent a year on the equity stakes they hold in the project companies" as soon as the building is complete and Trusts start paying up for the use of the new buildings.

Consultancy firms, too – architects, engineers and surveyors – are used to pocketing above average fees for work on PFI schemes. As

---

[106] Gaffney, D. Pollock, A.M., Price, D. and Shaoul, J (1999) NHS Capital expenditure and the Private Finance Initiative - expansion or contraction? *BMJ,* 319; 48-51 (3 July).
[107] House of Commons Public Accounts Committee 44th report (2011) *Lessons from PFI and other projects*
https://publications.parliament.uk/pa/cm201012/cmselect/cmpubacc/1201/1201.pdf

the *HSJ* article pointed out: "there is little chance of the construction industry losing interest in PFI hospitals." [108]

Fewer beds for the buck

The first wave of PFI hospitals were by no means as expensive to build as the later schemes were to become: but they became notorious for the scale of the cuts in bed numbers they represented, with reductions in front-line acute beds ranging from 20% to 40%. These bed numbers were based not on the actual experience of front-line Trusts dealing with current levels of caseload, or on any actual examples of hospital practice in this country, but on the wildly over-optimistic projections of private sector management consultants working for PFI consortia.

PFI planners wanted to axe almost 40% of beds in **Hereford** (from 414 to 250) and **North Durham** (from 750 to 450). The newly-opened North Durham Hospital was plunged into an immediate beds crisis[109].

Hereford Hospital was forced to hang on to its crumbling war-time hutted wards for years after the brand new, smaller hospital opened up next to them[110]. In Worcestershire the Health Authority forced through plans for a PFI-funded **Worcester** Royal Infirmary which would cut 260 acute beds –a county-wide cutback of 33%: it caused a desperate shortage of beds, while the PFI hospital forced the Trust deep into the red, problems from which health services in Worcestershire have still not recovered in 2018.[111]

In **West Hertfordshire** a plan was drawn up (but eventually never fully implemented) for a single site acute hospital with a 50% reduction in capacity from the four relatively modern hospitals

---

[108] *Health Service Journal* [1999] Profits for Industry, May 13.

[109] Smith, R.(1999) Perfidious Financial Idiocy, *BMJ* 318(3July).

[110] Lister, J. (2003) *Voices from the Frontline, the PFI Experience*, UNISON, London, available https://healthemerRencv.org.uk/pdf/PFI experience.pdf

[111] According to Trust Board papers Worcestershire Acute Hospitals Trust was over £40m in deficit in January 2018. See also the analysis for London South Bank University of the county's Sustainability and Transformation Plan by Boyle, S. Lister, J. and Steer, R (2017) available https://drive.google.eom/file/d/0BwNevFaFmi8bbilxaHV2UF9tbWM/view

covering the population. [112]

Lesser, but significant bed reductions were also involved in most of the PFI schemes that have been completed: **Bromley's** new £121m hospital had 13% fewer beds than the hospitals it replaced. The hospital went on to develop the country's largest-ever trust financial deficit at that time, and continues to represent a major financial liability: it has been a major factor in the £127m forecast deficit of King's College Hospital Foundation Trust, which took it over after the break-up of South London Hospitals Trust.[113]

After the findings of the NHS Beds Inquiry, commissioned by the Labour government to report on the adequacy of bed numbers, which concluded the NHS was well short of the necessary number of acute beds[114], Alan Milburn became more sensitive to the charge that PFI was further reducing front-line capacity.

After intervening to force the **University College London Hospital** scheme in central London to be expanded to include additional beds (at dramatically increased cost), Milburn insisted that new PFI schemes must at least match the existing numbers of acute beds[115]. This in turn led to a further escalation in the costs of the next generation of PFI schemes.

Staffing levels and privatisation

As Allyson Pollock and colleagues pointed out on the basis of the early PFI schemes, "The most common way of balancing the books is to cut the workforce." PFI business cases for the new hospitals in

---

[112] West Hertfordshire Health Authority (1998) *Choosing the right direction: a public consultation document.*

[113] Clover, B (2018) Teaching trust's deficit to top £100m this year, *HSJ* March 15, available (£) https://www.hsi.co.uk/kings-college-hospital-nhs-foundation-trust/teaching-trusts-deficit-to-top100m-this-year/7021928.article

[114] Available:http://webarchive.nationalarchives.gov.uk/20091106105122/ http://www.dh.gov.uk/en/Publicationsandstatistics/Publications/Publicati onsPolicyAndGuidance/DH_4006701

[115] Milburn, A. (2001) Commons statement February 15, available https://publications.parliament.uk/pa/cm200001/cmhansrd/vo010215/de btext/10215-08.htm

Edinburgh and in North Durham projected cuts in clinical staff of 17% and 22% for respectively. The Edinburgh plan assumed an 18% reduction in clinical staff; North Durham was expected to manage with 14% fewer qualified nursing staff. [116]

In Bromley's PFI hospital project, the Full Business Case projected savings in staff costs of £2.9m a year, which arose, among other things, from "the (13%) reduction in the number of beds and theatres." 136 jobs were to go, including 34 nurses and 8.5 doctors, while the reduction in qualified nursing was to be compensated by a higher ratio of health care assistants. However £3m of the money "saved" had already been squandered on management consultancy by 1997.[117]

But the cutbacks were by no means restricted to clinical staff: staff working in non-clinical support services in the first waves of PFI hospital schemes were routinely "sold on" to private contractors providing "facilities management" for the PFI consortium. Their pay and conditions were safeguarded only by the fragile TUPE (Transfer of Undertakings) rules, which protect only existing staff – leading to a 2-tier system in which new employees were recruited on different term and conditions – and which can easily be circumvented by unscrupulous employers. Persistent

After the 2001 Election, Alan Milburn – in the aftermath of nearly a year of strike action by support staff at **Dudley** Hospitals Trust fighting their compulsory transfer to a private contractor as part of a PFI deal – announced three "pilot" schemes, in which support services would be separated from the financing of the new building, and there followed negotiations with the unions on a Retention of Employment agreement, enshrined in regulation in 2006[118], by which NHS staff would be seconded to the management of the private sector. This now applies to staff working in a number of later PFI

---

[116] Pollock, A.M. Dunnigan, M.G. Gaffney, D. Price, D. Shaoul, J. (1999) Planning the "new" NHS: downsizing for the 21st century, *BMJ* vol 319 17 July pp 179-184)

[117] Lister (2001) *PFI in the NHS: A Dossier*, report for GMB, available https://healthemergency.org.uk/pdf/PFI%20in%20the%20NHS%20-%20a%20dosier%20-%20for%20GMB%20-%202001.pdf

[118] http://www.hrmguide.co.uk/law/retention-of-employment-model.htm

hospitals, including Mid Yorkshire Hospitals, as well as more recent schemes in Liverpool and the Midland Metropolitan Hospital in Birmingham.

However the inclusion of a Retention of Employment model is no guarantee that all of the existing staff will be retained in their jobs: for example in the Business case for the Midland Metropolitan Hospital 78% of the proposed cost-cutting "efficiencies" centre on savings on pay, with a near-halving of numbers of non-clinical staff.[119]

Squeeze on clinical staff

The inclusion of all non-clinical support services in rigid, legally-binding "unitary payments" effectively top-sliced from Trust budgets under PFI creates a new pressure on staff in clinical services.

Clinical services become the only area of Trust spending where Trust managers can seek the "cost improvements" and "efficiency savings" which they are required to make each year by government and by NHS purchasing bodies.

As the then **Wellhouse** Trust was told in the negotiations over the new **Barnet General** Hospital – where even medical records were to be incorporated into a PFI contract in a new computerised system:

> "Part of the price … has been to agree to an indexation regime which has no in-built cost improvement and is linked to the published RPI index … The Trust will not therefore be in a position to impose Cost Improvement Programme targets across most of its support and operational services. … The scope for future mandatory CIP targets will be limited to clinical services and to the few support services remaining under the management of the Trust." [120]

---

[119] Lister J. (2016) The Right Hospital and the Right Size? Report for Birmingham Keep Our NHS Public
https://healthcampaignstogether.com/pdf/Final%20update%20The%20Right%20Hospital%20-%20and%20the%20right%20size.pdf
[120] Green, B.(1997) *Deputy PFI Director Report to Barnet Health Authority*, 23July. London, Barnet Health Authority.

Poor quality buildings

Unveiling the latest round of PFI schemes receiving the rubber stamp, Alan Milburn argued that:

"For too long investment in NHS infrastructure has been a low priority when it should have been a high priority. Capital investment in the NHS was lower at the end of the last Parliament than it was at the beginning. The consequences are plain for all to see. Buildings that are shoddy, equipment that is unreliable, hospitals that are out of date. In too many places the environment that staff work in and patients receive care is simply unacceptable." [121]

But the experience since PFI has been NEW buildings which are shoddy and NEW equipment that is unreliable – at a higher price than before.

After just a few months of the first PFI hospitals coming on stream there were problems in Carlisle, in Dartford, in North Durham, and less publicised problems with the fabric and design of the building in many other PFI hospitals. Many of these are itemised by staff interviewed in PFI hospitals by this author in 2002.[122]

Smaller schemes can prove pro rata even more disastrous than larger ones, and the combination of PFI with mental health services has proved to be just as hazardous as the more routine deals in the acute sector.

In the autumn of 2003 a devastating report by private consultants for East London and City Mental Health Trust laid bare a whole raft of major problems that had hit a new £12.5m mental health unit in Newham built using PFI.

The report, a copy of which was later leaked to London Health Emergency, made it clear that the new building was too small, in the wrong place, poorly designed, poorly built, and suffered from poor quality support services from the private consortium.

---

[121] DoH PressRelease2001,as reported by Boseley, S. (2001) 29 new hospitals to be built, *Guardian* February16, available https://www.theguardian.com/uk/2001/feb/16/sarahboseley1
[122] Lister, J. (2003) *Voices from the Frontline, the PFI Experience*, UNISON, London, available https://healthemerRencv.org.uk/pdf/PFI experience.pdf

Almost every paragraph of the 36-page report from consultancy firm Hornagold & Hills pointed to another basic flaw in the process that had led to the Newham unit's completion:

- The bidding and negotiating process was delayed, but even after two years the contract did not adequately specify the obligations of the PFI consortium.

- No details were specified of acceptable room temperatures or lighting levels.

- The architects' full fees were not paid, and so the architects did not inspect works, certify completion or identify defects.

- No drawings existed of the finished building.

- The original design provided no office space at all – and the resultant reorganisation to squeeze in offices left some admin staff having to pass through wards to go in and out.

- The ward arrangement made gender segregation impossible.

- Cold water tanks on the ground floor meant that all water had to be pumped into the building, and at opening there was a 'total failure of water supply'.

- The wrong specification baths were used, but the proper replacements were too big to go through the doors.

- The wrong specification windows were used: standard windows are unsuitable for a mental health establishment, and have suffered damage and broken handles.

- A number of toilets were not connected to drains, "leading to obvious problems".

- The site was polluted and released methane, raising serious hazards for smokers.

- Floor coverings were defective, alarm and call systems unreliable, emergency systems non-functional, staff were ill informed and alienated, and the contractor has been 'uncooperative and adversarial'.[123]

Worryingly, managers clearly wanted to keep these real problems

---

[123] Hornagold &Hills (2003) *Post project evaluation report.* Prepared for East London Community and mental Health Trust, November 4, available https://healthemergency.org.uk/press/Newhamdocument.pdf

quiet, which would potentially prevent other PFI schemes from learning any lessons from the Newham fiasco.

Loss of additional income (car parking, shops, catering, etc.)

While private consortia may generously offer to carry the 'risk' that income from such sources as car parking charges and rent from shops, cafes and restaurants on the hospital site may fall below expected levels, the fact is that these streams of funding might previously have gone to the Trust, but under PFI become just another income stream for the consortium and its shareholders.

These are just some of the changes that will be ushered in when private firms own the hospital and its surrounding facilities.

Land assets stripped: NHS as tenant

Many PFI deals are part-funded by handing over to the consortium "spare" NHS land and building assets released as part of the new scheme. Although this defrays some of the initial costs – and therefore reduces the monthly "unitary charge" which it must pay, the Trust then becomes a tenant, renting its key acute facilities from the private sector.

This has important consequences for the future:

First, once the NHS assets – paid for over the generations by the taxpayer – have been passed over in this way, the Trust no longer has any scope to use them in future service developments. And at the end of the contract period, the NHS Trust is likely to be in a weak position to negotiate over a further extension of the lease agreement.

Second, the PFI deal effectively locks the Trust in to a long-term commitment to maintain services around the new hospital or PFI-funded facilities – no matter what changes may take place in local health needs, medical techniques or population over the next 25-60 years. The flexibility of owning land and buildings and being able to take decisions over how they should be used is seriously reduced.

And the third major problem comes when the package of land and property is traded in as part of a PFI deal at much less than its eventual market value: Edinburgh's Royal Infirmary PFI involved handing over property assets that turned out to be worth as much as the new hospital, but only a fraction of this value came back to the

Trust.[124]

Refinancing: another private sector rip-off

Huge bonus profits can be made by PFI companies which refinance the deal as soon as the most "risky" phase – of constructing the hospital – is complete.

Octagon, the consortium that financed and built the £220m Norfolk & Norwich Hospital refinanced the deal and scooped a bonus £115m – almost half the initial cost – in windfall gains. Just £34m of this was shared with the Trust, and that to be paid in the form of a £1.7m cut in the annual fees for use of the building and support services. The remaining £81m has no doubt been wisely invested in yachts, claret and caviar by Octagon's gleeful shareholders. The deal, later branded by the Tory head of the Commons Public Accounts Committee as the "unacceptable face of capitalism" was even more amazing when we realise that the five firms behind the Octagon Healthcare consortium invested just £30m of their own money in the project. [125, 126]

Other NHS hospitals which have generated a healthy hand-out for shareholders are **Dartford**, where a third of the refinancing gain was shared with the Trust, but the Trust found its 28-year contract extend to 35 years as part of the deal, and **Bromley**.

As more PFI hospitals come on stream, we can expect more refinancing deals to surface, within which the NHS Trusts will receive at best only a portion while shouldering much of the real risk, underlining once more how unequal is the "partnership" and "risk sharing" between public and private sectors.

---

[124] Lister, J. (2003) *The PFI Experience: Voices from the frontline*, UNISON, available https://healthemergency.org.uk/pdf/PFI_experience.pdf

[125] Monbiot, G. (2001) Bleeding the hospitals, *The Guardian* June 5, availablehttps://www.theguardian.com/politics/2001/jun/05/election2001.politicalcolumnists2.

[126]https://publications.parliament.uk/pa/cm200506/cmselect/cmpubacc/694/694.pdf

Part 2: the practice

Chapter 4

Laying the basis for PFI: from Pinderfields & Pontefract to Mid Yorkshire Hospitals Trust

The promise of a new hospital on the Pinderfields Hospital site in Wakefield dates back to the 1960s. In the early 1980s staff were being told that the building of a new hospital was imminent: it's fortunate none of them held their breath waiting. But the period under discussion in this book begins in 1992, the year the Private Finance Initiative was first formulated as a policy (and the year UNISON began to be formed from a merger of three major health unions, NUPE, COHSE and NALGO).

In that year both Pinderfields and Pontefract hospitals submitted separate bids to form NHS trusts in the aftermath of the 1990 "internal market" reforms designed at the instigation of Margaret Thatcher and implemented under John Major. Both of the trust applications (in common with so many other applications to form hospital trusts in that period) promised to increase 'local' involvement and local control of health services, and that the new trusts would borrow to build new facilities.

The air of unreality was underlined by the lack of any business plan or projected financial balance sheet for the new trusts. Ever since then such plans have been at best skimpy and misleading, and the subsequent emergence of a single trust covering Wakefield Pontefract and Dewsbury has simply expanded the scale of this weakness.

The Pinderfields application went as far as to promise to build a new hospital, "opening in 1998," which at that point appeared to have secured the support of the Regional Health Authority and an allocation from its capital programme (Application for NHS trust status, p13) – although of course we now know that no such money would be available. In fact the funding for the Pinderfields plan, along with many other NHS capital projects, was effectively supplanted after 1992 by PFI.

In blithe ignorance of the changes coming through, the

application document declared that the top "imperative" for the Trust would be:

"To progress the redevelopment of the Pinderfields site. ... Plans are well advanced, with the new hospital opening in April 1998" (p5)

These illusions were maintained during the limited consultation on the trust application, but soon afterwards were at least partly dispelled. By the end of the first full year of Trust status (1993-94) the Pinderfields Trust Annual Report noted:

"We suffered a setback with our plans for a new District General Hospital. Our innovative scheme was not given the go ahead despite its forward thinking, patient centred approach because of limited capital funding and a developing national policy encouraging increased patient care in the community." (p33)

Here again we now know that this was an inaccurate picture of the real priorities driving NHS policy: in practice even the proclaimed NHS commitment to care in the community was soon to be set aside in the quest for funding for a new acute hospital that effectively soaked up all the available capital and revenue resources in the area.

The trust application also stepped up the hypocritical professions of concern for NHS staff which have recurred at varying intervals, interspersed by policies that demonstrate very different concerns – not least of course the very submission of the application for NHS trust status without any endorsement from staff or their organisations.

This has continued right up to 2018, when we can see the same happy-clappy rhetoric attached to cynical moves to hive off hundreds of NHS support staff into a separate "Special Purpose Vehicle" company that would aim both to dodge VAT payments, and also undermine their NHS terms and conditions and step towards a 2-tier workforce).[127]

In 1992 the misleading rhetoric was quite shameless:

"Our staff will know that they are our most important asset,

---

[127] *Union Eyes* no 25, Winter 2017-18

and we will promote an environment which allows the skills and energies of our staff to develop and flourish and in which teamwork, personal growth and recognition of the value of the individual are encouraged; and that we will develop and introduce an Employee's Charter to demonstrate and increase this" (p7)

There was more in the same vein, plus an ominous threat to vary terms and conditions:

"A more distinct identity and philosophy will enable us to build an even better relationship with … staff. Trust status accords the power to vary Whitley provisions. This added flexibility will allow us better to reward good performance." (pp8-9)

However a later reference to the same point assured staff that:

"The Trust intends to reflect Whitley Council and Pay Review Body agreements for the purpose of determining pay, and does not intend to offer less than Whitley rates." (p27)

The application expressed such confidence that the range of services after achieving trust status would remain the same that the UNISON branch questioned the reason for 'opting out' in the first place.

However the inherent instability created by the competitive "internal market" regime that separated purchasers (the District Health Authorities and fund-holding GPs) from providers also emerges: despite all the illusions of autonomy, the new Trust would only be able to operate along lines supported by its main purchasers:

"Future developments will be dictated by purchasing intentions, the need to respond to changing patient needs and by operational capacity." (p13)

Market-driven merger

By 1994, just two years after separate applications for trust status, the extent to which the plans and services of the two trusts were being dictated by the purchasers was revealed when Pinderfields and Pontefract trusts published their plan for merger – entitled *A Health Strategy for Wakefield.*

As Wakefield's Labour MP David Hinchliffe pointed out:

"The proposal to combine the two health Trusts covering the Wakefield district amounts to an admission by the Health Authority that a health market cannot work at local level.

"All the MPs representing the Wakefield district recognise that such a move will lead to yet further cuts and closures in our local health service. "The answers to the problems facing the health service in Wakefield and elsewhere will not be found through mergers and rationalisation.

"We need to rid ourselves completely of the market approach and get back to the basic founding principles of the NHS."[128]

The UNISON response argued from the outset that the merger would simply be a prelude to a process of centralisation and rationalisation.

"The result of the merger would be to trigger a process of 'centralisation' and rationalisation which would lead to either Pontefract or Pinderfields hospital being reduced to little more than cottage hospital status—and, since this would not be financially viable in today's NHS market, closed down." (p2)

Rather than address these issues upfront, the consultation document led local people "around the houses" in an extended diversionary discussion of secondary questions. Indeed the branch complained of the lack of specifics and poor quality of the document, most of which was:

"little more than a 'fill in the blanks' identikit text on health promotion issues, apparently bought off the peg from the Department of Health, and currently doing the rounds under one title or another in almost every district in the country." (p2)

Like many areas, the most pressing concern for local people in Wakefield was not only easy and swift access to high quality primary care, but also access to acute and emergency hospital services which

---

[128] *A strategy for hospital closures*, a response on behalf of Wakefield Hospitals UNISON to the consultation document *A Health Strategy for Wakefield*, September 1994

can deliver treatment when required. This central public concern was not seen as a priority by Wakefield Healthcare: indeed it was not even mentioned in the 6 key objectives on page 7. The Branch was critical of the fact that:

> "Health purchasers in Wakefield and elsewhere, obediently following Department of Health guidelines, are clearly operating on an agenda which runs at a tangent to the views of their local population." (p3)

Not until page 24 of the Strategy did the document address the issues of 'centralisation' and reductions in local services which were implicit in any genuine merger of the Pontefract and Pinderfields Trusts. The UNISON Branch warned that:

> "The word 'centralisation' is itself a euphemism: it would be more honest to spell out the fact that what is under discussion in each case is the closure of one of the two current units. The drive towards a single site provision of acute services means the extinction of the other."

The health authority revealed on page 24 that it was planning "a reduction in the number of obstetric in-patient beds"—severely restricting a woman's ability to choose to have her baby in a hospital. A consequence of the proposed merger would be also to intensify the drive towards a single site for all births in the district, "a single, centralised maternity unit to serve the whole of Wakefield Metropolitan District."

However the centralisation of maternity also implies a centralisation of children's services. The Strategy confirmed that the health authority was examining: "... the future pattern of paediatric medical in-patient facilities.

This would involve consideration of the partial or total centralisation of paediatric services". The same review would also "take into account the need for paediatric support to accident and emergency services, children's surgery and neonatal services."

This pattern of 'centralisation' has since become grimly familiar across the country, and is continuing in 2018 with plans to "merge" services and for "Sustainability and Transformation Plans" across even wider geographical areas: the whole of West Yorkshire has now been bundled up into a single STP.

Reducing bed numbers

The Strategy indeed went on to question the need to retain the current number of acute in-patient beds (then 1,195 general and acute beds between the two trusts)[129], suggesting that instead there might be a move to shift services "from existing hospital settings".

UNISON questioned the assumptions implicit in these proposals, arguing that:

> "There is an automatic, unproven assumption that such changes would be readily accepted by patients; but there is also a hidden and doubtful assumption that the new model of providing care outside of hospitals is cheaper." (p4)

The 1980s had seen cash pressures and government policies wipe out almost all of the remaining cottage and community hospitals, using the argument that all such services should be centralised on general hospital sites.

However by 1994 NHS managers appeared to be turning full circle, arguing for cuts and closures in general hospitals – and for services to be dispersed once more to small community units.

Arguing that Pinderfields and Pontefract hospitals were "only 9 miles apart" the first draft of the Strategy began to move towards promoting a "centralisation of some services" – a phrase largely avoided in the subsequent "final document" produced after the consultation, in 1995. It was clear that the merging trusts would seek to 'rationalise' services onto either the Pinderfields or the Pontefract hospital site.

This was refined in the final draft into a series of 4 options which included "do nothing"; redistribution of specialties; separating out services into an emergency hospital and an elective site, and building a new hospital (which of course required "major capital investment"). (pp32-34) As we now know, the eventual outcome was a combination of the two, with a much reduced new hospital being built at Pontefract without acute in-patient beds, while emergency services and many specialist services were concentrated in Wakefield.

---

[129] *Bed availability for England 1992-93*, DoH, Government Statistical Service 1993

One major driver in this process as far back as 1994 was the growing financial pressure: the final draft referred to a "newly introduced capitation based formula for establishing health authority funding levels" which pointed to Wakefield being already funded at £7m above its new target level, and implied a squeeze to redress this. And more generally, as the first draft sums up:

> "Pressures already exist within the current situation, including almost £2m non-recurring support to contracts.... In view of the uncertainty surrounding allocations at the present time and the current economic climate, it does not seem appropriate to assume any growth in revenue allocations ..." (Strategy p5).

Nonetheless the merger process that had begun with the Strategy document in 1994 dragged on into 1996. In July 1996, with a formal plan for merger from the two trusts on the table, Tory Health Secretary Stephen Dorrell stated in the Commons that any trust merger proposal would be judged on the basis of how patient care was to be improved.

This proved to be a deceptive statement; the key driver in all these changes was finance.

A rebuilt Pinderfields – for £37m?

The proposal to merge Pinderfields and Pontefract Trusts was set out in a joint application document Working *Together for a Healthier Future*.

UNISON's response, an 8-page brochure entitled *A Blank Cheque for Closures*, was published in August 1996.

At the centre of the merger was a £37m scheme, to be funded through the Private Finance Initiative (PFI) to rebuild Pinderfields.

The estimated cost seems inconceivable now, and proved to be hyper-optimistic: but the first wave of PFI-funded hospitals did come in at an average of less than £100m per hospital, with South Durham costed at £41m and one which involved a rebuild on an existing site (Barnet General) at £54m[130].

---

[130] Sussex, J. (2001) *The economics of the Private Finance Initiative in the NHS,* Office of Health Economics,
https://www.ohe.org/publications/economics-private-finance-initiative-nhs

UNISON however warned that:

"Both Trusts have been following the rules of the government's Private Finance Initiative, and business consortia are being promised the opportunity to make lavish profits not only from the building projects, but also from associated land deals, retail opportunities and long-term contracts to provide support services." (p3)

The *Working Together* document admits that the financial pressures on the two trusts are a major factor forcing the merger:

"The two acute Trusts have faced significant financial pressures during the past three years. Increased demand for services, pressures to reduce waiting lists and the shift of resources from hospital services to develop primary and community care have all contributed to a growing problem. In the current financial year 1996/7 both Trusts are again faced with significant cost improvement measures in order to meet the statutory financial targets." (page 27)

UNISON emphasised this problem, and the fact that so far trust status had not delivered the previous promises:

"It should be remembered that this new Trust application takes place amid the wreckage of the hopes, promises and plans offered up in the original applications, submitted back in 1992.

"None of the promised advantages of Trust status has yet been forthcoming to either Pinderfields or Pontefract as an individual unit: and there is little prospect of patients or staff gaining any benefit from the latest package of proposals, which set out to obscure more than they explain."(p1)

The Branch questioned the significance of the Working Together document's claim to be "integrating" services. Noting that the proposals for ENT services almost certainly implied just one unit to serve the Wakefield Metropolitan District, it went on:

"The same proviso seems certain to apply to the plans for new "local" provision of MRl scanner services. It is most improbable that two such units are proposed: but it is obvious that whichever hospital were to be chosen as the location of the new MRl unit would be the prime favourite to

97

become the focus for other specialties and for front-line emergency services. This new, necessary investment could help trigger a new process of 'centralisation' between Pinderfields and Pontefract.

"Without such rationalisation of units, it is hard to see how the merged Trust could achieve its goal of "economies of scale" (page 27). This, too, implies running fewer, larger units, with the closure of services at one site or the other." (p3)

UNISON warned that the main targets if jobs were to be axed for efficiency savings were likely to be admin and clerical staff rather than surplus senior managers. The two Trusts had notched up deficits in the years prior to the merger plan, and were projecting a reduction in income of over 5 percent (£6m a year) by 2000, forcing plans to cut non-pay bills by 12 percent and the pay bill by 4 percent.

And the Branch pointed to another broken promise – of increased accountability – which would not be remedied by merging the two trusts:

"We are told that the new merged Trust would promise 'Greater public Involvement': "Openness and accountability will be the hallmarks of a strong partnership with all local communities. ... The Trust will use whatever opportunities it can to enable the public to meet the Trust Board, senior clinicians and managers ..."

"Of course we were promised all -this before: if those promises had meant anything, there would be no way the new Trust could now achieve more public involvement. But of course they didn't." (p4)

To add to the problems, the need to seek PFI funding for the Pinderfields redevelopment made other Trust promises null and void, notably the claims the trust would have "Direct planning of service developments, minimising delays in improvements to services."

UNISON pointed out the painful reality: "This apparent freedom has since been squashed by the bureaucratic nightmare of PFI."

So were hopes of "Direct ownership of assets, enabling the Trust to make the most effective use of land, buildings and equipment." These too were crushed by PFI, which would mean the Trust would have to lease any new or refurbished buildings, equipment and [if standard PFI contracts at that point were any guide] purchase support services from profit-seeking private consortia.

The next move by the Health Authority was to publish a "Green paper" in 1997 (in response to which local people made it abundantly clear that they saw the plans for rationalising services as a finance driven exercise.)

New government – same old problems

June 1997 of course brought a change of government, but for the first three years of New Labour there was no let-up in the financial squeeze on the NHS initiated by the Tories, while the new government was if anything even more enthusiastic in promoting PFI as "the only game in town" for funding new hospitals.

Also in 1997 Wakefield Health Authority brought in management consultants Newchurch & Co. to help draw up plans for service reductions – the first of a long succession of unsuccessful interventions that have taken place ever since from high cost management consultants.

The company's advice was to seek ways of treating fewer patients and reducing the number of beds provided, as well as centralising acute services onto a single site. Newchurch claimed that these measures, especially if land and estate could be released for sale, could help the trust cut its costs by between 8 percent and 14 percent. [131]

Following this advice, yet another strategy document was unveiled by the health authority in 1998, entitled *"Meeting the Challenge for Health Services in the Wakefield District"*. UNISON's 22-page response, published in the summer of 1998 was *The Closure Trap*.

Once more UNISON challenged the drive to rationalisation through the run-down of acute services which included closure of intensive care beds at Pontefract. The Branch noted the strategic aim of replacing both hospitals with a new single-site PFI-funded

---

[131] Price, D., Pollock, A. (2002) *Debts, deficits and service reductions: Wakefield Health Authority's legacy to primary care trusts.* UNISON, London

hospital, and warned that this could also have major implications for services in Dewsbury and as far afield as South Leeds.

And yet again, UNISON argued, the document offered no financial information:

> "The consultation document is exceptional in that it contains no actual financial information whatsoever, despite the fact that in his Foreword the Chief Executive states that one of the driving forces behind the plan is "a legacy from underfunding".

> "The consequences from this legacy of underfunding are not spelt out.

> [...]

> "Incredibly, the plans put forward for consultation have not even been costed in detail. The Authority dismiss such a notion by saying that: "Carrying out a full, costed option appraisal would be time consuming to prepare and would focus attention on detail...."

> "This is a stunning admission. The public are being asked to sign up to a set of proposals involving millions of pounds of tax payers' money, which have not even been costed!

> "In the same paragraph the Authority says that: 'It is important, however, to be confident that the proposals in this document are financially achievable....'

> "How does anybody know, if the proposals haven't been costed? You couldn't run a whelk stall on this basis let alone vital front line health services for 320,000 people." (p5)

Not only were financial numbers missing from the new plan: bed numbers too were completely missing, offering local people no guarantee of future local access to services. In view of the growing commitment to PFI as the route to funding the new hospital, UNISON's response pointed to research conducted by the BMA which had shown that not only did the PFI process result in an average 32% loss of beds, but during the planning process the costs of the PFI schemes escalate by a staggering average of 72 percent.

As we shall see, in Mid Yorkshire Hospitals the increase from the initial costings to the final PFI deal was much higher than 72 percent, soaring upwards from the hugely optimistic hopes of refurbishment and rebuild for just £37m to the eventual hefty £311m PFI deal for new hospitals in Wakefield and Pontefract – an increase of 840%.

The Closure Trap also pointed to the inevitable logic of downgrading Pontefract General Infirmary, and challenged the insistence by local NHS managers that the remaining service could still be regarded as an A&E:

> "The proposed closure of ITU beds at Pontefract is used as a justification for downgrading the hospital's casualty department and removing the acute medical beds. The closure of ITU beds would pull the rug from under Pontefract Hospital and the Health Authority know it.
>
> "It's a nonsense to suggest that a unit which cannot take blue light ambulances or provide ITU support or beds for medical admissions is anything other than a glorified minor injuries unit.
>
> "To suggest that such a unit could still be called an Accident and Emergency Department is both deceptive and potentially extremely dangerous.
>
> "If Pontefract loses its ITU, A&E and medical beds it is effectively killed off as a local district general hospital. The only way to prevent this sequence of events is to halt the closure of the intensive care beds on the site."

UNISON warned that the consultation that was taking place was misleading, since the long term implications of the proposals were a single site acute hospital – despite official denials.

> "Our fear is that if the proposals in the current consultation are pushed through they will be irreversible and will mean that a single acute site for the whole of Wakefield District becomes inevitable despite the fact that no work has yet been done on the implications for such a move for local people.
>
> "If the Health Authority is so keen on the single site option they should be consulting on that right now rather than the half-way house which this latest document represents.
>
> "Apart from our other concerns about the single site option it is simply bad planning to unleash an irreversible chain of events without assessing in advance their long term consequences. That is exactly what Wakefield Health Authority are doing."

It is quite shocking even now to note that the *"Meeting the Challenge"* document openly admitted that the health authority had done no work to assess the access issues raised by their proposals, stating: "We do not feel that it is viable to undertake a review of access issues until such time as potential changes are confirmed."

However, even without having done this work on the impact of their plans, the health authority were proposing a substantial diversion of A&E patients:

> "They suggest that Pinderfields would take around 80,000 out of the 105,000 current A&E cases, leaving the minor injuries unit at Pontefract with just 25,000 cases - a reduction of more than half, and leaving 26,000 people who would currently use Pontefract A&E to travel elsewhere." (*Closure Trap* p16)

UNISON argued an alternative approach; rather than continue to send 140 ITU patients a year out of the district, and further increase that number by closing the three Pontefract ITU beds, why not use the money spent on sending them elsewhere to expand the ITU provision at Pontefract to 5 beds? (p15). Of course this was the opposite of the advice the health authority was getting behind the scenes from their expensive management consultants.

The closure of the ITU beds also became the basis for the plans to centralise the main surgical services at Pinderfields – a possible greenfield site along the "M62 corridor" had been explored and rejected by the health authority in September 1998. In either case Pontefract would be left with no emergency surgical cover. It would be a scaled down facility, open on only a five day a week basis, dealing only with elective work and day cases.

Campaigning

UNISON stepped up the campaigning against these proposals, but the financial imperative, and management consultant advice, continued to push the trust and health authority towards a rationalisation and centralisation of services.

This continued despite the overwhelming rejection of PFI by local people in a referendum organised by the UNISON Branch early in 1999 through the local *Wakefield Express*. An astonishing 81% of local people voting said they would prefer to have no new local hospital than one funded privately through PFI.

The Wakefield campaigners secured the referendum by invoking a little-known clause in the 1972 Local Government Act 1972 to trigger a local referendum. The Branch had also enlisted campaigning comedian Mark Thomas to help build local awareness of the issues posed by PFI. The result did not deliver the size of vote the Branch and the newspaper hoped would take part, but nonetheless in the referendum vote 87% of people voting endorsed the principle of full public funding of local hospitals, while 72% supported the principle of only using public sector capital to build new hospitals.[132]

Nor was the Health Authority willing to learn from the rebuff by the Department of Health, which rejected the initial *Meeting the Challenge* proposals. A Strategic Outline Case for investment in the new single site hospital, submitted by the Pinderfields and Pontefract Trust with the Health Authority in 1998 was also bounced back in a letter from Health Minister John Denham, in the summer of 1999.[133] Denham dismissed the plans as insufficiently developed.[134]

The DHA however was undeterred by their repeated failure to convince ministers of either main party that their plans held water. Within a few months yet another scheme had been drawn up, this time a daunting 74 pages long: it also added a more unusual title, *Grasping the Nettle* (October 1999).

UNISON's response, published in December 1999, dismissed the plans as *Clutching at Straws*.

UNISON's was by no means the only critical response. The Health Authority itself conceded in its response to the consultation (p180) that the "apparent consensus" around the development of an acute specialist centre with supporting ambulatory care

> "must be tempered by consideration of the 2,000 or so pro-forma responses which raised key questions about the future of Pontefract and its hospital services."

Among the more concise and critical statements was the

---

[132] *Health Emergency*, Summer 1999, p3

[133] *Grasping the Nettle: Outcome of consultation*, February 2000, p4

[134] Price & Pollock (2002), p8.

Pinderfields and Pontefract Trust JTUC, whose Secretary Ian Stevens wrote a tough response in January 2000, which began by challenging the Health Authority's assertions that it was "working in partnership," and pointing out the reality:

> "The great majority of staff whom we represent in this partner organisation have no real involvement in decision-making"

The JTUC noted that the plans to reduce local bed provision came before any report had been published from the Beds Inquiry commissioned by Health Secretary Frank Dobson (which only became available in February 2000 after the consultation had closed), and highlighted the contrasting attitude between the NHS Confederation, representing health authorities and trusts nationally, pressing for more acute beds, while Wakefield's health authority and trust were arguing for a reduction.

The local Community Health Council's response from Chair Fred Walker also argued that:

> "the health authority has vastly underestimated the number of acute beds the district requires. Whilst there have been no bed numbers indicated in the plans for the intermediate care, we are faced with an increasing aged population who will require access to both acute and intermediate care. If all major trauma is to be dealt with at the acute specialist centre, then more beds will be needed not less."

The JTUC went on to warn of the implications of projected reductions in trust income of £12m (more than 10 percent) over the next 7 years: of course we now know this was one issue which did fundamentally change later in 2000, with the unveiling of the NHS Plan for ten years of sustained above inflation investment in the NHS. However in the final months of 1999 when *Grasping the Nettle* was written there was little to suggest this would be the case.

Intermediate care

Another important point flagged up by the JTUC response was that the proposed introduction of "intermediate care" required the health authority and local trusts to put a structure in place, and warned "there is not even a blueprint at present".

UNISON's response pointed out that yet again local people had been confronted with an inconclusive document, but warned that behind this were worrying issues:

> "At first sight "Grasping the Nettle" is not a proper Consultation Document at all: it makes no overt recommendation, and insists that it wants the local community to "tell us your thoughts" after studying the limited range of options as interpreted by the HA itself.
>
> "But a closer reading of the document shows how the information presented is selected and angled to urge the reader to accept as "inevitable" the same type of service rationalisation and the same single site option which local people overwhelmingly rejected last time."

Foreshadowing the concerns of the JTUC, UNISON also questioned the seriousness of the WHA plans which could involve the transfer of the equivalent of up to 40,000 acute bed days of treatment (equivalent to as many as 8,000 episodes of care) from hospital to the community or even primary care. UNISON comments:

> "The health authority offers no convincing explanation of how the necessary resources would be put in place to enable this new style of treatment to be carried out. We would ask for clarification on the following:
>
> • Where will the proposed "intermediate" beds be situated?
> • Where will staff be recruited and trained?
> • Who will be in charge?
> • Where will they work from?"

In similar vein UNISON also questioned whether the Health Authority had properly taken account of the pressures that would rise in Wakefield if emergency services were concentrated there:

> "Even if up to 20% of current caseload could be diverted to a minor injuries unit, a single A&E unit would, according to WHA's own figures in 1998, expect to deal with upwards of 80,000 first attenders – comparatively few of them minor cases.
>
> "Not only is this dramatically larger than either existing unit,

it would make the Wakefield A&E one of the largest in the country – creating a substantial requirement for acute beds on site, as well as posing new staffing issues.

"It is likely that up to 25% of A&E first attenders (20,000 a year) could require immediate admission to hospital, which at current English levels would require over 300 beds. Nurses and staff working in radiography, pathology and other support services would be under constant pressure.

"WHA does not discuss this aspect of its plan." (p3)

Reduction in funding

Also unexplained was the abrupt shift of policy in *Grasping the Nettle* compared with recent strategy documents in 1998 and 1999, which had shown spending on acute hospital services remaining constant for seven years ahead. We now know that this was the result of the Newchurch consultancy work and their recommended plan to scale down services to match resources. This meant a drastic change (as the JTUC also noted):

> "The new figures show that spending on acute hospital services is now expected to reduce by £12m (over 10 percent) in the eight years to 2006/07, while community and mental health service spending is projected to remain almost unchanged.
>
> "… cash allocated to the unexplained "Primary Care Shift" - which is not discussed anywhere in the Consultation Document - will rocket from zero to £9m.
>
> "This suggests that WHA expects the main burden of caring for patients to switch from hospitals **not** to community services but to **primary care,** in a new system that has not been explained in the Consultation Document.
>
> "There is no precedent in this country for such a major switch from hospital to primary care. UNISON is concerned that WHA appears to be offering an untested, experimental model of care which could prove unable to cope with the needs of local people." (*Clutching at Straws* p4)

UNISON notes the substantial expected increase in numbers of older people in the local population, and questions whether local GPs willing to undertake more responsibility for the care of frail elderly patients at home and for patients discharged more quickly from Hospital, asking "Do they have the time, the staff and the resources to do so?"

Clutching at Straws also pointed out that the consultation document was heavily loaded in favour of the two options the DHA wanted to secure:

> "WHA has set out to draft a Consultation Document which puts no explicit proposal, but which rules out in advance the most likely views of local people. The evidence is loaded in favour of two principal options favoured by the health authority, while the others are effectively dismissed out of hand - regardless of local views.
>
> [...]
>
> "Only Options 4 and 5 are regarded as meriting 'serious consideration', of which Option 5 'a new single district general hospital' is described by WHA as offering 'the most improvement in clinical safety and quality of acute services'."

The UNISON response went beyond criticism to point out positive alternatives, including proposals similar to those raised by Kidderminster Health Care Trust, which argued for a county-wide reorganisation of services to retain three general hospitals in Worcestershire, to be covered by "a single integrated medical workforce" – as an alternative to that health authority's proposals for a centralised service in Worcester, with the loss of local services in Kidderminster.

A joint document published by the BMA, the Royal College of Surgeons and the Royal College of Physicians had also suggested an alternative to centralising services in a single site district hospital:

> "Where possible neighbouring acute general hospitals could cooperate or merge to enable the provision of more comprehensive and specialist acute and emergency services."

In Scotland, too, (where government guidance has been very different from the pressure to rationalise and centralise south of the border) the findings of a major Acute Services Review published by the Scottish Office in 1998 was that:

"It is important to stress that concentration of services in larger acute hospitals is not the only way of achieving critical mass and increased volumes of activity in any drive of optimise the quality of care and outcomes.

"The managed clinical network approach is grounded on the premise that appropriate clinical skills, expertise and facilities are available across the network to provide high quality care."

By contrast the Wakefield proposals offered little guarantee of delivering the savings required, but a certainty of substantially increased costs. One of the first PFI hospitals, Carlisle had just revealed enough of its final business case for analysts to work out that the new hospital was costing the trust an extra £3.5m a year, but resulting in 25 percent fewer beds. The "savings" included the axing 70 nursing posts among 100 clinical jobs.

The projected cost of the new Wakefield Hospital had by this point already rocketed almost 5-fold from £37m to £176m in the 4 years since 1976. It was to rise even further before the deal was signed.

Brushing aside all of the concerns and questions over viability that had been raised in the consultation, the Health Authority response to the consultation, in February 2000, agreed four recommendations, the most important of which was the second one: to move ahead with an Acute Specialist Centre model based at Pinderfields – the Newchurch plan.

A management Team Brief revealed that in a token gesture to the many critics of the plan, the DHA would agree to "a limited delay in making decisions about short-term change to allow time for further work" (maybe filling in some of the many missing figures). The two other recommendations were a commitment to take national policy guidelines into account, and a vague commitment to a "collaborative planning process".

The DHA response also, interestingly gave "Categorical assurances" to the public in Dewsbury that "it is not our intention to have an adverse impact on services in Dewsbury District Hospital" (p17). Maybe it was true that this was not intended – so few of the potential knock-on effects had been properly taken into consideration

– but it's clear that the subsequent Trust merger with Dewsbury and more recent downgrade of Dewsbury's acute services have made a complete nonsense of that commitment.

The DHA was shifty and evasive in its response to the newly published National Bed Inquiry, promising only that "bed number projections will continue to be reviewed…" and that "plans for bed numbers will be sufficiently flexible": but the underlying resistance to revisit their assumptions was spelled out in the statement

> "Committing to excess bed numbers will mean fixed capital investment which will in turn mean less money for service elsewhere in the network". (p16)

The DHA had clearly forgotten that nobody was asking for them to build excess numbers of beds – simply wanting them to maintain and not cut provision. It was their plan that involved spending huge sums on a new hospital – and reducing bed numbers.

Merger with Dewsbury – the Mid Yorkshire trust is formed

However the delays turned out to be much greater than the DHA had hoped: in fact the new hospital project was not that much further along the line a year and a half later, when the proposal to merge the Pinderfields & Pontefract trust with Dewsbury hospital was put out for consultation towards the end of 2001.

Once again UNISON's response *A Pig in a Poke* (January 2002) focused on the wider and longer term implications of the merger, noting that:

> "UNISON's principal reservations over these proposals centre on the potential future implication that services may be further centralised after the merger has taken place. This would almost certainly create problems of accessibility to key services for local patients in the Pontefract or Dewsbury areas."

UNISON shared the wish to find ways to pool and make effective use of scarce reserves of professional and specialist staff, and to minimise unnecessary overhead management costs, but:

> "our strong support for the need for two fully functioning A&E units to service the Wakefield and Pontefract area has been well documented in previous consultation exercises. We are therefore concerned to ensure that any new mergers

with neighbouring Trusts are done in such a way as to consolidate and expand the local availability of services including A&E, and not in any way to reduce them."

This time there seemed to be some grounds for hope that the approach might be different. The chairs and chief executives of both merging Trusts declared in the Foreword that "When we talk about merger we mean bringing together our managements. We do not mean closing hospitals or cutting services." The management document also offered what appeared to be an explicit commitment:

"In the proposed merged Trust, acute services would continue to be provided on three hospital sites, i.e. at Dewsbury and District Hospital, Pinderfields General Hospital and Pontefract General Infirmary. Each hospital would retain a strong identity and local management and would develop close relationships with its local primary care trust." (p6)

Of course we now know that things have turned out very differently, and that these assurances were no more than tactical attempts to defuse opposition.

The consultation document explained that the proposed launch of the Primary Care Trust for North Kirklees, and the development of a specialist mental health services Trust would effectively strip away services [and therefore revenue] from the Dewsbury Trust, warning that these changes would: "significantly reduce the size of Dewsbury Health Care NHS trust, leaving it too small to maintain high quality services by itself."

UNISON noted that among the many omissions in the consultation document was "even the semblance of a business plan to demonstrate financial viability."

"The vagueness and lack of serious preparation of the merger plan are shown by the absence in the consultation document of any financial appraisal of the two merging Trusts, or any analysis of their recent record in measuring up to government financial targets."

In what proved to be a telling and prescient point, the Branch warned:

"UNISON is concerned that the merger may be seen by the

Pinderfields and Pontefract Trust board as a way of spreading the cost of the new hospital across a larger Trust with additional commissioning bodies and sources of income."

There were also concerns over the potential combined caseload an inadequate capacity if emergency services were centralised at a new Pinderfields hospital:

"If a single Pinderfields A&E unit were required to handle all of the more serious emergencies from the 177,000 combined A&E caseload to be expected in a merged Trust, it would require a substantial expansion in beds and other support services above and beyond the existing PFI scheme – which we have been told (p2) is not being changed as a result of the merger plan."

Not for the first time, the Branch sharply criticised the flimsy content of the merger plan:

"UNISON is concerned that such a flimsy and insubstantial consultation document is seen as sufficient to lay the basis for a merger of a Trust with £136m assets and an annual turnover of £207m."

Strategic Outline Case – shredded

In April 2002 UNISON published a detailed report on the developing situation in Wakefield, commissioned from two leading academics, David Price of the University of Northumbria, and Professor Allyson Pollock, then at University College, London. Entitled *Debts deficits and service reductions, Wakefield Health Authority's legacy to Primary Care Trusts,* it focused on the revised and resubmitted Strategic Outline Case, which had been drawn up two years previously by the DHA and the Pinderfields and Pontefract trust.

Many of the features of this SOC were already familiar: the plan to centralise acute services on the Pinderfields site; the plan to finance the new hospital through PFI; the downgrade of Pontefract, which would cease to be a District General Hospital, losing all its acute inpatient beds and become largely an outpatient and day case centre, as well as losing smaller hospitals in Castleford and Hemsworth (Southmoor) as well as Clayton in Wakefield. Acute bed numbers would be cut by 24% by 2007, with acute care to be re-provided in undisclosed "intermediate care settings" in North Kirklees, Wakefield and Pontefract.

> "'Intermediate care' is not defined in the SOC but is central to the strategy. The plan involves building 148 new intermediate care beds in the medium-term (i.e., by 2003-04), with a total of 328 intermediate care beds in the long-term (by 2006-07). However the SOC does not make clear where the new intermediate care capacity will be provided, how it will be staffed and funded, or whether it will be in the NHS or in the chargeable private and local government sectors."[135]

The SOC proposals were for a new building, costed at £176m. This is equivalent to £210m after inflation, of which the vast majority (£164m) was for the new Pinderfields Hospital, £17m was for Pontefract and £12m for intermediate care in North Kirklees. A further £20m would be required for investment in intermediate care. Some of this money was to be raised through sales of existing assets and sites, but 93 percent was to come from PFI.

Price and Pollock (p14) point out that while the SOC calculated that in the unlikely event of securing public funding the scheme would increase the capital value of the trust almost four-fold and result in an additional £21m per year in capital charges, there is no estimate made of the cost of the PFI contract "unitary charge".

Price and Pollock also argue (p15) that from previous PFI experience a costly element of the eventual cost is the additional costs of financing the loans required by the consortium during the construction phase of the hospital, which range from 25 percent to 35 percent of the costs: "These capital costs are unique to PFI: they would not be paid under traditional procurement."

Their report goes on to show how the SOC plans would seek to generate "savings" to cover the additional costs of the new hospital, through cuts in staff budgets (£6.3m, 45 percent of the total projected savings); moving patients to other parts of the NHS (the Newchurch report assumed caseload could be reduced by 14-18 percent, with 5-

---

[135] Price and Pollock (2002) p10.

6,000 more patients having to travel out of the area to access treatment) or out to social care; "estate savings" of £5.3m; increasing the costs charged to the Health Authority to raise an extra £6.6m (over 90 percent of the new money the DHA/primary care trust would be receiving from the government), and diverting money aimed at developing integrated health and care. (pp16-18)

Price and Pollock are also highly critical of the narrow focus of the SOC which make no attempt at any system-wide approach:

"The National Beds Inquiry recommended that "service reconfigurations based on assumptions of major acute bed reductions are unlikely to be safely attainable unless expanded intermediate and community services are put in place". And to this end it stated that health authorities and trusts take a whole system approach to care and review all aspects of service provision across health and social services. "However, the SOC relates only to current and projected bed provision in three hospitals. It does not provide an overview of current NHS and local authority provision across the districts as a whole and notably absent is a comprehensive account of long stay, intermediate care, and acute NHS beds and NHS day care. Local authority provision is also omitted ..." (p19)

They note that on the basis of local trend data "there is little evidence to support a 24% reduction in acute beds between 2001 and 2007." Table 1 shows bed numbers have remained relatively static in the six year period 1995-2001 indicating that in spite of the deficits and pressure to close services the Trust has not been able to do so.

Price and Pollock argue that even by 2002 there was already extensive evidence to refute the assumptions made in most first-wave PFI hospitals that acute bed capacity could be reduced by 30% without impairing service delivery:

"PFI hospitals in Durham, Carlisle and Calderdale are currently experiencing severe difficulties in accommodating inpatient admissions in general, and elective admissions in particular. The downsizing of acute capacity preceding the construction of PFI hospitals in Worcester and Hereford has resulted in severe shortages of acute beds in both counties." (p21)

Table 1: Average daily number of general and acute available beds, wards open overnight by trust, 1995-96 to 2000-01 (from Price & Pollock 2002)		
General and acute available beds		
	Pinderfields and Pontefract*[136]	Dewsbury
2000-01	1,000	408
1999-00	987	406
1998-99	1,001	393
1997-98	1,023	389
1996-97	1,046	398
1995-96	1,069	401

The SOC had not even attempted to provide any measures of need with respect to trends in caseload by specialty and type of admission or in unmet need for services in the community. It provided no community needs-based assessments. No caseload data were provided, and no detail of trends in length of stay, bed occupancy, or throughput and the feasibility of their performance measures.

The SOC also admitted that the investment and capacity needs of the 'care closer to home' model had yet to be developed, claiming, falsely, that "A detailed intermediate care strategy ... will be determined and consulted upon as part of this process in 2001"(p23). However the long term projections suggested the need for an extra 328 intermediate beds by 2006/7, with more to follow later. In other words the apparent efficiency of the new hospital would be at the expense of dumping a substantial caseload (and the related costs) onto other services outside of the trust.

Price and Pollock's report, published nationally by UNISON, added to the growing body of evidence that PFI was a costly and

---

[136] Bed totals summed from two separate hospitals, Pinderfields Hospital and Pontefract Hospital for 1995-96 and 1996-97 by Price and Pollock 2002. Sources: Department of Health, *Bed availability and occupancy for England, 1995-96 to 1999-2000*.

potentially dangerous gamble in which the only winners would be the shareholder of the private consortia coining in guaranteed profits.

Primary Care Trusts – with more of the same

There is no doubt this and other problems of evidence and viability contributed to the growing pressures on the Mid Yorkshire Trust and the health authority, which from 2001 handed over commissioning responsibilities to the newly formed Primary Care Trusts.

Two years later in 2004, with no deal yet finalised, the finances of the Trust, as UNISON had warned, had deteriorated drastically, with the deficit rising to almost £30m in 2003/4, and rising. Costly consultancy from ATOS/KPMG failed to offer any relief.

In the early summer of 2004, as the Trust became more embroiled in its financial crisis, private management consultants Secta were commissioned to review hospital services and look at ways to reconfigure services. On top of the other woes Secta warned of an £11 million "affordability gap" in the PFI scheme.

Their main proposal centred on seeking cash savings. Policies were proposed for both Mid Yorks Trust and local Primary Care Trusts to enable the hospital to reach the "65th percentile" for its performance – drastically reducing the use of hospital beds and average length of stay for in-patients. This, claimed Secta, would make possible a reduction of 238 beds from the 2004 bed complement – and effectively lop another 100 beds from the plans in what was now called the Hospital Development Project.

However the Secta report noted that such a large reduction would not be possible without local Primary Care Trusts (PCTs) putting in place new strategies to reduce admissions and manage the continuing care of patients discharged from hospital. Such decisions and allocation of resources were of course outside of the control of Mid Yorks Hospitals Trust.

Secta also noted that not one of the other NHS Trusts Mid Yorks was compared with, in a survey of similar hospitals around the country, had an overall performance as high as the proposed target. Nevertheless the Secta report accepted the decision of the Trust to adopt the "more challenging target", despite the lack of evidence that it could be achieved, and the potential consequences of an over-stretched hospital and inadequate patient care if it was not reached.

To reach the target required local PCTs to work to reduce admissions by 4,500 per year: but the Trust would need to meet the demand for admissions while using 100,000 fewer bed-days. This required a hefty 25 percent reduction in average length of stay.

Secta also warned the Trust that an even higher level of performance, the 75th percentile, would not be a viable possibility. The increasing population of elderly people requiring hip replacements meant that any attempt to reduce further the number of orthopaedic beds could lead to "a breakdown of the services and an inability ever to respond to changes in demand".

Moreover Secta noted that there were "large risks" involved even in the Trust's proposals, which could also leave it without sufficient beds and capacity to deal with emergency pressures. The result could be a disruption of elective work that would result in loss of contract income and a worsened financial crisis: but the attraction of such a gamble was that achieving the higher performance should mean that the size of the PFI hospital at Pinderfields could be reduced by "a whole floor".

Secta discussed additional reductions, including the outsourcing of pathology services, and some potential for cutting the numbers of rehabilitation beds, which they regarded as potentially problematic. The firm also warned that the scaled down proposals left no room for the future development of local services such as oncology and nephrology:

> "the shoehorning of facilities into an already 'tight ship' will present further challenges".

Financial health warning

In the autumn of 2004 the Audit Commission issued a 'public interest warning' over the Trust's finances, pointing out that the Trust had already accumulated a deficit of £21m, and that this was set to almost double to £40m by the end of 2004/5, leaving the Trust in clear breach of its statutory duty to break even.

This forecast was actually more optimistic than the report in the *Wakefield Express* in the spring of 2004 which warned of a possible £53m deficit, and the report to the West Yorkshire Strategic Health Authority, which had predicted a shortfall as high as £46m.

Nonetheless the Audit Commission referred the Trust's plight to the Secretary of State.

Subsequent details published jointly by the Audit Commission and National Audit Office[137] show that Mid Yorkshire Trust topped the league table of trusts receiving financial support of £10m or more in 2004/5, receiving £30m to bring its deficit down from a potential £49.9m to £19.9m. Its deficit was third highest of all the NHS trusts with deficits over £5m that year. As of March 31 2005 its cumulative deficit of £40.7m was the second largest in England.

The Trust's senior finance chiefs remained firmly in denial, pinning their hopes of achieving a staggering £46m through efficiency savings, and talked of achieving "balance" in 2005-6, despite the necessary details still not having been identified in June 2004.

Meanwhile the Trust, which had been rated as not deserving any stars on the league table of quality, was also being investigated by the Healthcare Commission, which at the end of the year took the unprecedented step of calling on the Secretary of State to intervene to address "systematic management failings over a number of years." Mid Yorkshire became the first Trust to be subjected to "special measures". In June 2005 a National Audit Office report[138] accused the trust of a "historic lack of adequate budget setting," a charge as inadequate as accusing Dracula of being "unusually keen on the taste of blood".

In the midst of this chaos and confusion the Trust decided to forge ahead with the PFI hospitals in Pontefract and Wakefield, and appointed Consort Healthcare (the health project arm of Balfour Beatty Capital Projects Ltd) as the Trust's preferred partner for developing these new facilities. The plan was to move forward with detailed negotiations on the design of the project, with a view to signing financial contracts by July 2006; but some initial

---

[137] NAO and Audit Commission (2006) Financial Management in the NHS: NHS (England) Summarised Accounts2004-05, Stationery Office, pp21, 25, 31.
[138] National Audit Office (2005) Financial Management in The NHS:NHS (England) Summarised Accounts 2003-04, p16: available
https://www.nao.org.uk/wp-content/uploads/2005/06/050660_l.pdf

developments were proposed to take place straight away on both sites to clear the area for the new hospitals.[139]

There was some abatement in the financial situation in 2005/6, reducing the deficit over the year to £14.6m, in line with the target set by the Strategic Health Authority.[140]

Rescoping review

In the spring of 2005, with the original scheme now described as "unaffordable", another "rescoping" review of the PFI scheme called for bed numbers to be reduced by 30% from the original planned total. This would leave them 40% below the 2004 bed numbers. The new plan also called for a huge 75% reduction in provision of "flexible" ward accommodation to be kept in reserve, from 128 beds to just 32.

The new building, according to the Project Director in summer 2005, would be much smaller, with have "less outer wall area". By September the Trust confirmed that Consort had been asked to carry out radical design changes to an "unaffordable" Pinderfields plan. The following month Consort made clear they would do so only if they could pass all the additional costs of changing what had then growing into a £280m scheme, including architects' fees for a major redesign, on to the Trust.

The redesign was linked with yet more vague suggestions of alternative services "in the community," the idea floated years earlier by the Newchurch review. This was theoretically to be provided by Primary Care Trusts: but in fact neither funding nor firm plans had been agreed for these promised new services, which, as UNISON had warned, never materialised.

In August 2005, Professor Sir Ara Darzi, Head of the Division of Surgery, Anaesthetics and Intensive Care at London University's Imperial College[141] was brought in to conduct an independent review

---

[139] Mid Yorkshire Hospitals Trust Annual report 2004-5. September 2005.

[140] Mid Yorkshire Hospitals Trust Annual report 2005-6. September 2006

[141] Later Darzi, working with consultants from McKinsey, was to formulate a major and highly controversial plan for reconfiguring health services in London on the basis of a new network of 'polyclinics,' and was then elevated to Lord Darzi and appointed as a Health Minister by the Labour government.

of the Mid Yorks project. In a low-key and amusingly under-stated report, Prof Darzi noted that:

> "Part way through the process of selecting the preferred bidder for the PFI the Trust got into financial difficulties. In addition, there is a significant affordability gap in the current proposals."

In fact the "financial difficulties" were so enormous that only a massive £30 million hand-out from the Department of Health salvaged the situation, averting a deficit which would otherwise have been almost £50m in the previous year. Prof Darzi concluded that as a result of this ticklish financial situation the Trust should attempt to steer round the difficult question of how many beds will be included in the new hospitals, since any focus on this "has been unhelpful in winning support for the proposals."

He also noted that the main overview consultation had been completed as long ago as 1999, proposing the separation of roles between the main acute ("hot") services at a rebuilt Pinderfields Hospital, while retaining Pontefract as a "cold" site offering short stay and day case surgery, diagnostics and outpatients.

Prof Darzi said the claims in 1999 that Pontefract would have "an A&E department that is medically led and open 24 hours a day" were "misleading". In fact all that was proposed was a GP-led minor injuries unit and not a full A&E. But he also noted the proposals to cut the cost of the project and reduce the £11.4m affordability gap, which involved acing 200 beds across Dewsbury, Wakefield and Pontefract hospitals. He expressed concerns that this policy was:

> "Too heavily reliant on primary and intermediate care services providing a significant volume of acute care. I do not believe the evidence yet exists to support this to the extent that will be necessary in Mid Yorkshire".

UNISON had raised identical points in responses to successive plans; Prof Darzi's comments were ignored in the same way. Prof Darzi also echoed UNISON's concerns when he highlighted the problems that can arise from concentrating all of the in-patient care on the Pinderfields site. He warned that with reduced bed numbers the hospital's ability to treat waiting list patients could be disrupted by the weight of numbers of emergency medical admissions. This would be worsened by the "choice-driven health economy" and the new system of payment by results which was to be introduced from April 2006. This meant that every delay or cancellation of waiting list treatment could result in the Trust losing the income for that work.

Prof Darzi therefore suggested the establishment of a 'medical admissions unit' in Pontefract, with appropriate consultant cover and critical care services. He admitted that this additional service would have cost implications, but argued that it would help the Trust minimise the numbers of local patients whose treatment was "sub-contracted" to the private sector, and retain resources within the NHS. Once again the Trust ignored this suggestion.

UNISON took issue with Prof Darzi when he suggested that the local concerns over the size and viability of the new hospitals project should be dodged by a communications strategy to ensure the debate was "steered away from the number of beds to be retained at each of the three sites, and towards a more rational view of which services should be retained and where". In the absence of any evidence that the Trust had developed a robust or viable plan to deliver adequate resources to meet patient need, UNISON and local campaigners continued to press for categoric assurances both on bed numbers and on the provision of sufficient alternative services in primary and community health care to support the new hospital configuration.

Consultation

The Trust blundered on regardless. On December 1 2005 they opened a "consultation" on the proposals even though much of the detail was still firmly under the wraps of commercial confidentiality.

In the spring of 2006, towards the end of that consultation, a special issue of the UNISON Branch newspaper *Union Eyes* was headlined 'Countdown to Chaos', arguing that management were not telling the unions or the public the full story of what they were negotiating behind closed doors on the new hospitals:

> "We have got used to Trust bosses using the consultation process to float a succession of half-baked and unacceptable proposals, dismiss and discredit alternative approaches, and claim public endorsement despite clear evidence that their plans are unpopular.

"UNISON has responded in detail to each of the consultations, noting each time that the Trust pays little heed to views and responses that do not echo their main proposals. "But we have also been critical of consultations that go through the motions of discussing policies without clearly identifying what questions they want local people to answer."

Union Eyes explained the problem:

"In the last couple of months people have been asked their views on a vague document proposing a new hospital in Pontefract, to be funded through the government's 'Private Finance Initiative' (PFI) at a time when the government has effectively frozen all large scale PFI projects and is conducting a review of their affordability.

"The Mid Yorkshire Hospitals PFI scheme is a large one … and even before the government review it had already identified an affordability gap of £11.4 million per year, and begun to reduce bed numbers and the size of the new hospitals to save money."

Towards the end of 2006, performance began to fall on a wide range of targets, despite improbable claims by the Trust 'Director of Turnaround' Toby Lewis, who told Wakefield council's newly-established and singularly supine Health Oversight and Scrutiny Committee that the previous quarter's performance figures 'highlight performance scores improvements'. The bare-faced cheek of this claim was shown by even the briefest look at the Trust's own Integrated Performance Summary at the end of November, which showed:

- The 'first breaches this year' of outpatient waiting time targets
- Another rise in the numbers waiting over 11 weeks for outpatient appointments
- An increase in the number of cancelled operations
- A drop in performance in thrombolysis 'call-to-needle' times
- A fresh rise above target in MRSA
- A rise in readmissions of patients discharged after treatment, with several departments recording
- Readmission levels on or above 10 percent.

- A drop below plan in inpatient treatment, day case treatment and outpatient attendances – all of which were potentially serious problems under the NHS 'payment by results' system.

The financial crisis faced by the Trust was also far from resolved. Department of Health figures a couple of weeks earlier showed Mid Yorks Hospitals projecting a worsening deficit of more than £15m (the same size deficit as the previous year, but 50 percent higher than the estimate three months earlier). However Mr Lewis was not challenged on his claim that the Trust was 'on target' to achieve financial balance by October 2007.

The financial situation had not been improved by the succession of highly-paid management consultants who continued to take it in turns to have a go at sorting out the Trust. With well over £1 million already spent on private sector management consultants, and the total rising every day, the Mid Yorkshire Trust's 'turnaround' process was intensified in 2007, with the unachievable 2-year target for £35m savings slashed to an even less achievable 18 months.

The Trust had declared a target of cutting the pay bill by 10 percent, and claimed that up to £22m of the £35m target would come from reduced staffing costs, with up to £17m from 'non-pay savings'. None of the figures seemed to make much sense.

However pressure from the union had paid off, ensuring that early fears that such drastic cuts in staff budgets would require compulsory redundancies proved to be wide of the mark. Instead the Trust became obsessively keen to avoid paying any redundancy money to staff, and seeking any and every way around it, resorting to identifying jobs at risk in batches of just under 100 – to avoid either consultation or additional redundancy entitlements.

Staff morale was systematically undermined, with individuals placed under untold pressure by a constant process of reorganisation, which also involved reducing staffing levels to the point that many staff feared for the safety of patients. The union voiced its concern that staff who had once enjoyed and valued their jobs were telling UNISON that they dreaded coming in to work and the start of each shift.

The unresolved financial situation was one of the factors in the continual postponement of signing the Private Finance Initiative contract. After being told for much of 2006 that the deal had to be signed by the end of November, it was once again postponed, to the end of February 2007. A weary UNISON Branch warned in *Union Eyes*:

> "Staff eager to hear news of the conclusion of the deal are strongly advised not to hold their breath waiting."

Eventually, on June 28 2007, after a charade of a "consultation" and extensive delays beyond the target for "financial close" the Full Business Case was signed off for the new hospitals, which now included a new small hospital on part of the Pontefract Hospital site, with just 60 rehab and assessment beds, 4 maternity beds and a scaled-down "A&E" service to deal only with minor cases.

Reduced capacity

As the work began in earnest on constructing the two new buildings, it's instructive to note that the hospitals within the Mid Yorkshire Trust had already been reduced in scale over the previous 15 years, from a total of 1500 beds for elderly care and acute services to just 1273 – a reduction of 16%, entirely concentrated in the drastic reduction of elderly care beds.

By 2007 day case treatment had grown as a proportion to total caseload: the Final Business Case shows it rising to 76%, although the PWC report in 2007 makes clear that this was the figure aspired to, one achieved by the top quartile of trusts: Mid Yorkshire's real figure was 69.7%. The plans assumed the expansion of day surgery could continue to reach 79% by 2015, while average length of stay could be further reduced by 15 percent, from 5.3 days for non-elective admissions to 4.5. This was seen as enabling a further reduction in bed numbers, but there was no real explanation of how it could be achieved.

In fact acute bed provision had slightly increased across the Trust: but the sharp reduction of more than two thirds of the specialist beds for older patients, without adequate provision of any alternative means of supporting older people in the community, resulted in growing numbers of front line acute beds being filled by older patients.

Their discharge after treatment tends to be more complex since it often relies on the availability of sufficient social care services, which from 1993 became the primary responsibility of local government social services – and subjected to means-tested charges.

Table 2: Vanishing beds in Mid Yorkshire[142]					
		Pinderfields	**Pontefract**	**Dewsbury**	**Total**
1992	**Type of bed**				
	Acute	455	315	287	**1057**
	Geriatric	155	189	111	**455**
	Acute & general	610	504	398	**1512**
2007		**Mid Yorkshire**			**Change from 1992 %**
	Acute	**1127**			6.60%
	General	**146**			-68%
	Acute & General	**1273**			-16%

Many older patients are admitted as medical emergencies, and while surgical treatment has substantially shifted towards the provision of a growing range of operations as day cases, the proportional acceleration of treatment and throughput of medical cases has not been possible. Older people admitted as inpatients for surgery also often require longer in hospital and more support on discharge than patients of working age: many have medical complications or live alone, which mean that they are not suitable for day surgery.

The problem for the Trust has been that every attempt to balance the books financially has further constrained the resources available to treat these vulnerable patients. Building a new hospital without taking these problems into account would result in older patients and those needing emergency services waiting longer for admission to overcrowded beds – even if they would be in a more modern and up

---

[142] Figures compiled from Department of Health: *Bed Availability for England*, Financial year 1992-93, and 2007-8 (Form KH03).

to date building.

Meanwhile the extra costs of the hospital itself, and the need to sustain the trust, have helped to divert away the in already limited extra resources that might have been invested in community health services and the intermediate care which has been promised so many times without ever being properly provided.

NHS managers continued to talk a good talk, but without ever indicating the political will or even a concrete implementation plan to walk the walk: in those circumstances reducing the number of front line beds could only lead to more patients queueing for the beds that were left.

Chapter 5

From signing the PFI to opening the new Pinderfields hospital

The PFI contract ("Project Agreement") was signed off in the summer of 2007. However this did not indicate all was well. Just three months later a report researched by PriceWaterhouseCooper for the Department of Health (available even now only in heavily redacted form) exposed the sheer scale of the ongoing financial plight of the Trust, which had "failed to achieve breakeven for each year of its operation". It confirmed that since its formation as a trust through the merger with Dewsbury, Mid Yorkshire Hospitals had generated an overall deficit of £63.4m. PWC warned that:

"we believe the likelihood is that the Trust will:

- Struggle to maintain financial balance up until 12/13
- Be unlikely to recoup its current accumulated deficit of £63.4m, and
- As assumed in management's Long term Financial Model, be unable to achieve repayment of any current loans in this period."[143]

The report went on to outline the scale of the problem. On top of the £63.4m deficit there was a need to address "the early repayment of its £77.3m of temporary Public Dividend Capital and the £21.4m of SHA support" – the extra money that had so far kept the Trust afloat. However all material assets and cash generation options had already been used up in the effort to agree the PFI business case, so "no further options exist to repay any loans".

PWC concluded that the only viable option was not further loans, which would in turn bring extra long-term costs: instead they called for a "full cash injection of £85m".

---

[143]PWC (2007) Independent Assessment of Financially Challenged Trusts, Stage 2 – Draft Report Mid Yorkshire Hospitals, Department of Health, September, available (redacted)
http://data.parliament.uk/DepositedPapers/Files/DEP2009-0402/DEP2009-0402.pdf

The Trust had already identified "savings opportunities" totalling £36.5m, although one of these, to make large savings from outpatient departments, was rated as no more than 50% probable to release the full sum. Other cuts/savings proposed included speeding throughput of patients to close another 133 beds; increasing the usage of operating theatres; and £6.3m of savings from supply chain and non-pay items.

However the Trust's 5-year plan was already based on a hugely ambitious 5-year improvement plan, assuming cost improvements of £74.2m – upwards of 4.3% per year. Even PWC argued that

"the current year plan is achievable but remains challenging. There is little evidence of other Trusts being able to sustain the level of CIP savings expected by the Trust over the requisite time frame." (p21)

Among the additional suggestions from PWC was to "reconsider centralising acute medicine and major A&E activity at Pinderfields and close the infrastructure in Dewsbury," although one constraint would be "the bed capacity at Pinderfields" (p26). This of course is what subsequently has been done in the last few years.

So the PFI deal, which committed the Trust to substantial extra spending, was signed in the midst of the developing banking crisis, and at a time when the Trust itself was consistently failing to balance its books, and so mired in deficits it needed an £85m cash handout to pay back some of the loans that had propped it up.

The plans to balance the books hinged on very ambitious targets for improved performance – and a reduction in bed numbers. It was unstable from the outset.

Most of the hard details of the plans that were hatched up to argue that the PFI could be justified had been worked out behind closed doors, and remained closely guarded secrets until well after the deal had been signed.

Only a prolonged battle by the UNISON branch eventually ensured a (heavily redacted) version of the Full Business case was published.

The Trust had good reason to avoid any genuine scrutiny of their deal: it was flawed in so many ways. Even the sections that escaped the censor's indelible marker underlined two key concerns about the scheme, which had been raised throughout by UNISON:

- The price – and therefore the resultant ongoing cost – of the PFI contract
- The capacity of the new hospitals and their ability to meet levels of demand for emergency and elective care

By the early 2008 parts of the Full Business case had been grudgingly released by the Trust, and the Branch newspaper *Union Eyes* headlined 'Pure Financial Incompetence'.

The cost

The expectation was that the full revenue costs of the first year of the new hospital (2011-12) would add up to £41.2m. This combined the unitary charge (estimated at £35.3m) with additional costs for ICT (£900,000), loss of income to the trust from facilities management (car parks, shops, catering, etc.) of £3.3m (since these services would become part of the income stream for the PFI consortium), and another £1.7m of costs (FBC Appendix 10-B).

This was to have been covered by various means including support from the commissioners (then the Primary Care Trust), £16.6m of expected savings from the previous hospital budget, and £19.7m in Cost Improvement Programmes (CIPs). However it is not clear whether either large target for savings was fully achieved.

Moreover the cost was inflated from the beginning by higher than expected inflation, which pushed up the unitary charge to £43m. As a result the Trust was struggling from day one of the new hospitals opening, and the gap quickly grew wider. The calculation of the relative cost compared with the income of the Trust was bizarrely carried out using 2005-6 figures (Appendix 10-E). The experts came to the conclusion that the unitary charge would be a whisker under 15% of the turnover of the Trust.

The actual figures show that with the higher unitary charge and lost income, the combined revenue cost to the Trust in year one was more like £46-£50m. The Trust turnover in 2011-12 was estimated at £444m, of which around £40m was directly linked with the community health services in Wakefield, and so not part of the revenue base servicing the PFI. So from the outset the real, rather than hypothetical revenue costs of the PFI itself added up to 11.5-12.5% of the turnover of the acute services.

However to calculate the complete cost, on top of this must be added the continuing payments on the "Public Dividend Capital" (PDC) on the value of Dewsbury Hospital and other publicly-owned assets retained by the trust's community services, which are not part of the PFI. The increased cost of PFI is the difference between the original capital charges and the combined PFI charges, lost income, finance charges and residual PDC payments.

Trust annual reports prior to 2007 showed that these payments varying over the years, from a high point of £9.7 million covering all of the trust's assets in 2007-8, reducing to £5.7m in 2009-10 and £3.1m in 2011-12: however the additional 'finance costs' driven by the PFI rose sharply, from £1.5m in 2008-9 to £11.6m in 2011-12. Between them these two payments stacked up to a combined additional outlay of £14.7m on top of the PFI unitary charge.

PFI and other capital and finance costs together in 2011-12 therefore added up to almost £60m, equivalent to 13.5% of the trust's total turnover. This was substantially higher than the national average of 10.3% capital costs for other trusts with PFI projects.

Indeed the costs of capital for hospitals with major PFI schemes are in general much higher than the notional figure of 5.8% of trust income payable by trusts on their public dividend capital and depreciation (public sector assets). That is the figure used as the basis for the costing of average services, from which the 'payment by results' tariff of prices is calculated, fixing the fee paid to hospitals for each item of treatment they deliver.

If MYHT had been spending this (much smaller) share of its income on capital costs the Trust would have been paying out around £26m a year on capital charges instead of £60m – leaving it a massive £34m a year better off than actually was from 2011.

The dead weight of PFI and all of the related additional costs faced by MYHT as a result of the contract therefore became a significant factor in the worsening financial situation.

The details emerge

In other circumstances staff might have been expected to be excited by the prospect of a new building: with any enlightened approach they might have been drawn in, and their hands-on experience of delivering the various services could have been used as a valuable resource to help design and develop plans.

Instead, the way management conducted the preparation served simply to alienate staff and their representatives. Far from eager anticipation or excitement, the prospect of a new hospital was seen with considerable foreboding.

One key factor in this was the continued obsessive secrecy. It was a battle to get any information out at all on what was happening. As a result, *Union Eyes* warned:

> "If the finances or organisation of the new hospitals now being constructed in Wakefield and Pontefract go horribly wrong, managers will have only themselves to blame.
>
> "After nine years of furtive and secretive negotiations, half-baked "consultations" and inadequate information they are pressing ahead with a Private Finance Initiative scheme that has more holes in it than a Tetley teabag.
>
> "UNISON battled long and hard most of last year to extract a copy of the Full Business Case for the new hospitals: this is despite the fact that a condition for Department of Health approval for the FBC last summer was that it should be published in its final form within a month of completion.
>
> "However the complete report is still not available for scrutiny: when the massive collection of documents was eventually grudgingly handed over it was studded with deletions of information which managers claim is commercial and confidential.
>
> "Simply listing the omissions, with a few sketchy and formulaic arguments on why they have been omitted, requires 13 pages of A4 ..."

Among the subject areas the Trust or the PFI consortium believed were too sensitive to allow staff or the public to know the details were:

• Figures on the rate of return (profit) to be generated by the consortium

• Numerous details on the treatment of non-clinical support staff under the TUPE (transfer of undertakings) arrangements, through which they would be seconded to work under the management of the consortium, while remaining NHS employees

• A whole appendix analysing the transfer of staff to the management of the consortium

• Details of any additional borrowing to be carried out by the consortium

• Details on the time that was to be allowed for rectification of problems – a significant component of the accountability and monitoring of the PFI contract

• Letters from some of the long list of high-cost financial and legal advisors who had given their view of the contract and its financial implications, and allegedly supporting the project.

A backdrop of PFI deals in crisis

Among the worrying details included in the FBC were projections on bed numbers, and caseload which the UNISON Branch had consistently argued were hugely over-optimistic.

The 32-year PFI contract was also signed off in the shadow of the public revelation just two years earlier that one of the early PFI hospitals, Queen Elizabeth in Woolwich, was already "technically bankrupt" as a result of escalating PFI costs[144]. Others were also facing major financial problems. And the hospitals were proving to be poor quality buildings, badly designed, and stressful to work in. UNISON nationally had published two major studies of the views and experience of staff in a number of PFI hospitals, underlining the concerns[145]. *Union Eyes* warned:

> "The same PFI consortium that is building our PFI hospitals was also responsible for the University Hospital of North Durham, in Dryburn, which Trust bosses have admitted was too small to cope with demand, and the Edinburgh Royal Infirmary, which has been a chapter of disasters and

---

[144] https://www.theguardian.com/uk/2005/dec/16/publicservices.topstories3
[145] UNISON's April 2003 Press Release is
at https://www.unison.org.uk/news/article/2003/04/pfi-hospitals-fail-patients-and-staff-speaking-out-in-unison-against-pfi/. This report is available at https://healthemergency.org.uk/pdf/PFI_experience.pdf . Also *Not So Great, voices from the frontline at Great Western PFI Hospital in Swindon* available: https://issuu.com/repzone/docs/pfi---not-so-great

financial problems since it opened in 2003.

"UNISON notes with concern that while the private consortium is designing the hospital, the Trust is responsible for the clinical effectiveness of the designs – leaving the Trust holding all of the risk when it becomes clear that they have got their sums wrong."

There seemed to be reason to believe the sums were seriously awry on the Wakefield PFI finances. Mid Yorks Trust admitted that the increased cost of the new hospitals would be an additional financial challenge on top of the current "headline financial challenge of £77m". That figure rested on the false assumption that from 2008 onwards the Trust would only be expected to generate 1 percent of "cost improvements" each year, compared with 2 percent or more in every previous year.

The Trust Board heard – but appears to have ignored – worrying projections that if the cost improvements were fixed at the higher figure of 2.5% in future years the Trust's headline financial challenge would increase to £90 million. In addition there was the not insignificant "net revenue impact" (i.e. additional cost) of the scheme – £17.7m a year at 2006-7 prices: it was clear at once that there was a substantial affordability issue.

Nonetheless the Board meeting rubber stamped the PFI scheme (with extensive sections of documentation withheld even from Board members, as UNISON later discovered).

Hopes of increased income

To make it look as if the sums all balanced up, the Trust assumed a large (29 percent) increase in total clinical income, with little if any related increase in costs. But there was absolutely no guarantee at all that this money would materialise. Under the Labour government's newly-introduced 'Payment By Results' system, Trusts were only paid for the patients who turned up and received treatment – so if the commissioners did succeed in their mission to divert more patients away from hospital care and into community and primary care services, this would inevitably scale down the income of the Trust.

However the requirement to pay the PFI rent, or 'unitary charge,' would not be reduced. Instead it would definitely go up, year by year, by a minimum of 2.5 percent, or the rate of inflation if that was higher. Significantly the risk of the Trust running out of cash altogether and facing eviction from the new hospitals had not been one of those discussed and costed in the various working party discussions.

Yet previous reports from the Audit Commission (Public Interest Report 2004) and the Healthcare Commission (2005) had made clear that there was no local solution to the Trust's historically accumulated financial difficulties. The Audit Commission's findings summarised by the National Audit Office[146], noted the long-running financial instability of the Trust:

> "In 2003-04, the Mid Yorkshire Hospitals NHS Trust reported an in-year deficit of £18.6 million, the largest deficit of all NHS bodies in 2003-04. The Trust and the local health economy have long-standing service and financial issues, which the Trust had been able to manage in previous years through the receipt of one-off financial support and a variety of other non-recurrent solutions. However, these measures did not address the underlying problems.
> …
> **May 2003** Trust Board approves budget for 2003-04 which identifies savings requirement of £19 million to achieve financial balance.
> … **October 2003** Director of Finance's review of financial position shows that year-end deficit could be as high as £34 million.
> … **February 2004** Auditor writes to Trust Board outlining actions to be taken by June 2004, and stating that if the actions are not taken by June, he will consider exercising the special reporting powers set out in the Audit Commission Act 1998.
> **July 2004** The Trust's 2003-04 annual accounts show a deficit of £18.6 million (£30.6 million if external support is removed)."

---

[146] NAO (2004) *Financial Management in the NHS*: NHS (England) Summarised Accounts 2003-04, London, https://www.nao.org.uk/wp-content/uploads/2005/06/050660_I.pdf, p16

MYHT was unable to reach its statutory breakeven duty, and had so far been bailed out with £77m in cash support. The PWC which proposed the £85m cash handout to clear these cumulative deficits did not appear until after the PFI deal had been signed.

In the event the Trust signed up for a PFI project that was set to cost a staggering £1.6 billion over 32 years. It was hoped that a series of local level cost savings could nevertheless somehow bridge the gap and put the Trust's budget into balance.

This level of optimism was perhaps understandable: the plan was drawn up at a time when NHS spending was still rising year by year, and the banking crash had not yet even begun. However the PFI contract was to run for 32 years, and signing up to such a large-scale and long-running, increasing cost as first charge on the Trust's finances had to be a gamble.

Of course we now know that the economy would be plunged into crisis in 2008-9, the growth in NHS spending halted abruptly in 2010-11, and the cash squeeze has tightened on the NHS ever since, making the plans seem even more irresponsible..

Intermediate and community health services

Back in 2000 UNISON's response to the consultation document *Grasping the Nettle* asked:

> "Where will the proposed 'intermediate' beds be situated? Where will staff be recruited and trained? Who will be in charge? Where will they work from?"

UNISON the underlying question: how would such a service be financed? There were no answers. The publication of the Final Business Case also raised a fresh question: why had the much-vaunted and long-planned switch of hospital- based care to the community not been factored in to the Trust's financial projections?

According to the Full Business Case (FBC), the basic assumption underlying the service planning for the new hospitals was based on "a visible shift towards healthcare in primary and community care settings" (Executive Summary 1.4). It argued that:

> "future investment is intrinsically linked to a shift of resources to these settings and consequently is based on a preventative model for care." (Executive Summary 1.4)

The FBC went on to claim that the proposed reduction in

134

acute bed numbers was

"the result of the analysis of the total PCT projected activity for 2010/11 (including taking into account the most recent guidance on reduction to emergency admissions."

It also claimed – as usual without offering any evidence – that:

"Studies … have shown that alternative intermediate health care provision would best serve around 30 percent of patients currently admitted to the acute hospitals". (1.5.3)

However it was immediately obvious from the plans and the financial costs of the scheme that this was simply a form of words, paying mere lip-service to a new model of care. Had the policy been applied in practice, the reduction in hospital caseload and income would have pulled the financial rug even further from beneath the Trust, which was tied in to a hefty, long term capital investment in traditional hospital care.

Yet a curious aspect of the FBC was that there was no indication of how these assumptions had actually shaped the proposals and projections of the PFI project: far from dropping by 30 percent, projected inpatient demand was expected to dip by at most 15 percent, before increasing again (Appendix 3D).

Far from showing a substantial switch to primary and community services, the figures showed that the Trust apparently expected no real change in its elective (waiting list) income, which was thought to be the same in 2012 as in 2005: they also expected a continued substantial year-on-year increase in income from emergency admissions (to a new peak in 2012, 30 percent *higher* than 2007-8).

This not only questioned the general rhetoric about the possibility of reducing bed numbers while the population and demand increased, but also raised the question whether the new hospitals, which were supposed to have 15 percent fewer beds than were then currently available in Wakefield and Pontefract, leaving no frontline acute services in Pontefract to share the load, would have enough capacity to cope with the level of demand. Would the new set-up be clinically viable? If not, what was the Plan B? How far would local patients have to travel to access appropriate hospital care?

Indeed the Executive summary also included a contradictory (and exceedingly optimistic) passage in a table, which (despite the earlier decision to axe the additional "shelled" capacity in order to cut the size and cost of the project) claimed that:

> "Should the Trust prove popular in the market there is scope within the scheme for productivity growth to support higher volumes" (p1-5)

This made it clear that the Trust was not really expecting any diversion of patients from hospital: but they felt obliged to echo the trendy rhetoric of the times and also find some way to explain away the reducing numbers of beds that would be available. The Hospital Development Plan proposed to cut bed numbers from 1,388 to 1,176, with the biggest drop of all being the massive reduction at Pontefract from 388 to just 64 beds. Dewsbury provision was expected to remain unchanged.

It was a puzzle. What really were the planning assumptions?

UNISON was not alone in raising concerns over the capacity of the new hospitals: these also featured prominently in the Risk Register developed by the Trust and its advisors, and published as part of the FBC.

Six of these risks were summed up as having the potential impact of clinical facilities being constructed that "are not aligned against revised clinical care paths and capacity modelling", while five posed the possibility of requiring extra capital costs as a result of revising the plans for PFI facilities.

In the event, both of these major fears proved to be justified. The plans had to be not only substantially revised after the contract was signed: but the mismatch between capacity and actual patterns of clinical care remained a major, chronic problem for the Trust. Despite all the optimistic projections, emergency caseload rose by 12.7 percent in the ten years from 2001-2, while elective caseload remained almost constant. This resulted in an overall increase in admissions of 7.4 percent, maintaining heavy pressure on over-stretched hospital staff and facilities. These figures show no sign of any impact from "alternative intermediate health care provision," which remained at the level of empty rhetoric.

One reason for this was no doubt the cost of the capital investment in the new hospital buildings, which drained and largely exhausted available resources that might otherwise have been invested in expanding community based health care and primary care services. Indeed the 'payment by results' formula for funding trusts[147] meant that once the PFI hospital was in operation, any substantial expansion of community health services that did succeed in switching patients (and revenue) away from the hospitals would trigger an even more severe financial crisis for the Trust, since its core capital costs would remain unchanged – while the revenue to pay them would be reduced.

Far from being part of a scheme to develop new, integrated services and greater provision of care outside hospital, the PFI scheme immediately became a major obstacle to any such plans in the future, and a substantial burden on the local health economy.

Staffing cuts – across the Board

While many have recognised the frequent link between PFI schemes and cuts in staff to reduce costs, the Mid Yorkshire FBC indicated how this pressure can result in plans for cuts across the board, not by any means just in the non-clinical staff employed by support services that are covered by the PFI deal itself. The FBC explains that to meets its "turnaround" targets to balance the books and prepare the ground for the PFI project, the Trust had to reduce staffing costs by the equivalent of 450 whole time equivalent posts, to generate savings of £18m. The planned reduction in the workforce was to be 17% over four years, from 6,508 to 5,392.

The heaviest cuts were to be in nursing, which accounted for 38% of the job cuts and faced a 16% reduction in the five years from 2,620 whole time equivalent posts in 2006 to 2,198 by 2010-11. Costs were to be reduced by diluting the skill mix: using more vocationally trained health care assistants in place of professionally qualified nursing staff.

The next largest group under the axe was admin and clerical staff (192 posts to go, equivalent to 17% of the 2006 staffing); scientific and technical staff were to carry 12.5% of the total cuts, losing 22%

---

[147] Based on numbers of patients treated, and paying a fixed tariff for each treatment, in place of the previous "block contracts".

of their 2006 total (139 jobs); and even doctors were not safe. Medical staff cuts were to make up 11% of the job losses, with 18% of doctors losing their posts (127) (Table 7-1).

Where would all the money go?

It is a fitting irony that the PFI deal in Mid Yorkshire should be signed in 2007, the year the banking crash and credit crunch began in earnest in the USA, and soon had its devastating knock-on impact on the British economy. Later in 2007, Northern Rock, the first of the British banks to fall victim to the "sub-prime" lending crisis, to be nationalised the following year.

The initial winning PFI consortium, collectively known as Consort Healthcare, had defeated a rival bid by New Hospitals (Taylor Woodrow/ Innisfree) to become the preferred provider in the autumn of 2004, although the process had been repeatedly delayed by further discussions aimed at squeezing down the cost of the project in response to the Trust's ongoing and unresolved financial problems.

Consort's partner companies in the early stages were Balfour Beatty Infrastructure Investments Ltd (with Haden Young delivering the construction side and the subsequent maintenance services). Balfour Beatty was to cover the non-clinical support services. However in Mid Yorkshire the support services staff were to be retained as NHS employees, (supervised and managed by the company). Royal Bank of Scotland (Royal Bank Project Investments Limited) were the financial advisors and main additional organisers of the capital required.

Over £352 million was raised by the consortium on the strength of the Mid Yorkshire PFI – more than £40m above the costs of the new buildings. But just 9 percent of this money was actually put up in equity and 'subordinated debt' by Balfour Beatty and RBS, leaving the remaining 91% to be financed as debt, borrowed on the basis of an index-linked Bond for £171m and an index-linked loan from the European Investment Bank for another £150m.

In explanation the FBC argued that debt is a cheaper way of funding than equity. The financial model for the contract was drawn up by the Royal Bank of Scotland, and checked out on the Trust's behalf by PWC.

Taking the profits offshore

However in 2011, with the most "risky" phase of the project nearly complete, RBS – which had to be massively bailed out by the British government following the 2008 banking crash and was by then 84% owned by the taxpayer – sold on its 50% share of the deal to the Guernsey-based HICL Infrastructure, an arm of the HSBC bank.

As a result, all the payments that previously would have flowed to the RBS were from then on to be funnelled instead into the offshore coffers of a bank that pays no UK tax, and therefore none of the surpluses it accrued would flow back in any way to the NHS or public services. The offshore bank was free to simply cream off a profit from the PFI and distribute this to its shareholders, leaving the NHS and the taxpayer to foot the rising bill.

The FBC (Chapter 5) also confirmed that back in 2005 Consort Healthcare, as preferred bidder, had undertaken a further five month "rescoping" exercise to squeeze costs down still further. This was in response to proposals issued by the Trust in March 2005, and included further revisions to the number of adult inpatient beds at the Wakefield site and much greater use of existing estate rather than the new build.

Who carries the risk?

The Full Business Case tried to argue that funding the new hospital buildings through the Private Finance Initiative (PFI) represented "value for money", despite the evidence from projects elsewhere that the NHS was already set to repay a staggering £53 billion for use of buildings and support services on PFI projects with a total value of just £8 billion, resulting in a thumping great guaranteed profit stream for the private sector for a generation to come.

To make the cost of PFI seem less extortionate, the Treasury and Trust bosses have concocted a completely deceptive system of "comparison" between the PFI scheme in question and a purely theoretical "Public Sector Comparator".

Of course nobody wanted or expected ever to build a hospital based on the Public Sector Comparator (PSC): there was no public sector capital available to build one even if it had proved cheaper and better.

So the PSC never proves to be simply the same hospital project, but funded through public sector borrowing at government borrowing rates: it is always a much less attractive and less interesting project, generally involving the refurbishment of old buildings rather than construction of shiny new ones.

However the fiddles don't stop there: one problem in selling the idea of PFI is that the PSC, because it involves less new build, can often come out at close to, or even below, the cost of the PFI scheme. That's not what they want to see, since they are trying to argue PFI is better value. The Wakefield and Pontefract PSC, according to the Full Business Case, came out as less than one tenth of one percent (0.1%) more expensive than the PFI over 35 years.

So to make a case for PFI representing better value for money, the PSC has to be made to appear far more expensive than it actually is – and this involves an elaborate argument that the private sector is shouldering a large amount of "risk" under the PFI contract, whereas in reality that risk would remain in the NHS under a PSC.

So what is required in this fictional scenario is to make up a suitable cash value for the "risk" … so PFI can begin to look like a bargain. In the case of the Mid Yorkshire PFI scheme, the FBC chose to assume that the PSC would leave the NHS carrying a huge "risk" of up to £120m, while the PFI was presumed to reduce that to just £54m (Table 1-4). This may sound significant, but few of the hypothetical risks actually become liabilities (hence the enthusiasm of the private sector to sign more PFI deals, and the hefty profits they pile up from doing so).

In exchange for escaping a theoretical (and improbable) short-term risk, the NHS is persuaded in this way to fork out a hefty long term guaranteed payment. It's like taking out an insurance policy on a household object, but paying a disproportionately large amount for the policy – it would probably be cheaper to pay for repairs or buy a new one.

Despite even this element of book-cookery, when the Mid Yorkshire scheme is looked at over the 35-year contract period, the claimed "saving" from using PFI added up to just 1.6% of the total outgoings.

At the end of the day the figures were of course just make-believe, a flimsy fig-leaf to protect the modesty of the Trust as it signed up for a deal that was going to commit the Trust to paying out a total in excess of £1.4 billion for a hospital costing £311m to build. The building costs could have been financed so much more cheaply.

As is so often the case, the fantasy and fiction was hidden from almost everyone under a dark cloud of secrecy. Union reps were frustrated at the lack of transparency in the process. However UNISON was shocked to discover that it was not just the unions and the wider public who had been kept in the dark by the failure to publish the full details of the PFI Full Business Case: the Trust Board too had been left to guess at the content of missing sections, and as a result were effectively persuaded to sign up for a £1.4bn pig in a poke.

Looking at the shambolic, vague and inadequate paperwork that has subsequently been published, it is amazing that Board members were prepared to vote through the project with as little information as they were given. It's hard to believe that a regular bank would regard that level of documentation, with all its inconsistencies, as sufficient to back a development loan for a whelk stall, let alone £311m worth of new buildings, to be financed on a 35-year contract by a Trust already deep in deficit.

Immediate problems

Just eight months after the PFI contract was signed in June 2007 the Trust announced plans to close 92 more acute beds in addition to the 125 that had already closed since 2006 – allegedly as part of a £4.4m "investment" in community health care. The announcement in February 2008 came just a week after figures revealed that 92% of the Trust's then total of 1268 beds were occupied across all three hospitals[148].

But even as they defended the decision, Trust bosses were having to explain why two years after previous announcements that services were going to be reorganised to reduce length of stay in hospital and

---

[148] *Wakefield Express* February 11 2008

enable more patients to be treated in fewer beds, none of the predicted reduction in demand for beds had taken place. In fact numbers needing hospital care were still increasing. The Trust was having to open up additional spare capacity in hospitals and recruit additional staff to cope with the caseload.

Among the new proposals were the establishment of 25 rehabilitation beds for those who did not need a front-line acute bed but were not ready to be discharged; a community respiratory service to treat people "in the community" and avoid hospital admissions; a scheme for supported discharge of stroke patients who would receive the remainder of their care "at home or in the community"; and the investment in more community based therapists.

Still elusive was any definition of just what was meant by the phrase "in the community" and where any community facilities were to be located.

In the spring of 2009, with the new hospitals still being built, the collapse of Royal Bank of Scotland, and resultant massive government intervention to prop it up, *Union Eyes* was quick to point out that this meant the government effectively owned the lion's share of the bank that had loaned the money for the Mid Yorkshire PFI project. The UNISON Branch stepped up its campaign for the Mid Yorkshire scheme along with other PFIs to be nationalised. *Union Eyes* put the case, which also formed a Branch motion to UNISON's Health Conference in 2009:

> "What is the point of our Trust continuing to pay a massive, index-linked "unitary charge" to RBS for the next 32 years – shelling out £1,200 million for hospitals valued at £353 million – when the government now owns the bank?
>
> "Why should we squeeze down staffing levels by 1,100 in this Trust alone, in order to line the pockets of the remaining RBS shareholders?
>
> "Even now the government has become its majority shareholder, RBS has remained as secretive as ever on the fine detail of the Final Business case they signed with the Trust.
>
> […]
>
> "despite the fact that there is no legitimate argument for the

142

missing details to be kept confidential, despite the fact that it's now effectively OUR bank that is refusing to publish the details, and despite the fact that MPs in our local area include two leading government ministers, we – and local people – are still being kept in the dark.

"The bail-out for the banks has effectively nationalised the losses and the "toxic" debt, while leaving the bankers free to privatise the profits – which include milking millions from our local PFI project."

However there was no let-up in the drive to implement the flawed PFI. The cutbacks continued. On June 4 2009 the update forward plan presented to the Trust board stated:

"The Trust is at significant risk of not meeting its financial targets for 2009/10."

This report highlighted a requirement to make substantial savings, as the Trust headed towards the implementation of the new Hospitals Development Project (HDP).

In addition the PFI consortium were looking to maximise their profits by squeezing down the terms and conditions of the NHS staff they were to manage under the contract.

UNISON members in facilities and estates waged and won a dispute challenging the attempt to introduce new Balfour Beatty Workforce (BBW) downgraded jobs. A massive 95 percent of more than 400 members affected voted to support industrial action against this imposition. After months of management insisting that nothing could be done, since the changes were legally binding under the HDP contract, on September 3 BBW withdrew their new job descriptions and agreed to provide staff reps with copies of the Project Agreement.

During the industrial action consultation meetings, UNISON recruited over 70 new members, increasing its trade union density to well over 90% in the areas affected, and ensuring the Branch had a mandate to proceed immediately with industrial action ballots in the event of further attacks on pay and conditions of any members in those areas.

Branch Secretary Mick Griffiths warned in his annual report in *Union Eyes* early in 2010 that:

"The long-term debt problem of our Trust has not gone away: it has merely been absorbed into the exorbitant long-term cost of the Privately Financed (and commercially secretive) new Hospitals Development Project.

"The problem will be further exacerbated by whoever wins the next general election, as all the main establishment parties are promising to slash public spending – and freeze NHS budgets for years to come.

"While Labour, Tories and Lib-Dems are proposing to squeeze £10-£20 billion worth of cuts from the NHS, the International Monetary Fund is demanding that cuts of nearer £200 billion need to be found. This potentially puts the entire welfare state under threat."

Pontefract hospital opened – staff confront new problems

In February 2010, as the end of the decade of big annual above inflation increases in NHS budgets came to a close, the new Pontefract Hospital opened. Far from joyous celebration that the old buildings had been replaced by a shiny new (if much smaller) hospital, there was an immediate storm of protest from staff working in the new building. Staff who were about to move into the new hospital had been told they could not take their departments' kettles or fridges with them into the new building as they were deemed to be "health and safety hazards"! This ridiculous instruction was made worse for the staff when they eventually moved into the hospital – only to find inadequate rest facilities and high-priced food in the "franchised" catering outlets. During the building of the new hospitals the unions had been assured that there would be adequate rest and catering facilities in the new hospitals.

Staff demanded to know why they were no longer allowed to make their own hot drinks and keep a packed lunch cool in a fridge, as they had done safely for many years before. Why should they be forced to pay 80p for poor quality vending machine drinks, or £1.60 at the BBW café? Why should they have to use the café, which was charging £3 for a baked potato? Why were there only approximately 30 seats in the restaurant area, which was also to be used by visitors and patients? Why did the designated staff room have no chairs or equipment when the hospital opened? After all, the Trust had had years to purchase the furniture and fittings.

And to cap it all the cold water fountains had been removed from the wards and departments without notice on the weekend of 6/7th February.

Management had not warned that kettles & fridges would not be allowed in offices and departments: the unions could see no valid justification for them being banned – other than as a means of forcing staff to pay inflated prices in the new privately-run catering facilities, further boosting the profits of the consortium. *Union Eyes* stated firmly that the union would not accept this:

> "It is clear that what is happening at PGI will happen at the new Pinderfields when it opens, this year and next. We will then be in the ridiculous situation where staff at Dewsbury and other buildings still run by the Trust will continue to have their kettles and fridges – unless of course the Trust has already made the decision to ban them Trust wide?"

Questioning whether the same "health and safety" concerns over kettles and fridges also applied to management offices, UNISON went on with tongue in cheek to publish its own "warning" to management who might fall victim to "killer kettles":

> "UNISON welcomes the Trust and Balfour Beatty's attempts to save staff from these dangerous, life threatening machines.
>
> "We look forward to seeing the kettles and fridges which have been threatening the lives of our esteemed Directors in Rowan House thrown into the dustbin – and trust that our new "PFI partners" Balfour Beatty – who are so zealously protective of our health and welfare – will be providing free hot drinks and meals to replace our tea bags and lunch boxes?
>
> "UNISON is now demanding a full-scale inquiry into the health and safety hazards posed by other apparently innocent office and ward equipment including
>
> staplers (danger of accidental impalement and possible rust inhalation),
>
> ball point pens (hazardous if swallowed, inserted sideways into the mouth, or if either end is used to scratch the ear passage)

waste paper baskets (can easily become stuck on heads, or disturb the balance of a member of staff who accidentally stands in one)

photocopiers – a known hazard for staff who are tempted to sit upon the glass.

"If you have encountered other hitherto unrecognised dangers in your workplace please let us know. It's better (but sometimes a lot more expensive) to be safe than sorry.

"You know it makes sense!"

Change of government: austerity old and new

As many had feared, the June 2010 election brought a defeat for New Labour. Many of those who had been angered alienated by many of New Labour's reactionary policies, including PFI and privatisation, and had more or less concluded there was now little difference between the two main parties, were confronted by the grim reality. David Cameron's Tory-led coalition came to office, and within six months had slammed the brakes on almost any further real terms growth of NHS funding, begun outright cuts in local government and welfare budgets, and swiftly brought out a "White paper" and then a Bill outlining what became a massive top-down reorganisation of the NHS to entrench a full-scale competitive market system, with an ever-growing range of clinical services to be put out to tender.

However in Mid Yorkshire the change of government brought no significant immediate change of policy: the cuts were already under way. The focus shifted to Dewsbury Hospital as the Trust announced that plans to invest £29m in building a new 60-bed specialist cancer wing had been scrapped for lack of cash, raising wider concerns of the future of other services at Dewsbury. New investment appeared to be increasingly centred only on Pinderfields.

Eight months later in October these fears were reinforced when another round of "centralisation" led to the decision to axe trauma care, inpatient children's surgery and neo-natal intensive care at Dewsbury, once again transferring services to Pinderfields. In exchange for the loss of these specialist services, Dewsbury was to become the dumping ground for more "general medicine" cases that would otherwise have been treated in Wakefield. An extra 1,400 medical patients a year were to be diverted to Dewsbury at peak points of peak demand.

In 2011, as the consortium neared completion of the new Pinderfields Hospital and RBS sold on its share of the project to the tax-dodging HSBC subsidiary HICL Infrastructure Investments, Mid Yorkshire Trust chief executive Julia Squire was forced to admit that the Trust was in serious financial trouble as a result of the PFI contract.

It later emerged that the Board had been warned of this the previous November, when members were told that they had made "inaccurate financial assumptions". Months later Ms Squire told the local Dewsbury paper *The Press*:

> "The contract was assessed as affordable, but the way it is structured does increase the trust's savings programme year on year. In the new economic climate this is a pressure."

Pinderfields opens – pressure on Dewsbury

The services finally transferred into the new Pinderfields in March 2011. As a result of the opening of the new hospital, as *Union Eyes* in June 2011 pointed out:

> "We have two brand new gleaming hospitals: but we still have the same old financial miseries, now compounded by the steadily rising cost of payments on the £311m PFI contract which hangs like a millstone round the neck of our Trust."

And despite the hefty price tag, which should have secured a top class building, staff immediately came up against the same poor level of facilities that their colleagues in Pontefract had already faced in their new building. One angry nurse summed up:

> "It's a state of the art hospital, they tell us, but there are no lockers for staff, and no changing rooms. We have to leave our clothes on the floor when we change into our uniforms."

The new Pinderfields had also followed the Pontefract model by opening despite an unresolved problem with the water supply, resulting in strict instructions not to drink water from the tap (hence the mysterious and abrupt decision to remove water fountains from all of the wards prior to opening). Some staff joked that the bug may be transmitted not through plumbing glitches and the water supply, but by Balfour Beatty, the PFI contractors, who appeared to be the only common factor between the two new hospitals 11 miles apart.

The problem with water supplies delayed the opening of the Pontefract hospital, and taps in both hospitals had to be fitted with special filters. The new Pinderfields also suffered two major leaks in plumbing before it opened. To make matters worse, a basic flaw in the design of the plumbing system meant that security staff at Pontefract were obliged to work around the hospital at night turning each tap on for half an hour at a time to keep the water circulating.

> "We're told this will always need to be done," a member of the security team told *Union Eyes*. "It is the equivalent of a full shift's work." Other security tasks had to take second place to this tedious new routine, which was set to consume valuable staff time for decades to come.

But staff frustration at the inadequacies of the costly building were compounded by anger at the attitude of high-handed and Dickensian management, who told nursing staff that they were not allowed their mid-morning cup of tea that had been part of the routine in the old building. One member of staff commented:

> "From the outside it looks like a 21st century building: but walking in there is like stepping back in time: domestics are being required to clock on again, like it's the 1920s."

> "Nursing staff are being told that they have no right to a tea-break, with inappropriate EU regulations being quoted, regardless of the impact on morale. The matron has decided that they can have neither tea nor coffee, only water to drink. But we know that we can't even drink that from the tap!"

'Unitary charge' payments from the Trust to the PFI consortium began in 2011 at £27m a year, but rose each year, regardless of the Trust's level of income and other pressures on it. They were scheduled to reach £55m in the final year of the contract. Staff facing such miserable working conditions immediately asked how such a costly building could be justified as value for money.

Financial woes continue

In April 2011 Mid Yorkshire Hospitals was named by the Department of Health as one of 22 hospital Trusts with high cost PFI schemes whose financial situation made them unlikely to achieve

Foundation Trust status. Trusts like Mid Yorkshire were desperate to meet Andrew Lansley's deadline to become a Foundation by 2013. If not, the threat was that it could be "franchised out" to private managers or broken up and taken over by other Foundation Trusts. The DH feared Mid Yorkshire and similarly-placed trusts might reduce staffing to dangerously low levels in order to cut costs.

This had happened a few years earlier, in the disastrous failure of care at Mid Staffordshire Hospitals. Mid Staffs had been rubber-stamped by the regulator, Monitor, to become a Foundation Trust despite appalling failures of care that were bringing misery to patients in A&E and on the wards. Managers had slashed nursing staff and medical staff to well below basic levels in a drive to cut spending by £10m a year. Subsequent warnings in the 2013 Francis Report proposed the establishment of minimum safe staffing levels, although there are signs that under pressure trusts have since then began again to disregard basic safety issues and to fall back on staffing cuts as a way to address deficits.

The Mid Yorkshire Trust in 2011 faced pressure to cut *six times* as much as Mid Staffs had cut – £60m (more than one eighth of the Trust's annual budget) – over two years to stay afloat. The detail was tucked away in the flowery wording of an April 12 Trust 'Team Brief', but it was official. Half of the savings (£32m) were to meet the government's massive 4 percent per year target for so-called "efficiency savings": the extra £28m was to deal with additional "cost pressures" plus the hangover from the previous year's failure to hit savings targets.

The Team Brief also made it clear that the Trust had little or no idea of how such massive savings could be made. Unions could not even work out if the Trust had one committee looking at this, or two separate ones.

The Team Brief talked confusingly, almost incoherently, in two successive paragraphs about a "Health Economy Foundation Trust Board", and then a "Financial Service Recovery Board" which were apparently "working up schemes". The question was which of these was really in charge? And why did the Trust need two bodies, when it was clear that because so much of the Trust's routine non-clinical budget was now committed to ring-fenced PFI "unitary charge" payments, all of the cuts had to fall on clinical budgets, "corporate" and supplies?

The Team Brief argued that "expenditure had to reduce by 8% for clinical service groups and 10% for corporate": this they said could mean "outsourcing" some services, sharing some others, and "developing new partnerships". It was terribly vague and unconvincing. There were immediate fears that – having recently taken over local community health services previously run by the PCT – the Trust would immediately try to squeeze some of these for savings, and milk resources from this sector to prop up its hospital budget. However reducing community health services would be especially counterproductive if the Trust also wanted to speed up the discharge and shorten the average length of stay in hospital.

The Team Brief said that the Trust was spending £20m a year on temporary staff, overtime, waiting list initiatives and locums. UNISON pointed out that to stop this they would first have to plug the gaps that the temporary staff were helping to fill. *Union Eyes* argued that staff could quite easily turn all these questions round to question management's seriousness:

> "WHY is the agency and overtime bill so high? WHY is our average length of stay so high? WHY are so many outpatient clinics cancelled? WHY are theatres so poorly utilised? And WHY has the PCT not been paying us the right amount for the treatment we have delivered?"

The answer to all these questions of course lay in flawed systems and management failure. If these were not put right, no amount of sacrifice by individual members of staff could solve the problem. *Union Eyes* in June 2011 summed up the union's stance:

> "The Team Brief tells us that they are looking at improving ward stock control to "save £2,000 over year" on each ward. They want improved discharge planning – at a time when social services are again being savagely cut back. They want us to make full use of electronic systems, reduce waste, and avoid penalties for missing targets.
>
> "But even achieving all of this would leave the Trust miles adrift of a £60m cuts target. So what are their real plans?
>
> "Whatever emerges from this confused management, you

can be sure that UNISON will be with you, our members, every inch of the way, as we fight to ensure as best we can that your jobs and conditions, and your ability to give quality care to patients are not put at risk by irresponsible cuts.

"We will not tolerate a Mid Staffordshire disaster here."

As UNISON had warned repeatedly, even as it opened Pinderfields was already too small, and could not cope with additional patients from outside its immediate catchment area.

The new state of the art hospital was consistently failing by some margin to meet its performance target of seeing 95% of emergency patients within four hours, delivering just under 89%, with reports of seasoned nursing staff being reduced to tears by angry patients waiting for treatment. It was the only Trust in the region, and one of only ten in the country to miss the A&E targets at that time.

Yet more miscalculations by Mid Yorkshire Board

By June 2011, just three months after the new Pinderfields Hospital opened, it was already clear that the Trust had again got its calculations badly wrong, not long after closing 250 acute beds as part of the PFI project, the MYHT board began discussing the need to reverse some of its recent decisions – and reopen 76 beds it previously closed in Dewsbury.

Pressures on Dewsbury Hospital were also highlighted by an inquest verdict castigating management at Dewsbury Hospital for not improving its procedures. This was 11 months after a baby had tragically died as a result of a 61-hour delay in a caesarean operation because midwives had been overloaded with work.

The Primary Care Trust – perhaps belatedly aware that the level of demand was linked to the PCT's own continued failure to deliver promised improvements in primary and community health care – agreed to fund additional emergency admissions at the full tariff price, rather than impose a reduced rate on numbers above the contract level.

Barnsley Hospital 11 miles away agreed to take on some of the additional elective patients, many of whom were being diverted into private hospital beds to reduce the waiting list backlog at MYHT, where beds were clogged with emergencies.

The MYHT Board had grudgingly admitted to its failure to take inflation or VAT into account when calculating the costs of the new buildings. To remedy this incompetence it set a massive £60m target for budget cuts over two years in a desperate attempt to balance the books.

The regional efficiency plan published by Yorkshire and Humber Strategic Health Authority warned that the first full year of the PFI unitary charge at MYHT would, together with the national target of efficiency savings, require a further £45m of savings in 2011-12.

Inflation had helped to push up running costs by £6m a year above previous projections, and the Trust was facing penalties of up to £5m for exceeding permitted levels of readmitting recently discharged patients to hospital. It was already falling £14m short of its new savings target.

Yet another firm of private management consultants, Finnamore, were brought in to draw up plans for "reconfiguration" of services to cut spending in the hopes to achieving foundation trust status. Potential cuts at Dewsbury included cardiology services, A&E and the children's ward.

In July 2011 the Trust's auditors warned that "it is recognised that the trust is dependent upon future financial support to achieve statutory break-even in 2011-12". Discussions on such support were "yet to be concluded". By September 2011 MYHT was the only hospital declaring a deficit in Yorkshire and Humber. A month later it was missing its 18 week Referral To Treatment target for seeing elective patients within 18 weeks of referral, getting to just under 80% of those referred within the target time, rather than the required 90%.

Staff could be forgiven for feeling that the change of hospital building had simply intensified the problems they had faced for years and intensified the financial pressures on the trust. Dewsbury, with no PFI hospital, was in effect being sacrificed service by service to feed the beast of PFI, cut costs and keep the trust afloat, losing locally accessible services.

PFI could truly be understood to be not so much an investment as a new and insatiable liability for the Mid Yorkshire trust and many more like it throughout England.

Before and after ... the two hospitals

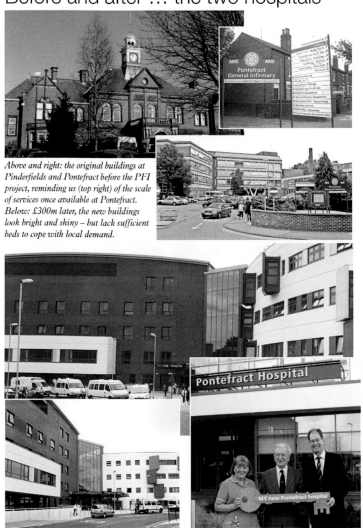

Above and right: the original buildings at Pinderfields and Pontefract before the PFI project, reminding us (top right) of the scale of services once available at Pontefract. Below: £300m later, the new buildings look bright and shiny – but lack sufficient beds to cope with local demand.

153

The prelude: 2004-2006

Nov 2005 public meeting in Pontefract Town Hall against the loss of services

Above and right: A vigorous lobby of the trust board in 2006 against the threat of redundancies resulting from the "turnaround" plans

2006: Frickley Colliery Brass Band helps lead a march to save Pontefract General Infirmary. Below: early issues of Union Eyes warn of defective plans

155

Admin & clerical staff strike back

The strikes against downbanding admin and clerical staff in 2012 and 2013 mobilised large numbers of angry women who had not previously been active. They refused to be intimidated into signing new contracts – and burned them instead.

Right: a mass meeting in Wakefield Town Hall

Above: Medical Laboratory Assistants were also moblised, and joined the 5-day strike against staff shortages in October 2015

156

Large numbers of women who had never previously taken action joined pickets and lobbies during the strikes and the ongoing admin and clerical dispute

Memories of EY, Stephen Eames …

Chief executive Stephen Eames arrived on a monster salary, but also ran up huge bills with management consultants, most notably Ernst & Young – whose lavish fees were ridiculed in a Daily Mirror cartoon.

…and the chaos they left behind

Up to date in 2018 – no to the WOCs!

Repeated strikes at Wrightington, Wigan and Leigh forced their Trust to drop WOC

Mid Yorkshire staff had been alerted to the danger of WOCs from the late autumn of 2017, and were well prepared to win a ballot vote by a massive margin and threaten strike action. After one false start and the threat of a 3-day strike management eventually agreed to drop their plans.

Our Message to our members and the Trust is:
WE ARE AND WILL REMAIN
100% NHS

Above and middle: Standing together against privatisation: staff rally outside Trust HQ against Mid Yorkshire WOC: (right) UNISON Branch Secretary Adrian O'Malley

Union Eyes kept telling the story …

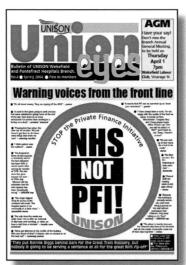

Chapter 6

Life after the new hospital

Mid Yorkshire Hospitals Trust's financial situation worsened abruptly as 2011 ended. A Leeds employment tribunal ordered the Trust to pay a massive £4.5m compensation to a hospital consultant who had suffered mental trauma after colleagues campaigned to get rid of her following maternity leave. Dr Eva Michalak, who worked at Pontefract General Infirmary, won claims for sex and race discrimination and unfair dismissal against the Trust and three of its senior staff members.

The tribunal panel, awarding what was a record-breaking high payment, had been "positively outraged" at the way the employer had behaved, and concluded the Polish-born doctor would never be able to work again.

By January 2012 the Trust's deficit had grown even further, and was forecast to be just under £20m by the end of the financial year – enough to tip the entire region into the red. A team of accountants from yet another consultancy, Ernst & Young, uncovered 'significant shortfalls' in the planned £31m savings programme.

There were warnings that the Trust may have to be dissolved and its services split up between other nearby trusts. The Trust even revealed it was investigating the possibility of using Army medics to staff the A&E at Pontefract, but eventually rejected the idea.

In February 2012, with Pontefract A&E still closed at night, Channel Four News ran a major exposure of the "flagship PFI hospital turning away patients arriving in ambulances because of lack of capacity", and quoting figures showing 87 such "service transfers" in 2011, with patients sent to Dewsbury instead.

A change of leadership

By the end of January 2012, with their management regime discredited and their financial projections in ruins, desperate problems staffing emergency services, and the Trust facing an increasing struggle to survive, Chief Executive Julia Squire resigned, swiftly followed by the Trust chair.

Squire was replaced on an ad-hoc basis by Stephen Eames, until then chief executive of County Durham and Darlington Foundation Trust – who took office in March, with a salary package that swiftly rose to cost MYHT an inflated £300,000 per year.

Stephen Eames' arrival at the trust was swiftly followed by the announcement of a plan to make £23 million 'cost improvements' in 2012-13, once again focused above all on reducing the cost of the workforce. These included reduced hours and offers of unpaid leave for staff. There was a fresh emphasis on the notion of "integration" of services, and talk of possibly downgrading Pontefract's already downsized A&E to a minor injuries unit.

The scale of these cutbacks may well have been fuelled by dire warnings that the trust faced "massive challenges" if it was to turn its finances around, apparently based on findings by costly management consultants Ernst & Young, who had been wheeled in by Yorkshire & Humberside Strategic Health Authority.

Ernst & Young (later renamed just EY) declared themselves alarmed by the financial problems they had uncovered – a "black hole". They claimed that growing numbers of local patients were no longer being treated in Mid Yorkshire hospitals, but were instead being referred by local GPs to hospitals as far afield as Goole and Barnsley.

The Trust was told it needed to strip out 20% of its costs (saving £2 for every £10 of spending) and concentrate on its 'core services'. This could even mean moving the regional burns unit (which was seen as a loss-making service by the PWC report back in 2007) out of Pinderfields to another Yorkshire trust, despite the costs and loss of revenue of such a massive change.

Now you see it, now you don't: the Mid Yorkshire "black hole"

However as 2012 went on and staff reps tried to get more details of the financial "black hole" it vanished as swiftly and mysteriously as it first appeared. It was first reported at the beginning of May. But by the June Joint Consultative and Negotiating meeting with staff side it was no longer being discussed, and in July new figures were presented which stressed the need for a colossal £80m in savings by 2015 and a reduction of 1100 whole time equivalent posts to scale down the workforce.

Early in August UNISON's secretary Adrian O'Malley asked what had happened to the "black hole", but no answer was forthcoming. The Trust had confirmed its lack of any rational priorities by appointing a new 'Associate Director of Organisational Wellbeing' – while seeking cash savings that undermined the wellbeing of low paid staff.

By September of 2012 more questions were being asked about the black hole, which management no longer mentioned in discussing the financial situation. Instead they made clear the objective of saving £20-£23m a year through Cost Improvement Programmes for each of the coming 3-4 years.

As the black hole came and went, management were repeatedly questioned on the value for money of employing Ernst & Young and other costly management consultancies when the plight of the Trust had not been improved by any of the many previous consultants' reports. Staff side argued that since public money was being spent on consultancy work, the details of the contracts with Ernst & Young and others should be in the public domain. The few details that were published showed that in the first nine months of 2012 the Trust had forked out £2.65 million in fees to Ernst & Young, but without setting them any apparent targets, and no value for money assessment of the work they did for it.

MYHT later revealed that the decision to award the contract to Ernst & Young had been made in a secret meeting of the Trust Board, and not put out to competitive tender. There was no fixed timescale for the contract, which could therefore potentially be eked out for many more months by the consultants, who were getting paid by the day, but had been set no savings targets and were not being paid by results.

There was no incentive for them to finish, and every incentive to milk it as long as they could. Unsurprisingly given this generous approach there have been no attempts to benchmark the spending on consultancy in MYHT against the levels of spending in other NHS Trusts.

One reason information on the finances was so hard to obtain was that the previous finance director, on whose watch any "Black Hole" may have developed, was no longer around to answer any questions.

He had unaccountably been declared "redundant" (although how a finance director can genuinely be "redundant" – rather than just ineffective – was a question that was not answered) and left on MARS (the ultra-generous Mutual Agreed Redundancy Scheme which seems primarily to have benefited senior managers).

And as further evidence that the Trust had its eye on the ball, as PFI costs drove the Trust deeper into crisis, the director of estates, who was also in charge of PFI, was also absent, on "gardening leave".

Screwing savings from the lowest-paid

In May 2012 the Trust launched the Workforce Challenge – as a means to make savings by reducing staffing and the pay bill. This began with the assertion that the Trust's deficit for the previous last year was likely to be £19.7m, and that the underlying deficit was estimated at £37m.

The argument was simple: since there was a hole that big in the finances, and 70% of the Trust's income was spent on staff, staff had to carry the lion's share of any savings to balance the books. The document said as much:

> "While staff are at the heart of our patients' experience, the burden of meeting this challenge will impact most on our workforce."

The working assumption was that the Trust needed 'cost improvements' of £24m by 2013, but the Workforce Challenge admitted that only £14m of potential savings had been identified. Towards this target no less than ten reviews were set up, the most significant from UNISON's point of view being the Admin and Clerical review and the review of Clinical Nurse Specialist arrangements.

The Admin & Clerical review set out to cut the equivalent of 40-80 jobs to save £1-£2 million, primarily from medical secretaries, booking teams, coordinators and facilitators, and ward clerks. The main focus was on staff below Band 7.

This was the review which led to the ongoing industrial dispute that brought repeated strikes as admin and clerical staff resisted downbanding that threatened to cost some staff up to £2,800 a year in lost salary.

There was also to be a separate review of management, which by contrast was seeking to cut no more than 2 to 6 jobs, even while admitting that management costs in the Trust were higher than comparable Trusts elsewhere. A review of nurse management also set out to cut 2-6 posts, as did the review of Clinical Nurse Specialists review which also wanted to cut 2-6 posts (from a staff of 197, including staff transferred into the trust as a result of the takeover of community services).

Yet another review of estates and facilities management set a target of cutting 40-80 staff to save £1-£2 million. The Trust stated that this was partly based on recommendations from the PWC review of the PFI contract, which – in keeping with its policies on transparency and engagement – the Trust refused to release to the unions or to the wider public.

On top of this the Workforce Challenge included reviews of Operating Theatre productivity (seeking to save £1.9m in 2012-13); Out Patients productivity – based on more consultancy, this time from Ernst & Young – and aimed at saving £1-£2 million; and procurement practices, with no immediate threat to jobs.

In other words the Workforce Challenge was consistently aimed at seeking savings from the lowest paid and least senior staff, while leaving in post the managers whose systems appeared to be seriously deficient in comparison with other Trusts, and whose extraordinary financial incompetence had brought soaring bills for consultancy and of course the signing of the PFI contract – with all the consequences we have seen since.

Admin and clerical staff in revolt against pay cuts

The Trust's efforts to secure savings by cutting the pay of support staff met strong resistance from the 400 or so members affected. The previously untapped militancy of this group of mainly female staff clearly took management by surprise: among the most active and vocal during the dispute were a large number of receptionists.

However by this point the Trust was clearly embarking on the first of what was intended to be a series of exercises in downbanding staff, reducing their standing on the Agenda for Change pay banding system, to save money from payroll. Reasoned argument and negotiations from the trade union side proved fruitless, the membership showed a solid response, backing a ballot for strike action and in November a one-day strike, followed by a further 3 days of action confirmed their determination to hold on to their hard-won national terms and conditions.

Angry rallies of admin and clerical strikers held in Dewsbury and Wakefield Town Hall voted unanimously to escalate the strike action if the Trust implemented its plans for downbandings. They concluded, quite reasonably, that since the Trust had up to then refused to negotiate on the issue, it was likely they had more downbandings planned for other groups of staff in the future. And since Ernst and Young had been heavily involved with the review of Clinical Nurse Specialists, there were real concerns that they too could be targets for downbanding, and other groups of staff were also hearing rumours about their pay bands being at risk.

The Trust would not listen to common sense arguments. They insisted that staffing costs (i.e. wages) had to be cut to address the deficit. This was completely unacceptable to UNISON and the staff side. *Union Eyes* November 2012 issue in its front page lead article argued that

> "It may therefore be necessary to widen the numbers involved in the dispute or go for a Branch wide ballot for industrial action. If that happens we urge you to vote yes. If a ballot of UNISON members takes place it will only have been announced due to the refusal of the Trust to withdraw its plans for mass downbanding of A&C and other staff."

In the event the dispute dragged on into 2013, with a 5-day strike beginning on January 28, supported by 120 pickets outside Dewsbury, Pinderfields and Pontefract hospitals. By then staff resistance had been hardened further by the bullying management tactic of sending out dismissal and reengagement letters to as many as 300 affected staff, setting a deadline for them to sign to register their acceptance of new contracts on lower pay bands.

"Normal practice" at MYHT

The HR director Graham Briggs, who on behalf of Chief Executive Stephen Eames had effectively created the dispute, confirmed how bad things had got in the Trust when he argued in the local press that:

"Dismissal and re-engagement is perfectly legitimate and normal practice for changing terms and conditions of service when negotiations and consultation have broken down."[149]

Many who had received these letters joined together on the Thursday of the strike to ceremonially burn them outside the Trust HQ in a display of defiant solidarity. The next day the strikers were visited on the picket lines by UNISON General Secretary Dave Prentis who promised to support them if they won a yes vote in a branch-wide ballot of all 3,000 members.

A rally at Wakefield Town Hall voted unanimously to carry out such a ballot, a step that would escalate the action to a new level. They heard that the branch had received a massive £27,000 in donations from fellow trade unionists all over the country.

During the strikes Stephen Eames claimed he was ready to meet with UNISON "any time any place, anywhere". It seemed he was simply echoing singing the words of the old Martini advert, especially since Mr Eames had been conspicuous by his absence from all of the key meetings and negotiations, and consistently refused UNISON requests for a meeting.

Branch suggestions for big savings

The branch nonetheless responded to the challenge by the Trust to come up with alternative ways of saving the Trust money. Among UNISON's many suggestions was that the Trust should stop throwing money at private management consultants such as Ernst and Young, who had picked up a hefty £2.6m out of the £3.4m squandered on consultancy since March 2011 – at a time when one of the Trust's claimed financial targets was to reduce the amount they spend on agency staff. Ernst and Young were the ones recommending the downbanding of Admin and Clerical staff.

The Trust response was that they had "budgeted" for these

---

[149] Mort, D. (2013) Union to ballot 3,000 members in bitter dispute at mid Yorkshire Hospitals Trust, Wakefield Express, February 1, https://www.wakefieldexpress.co.uk/news/union-to-ballot-3-000-members-in-bitter-dispute-at-mid-yorkshire-hospitals-trust-1-5376585

additional managers. Admin and Clerical strikers were outraged and insulted by these comments. The Trust was cutting their pay to save £650,000 – while handing over four times that amount to E&Y.

A second suggestion which the Trust failed to take up was to renegotiate the PFI, which had risen with inflation and was costing the Trust over £40 million a year. Other Trusts with massive PFI debts who were facing financial meltdown were being given financial support from the government to tide them over. UNISON asked why this hadn't happened in Mid Yorks, and called on Stephen Eames to use his management expertise to argue for extra income into the trust rather than cutting income of UNISON members.

A third suggestion was to start at the top. Why didn't the trust decide to employ its own Chief Executive rather than paying £27,000 a month to County Durham and Darlington NHS Trust for one on loan? Also why was the Trust employing more Directors when money was allegedly so short? *Union Eyes* posed the further, obvious question:

> "If we need so many Band 8 and above managers in the Trust, why were they all able to drop their vitally important work to cover our Band 2.3 and 4 A&C members on the 4 strike days?"

There was no reply. Attempts at further negotiations after the January strike brought a Trust offer of 18 months of pay protection for the staff set to lose income, plus six more months paid as a lump sum, apparently to "help the individuals affected to adjust to the change". As part of this offer the date for return of dismissal and re-engagement letters was pushed back to March 28.

These offers did not placate the angry staff, who were not only facing a pay cut but also expected to continue to do all the same work they had previously on a higher band. The relations between Trust and unions continued to worsen.

An exchange of emails between UNISON and Chief Executive Stephen Eames indicated the gulf between the two sides: UNISON Branch Secretary Adrian O'Malley pointed out that:

> "Mr Briggs says he is disappointed […]. His disappointment is tiny compared to that of our low paid members who, unlike the Directors of the Trust, are facing massive pay cuts

whilst at the same time having to cover the work of dozens of their colleagues who have left the organisation."[150]

With no progress in negotiation, UNISON decided at the end of April 2013 to hold the ballot of all 3,000 members and potentially escalate the dispute. Adrian O'Malley explained to the local press:

"As we expected the Trust is pushing forward with more downbandings and job losses in other departments. Clinical Nurse Specialists, Dental Nurses and more Admin staff are at risk of job and pay cuts. At the same time the Trust is employing more senior managers and has given over £4 million to private management consultants Ernst and Young.

"We have been forced into balloting our whole membership as the Trust is unwilling to discuss any alternatives to the downbandings (pay cuts). The Trust is holding a gun to its staff's heads and saying "take a pay cut or you're sacked". We cannot allow this to continue. Industrial relations within the Trust have broken down due to the senior management's bullying."[151]

An agreement, or not an agreement?

In the event a legally binding agreement was signed with the Trust that stated that every downbanded worker's Job Description (JD) would be revisited after six months and jointly agreed before going to job evaluation.

Following months of management dragging their feet, the JD for Central Waiting List Office Staff was finally agreed. It confirmed that the CWLO staff were still working at Band 3 levels, and not to the Band 2 JD they had been forced to sign or lose their jobs

---

[150] These emails and other details summarised here have been published by UNISON and are still available at:
https://www.facebook.com/275200775915924/posts/dear-mr-eamesbelow-are-emails-between-myself-and-stephen-eames-chief-executive-f/319752938127374 (accessed August 29 2018).

[151] Pantry, L (2013) Unison to ballot 3,000 members at mid Yorkshire Hospitals Trust, Wakefield Express, April 29,
https://wakefieldexpress.co.uk/news/unison-to-ballot-3-000-members-at-mid-yorkshire-hospitals-trust-1-5626886.

But not until November 2014 did the downbanded waiting list staff in the department finally get their original Band 3 pay bands reinstated by the Trust's joint staff side/management internal Agenda for Change Job Evaluation panel. UNISON immediately pressed for agreement on updated JD's for the remaining staff including Receptionists, Medical Secretaries, Fast Track, Call Centre and Office Admin staff who had also been downbanded and who were still working to their old job descriptions.

Nor was that the end of the process; in April 2015 UNISON was still having to report to members that the Trust was dragging its heels and failing to implement the agreement they had signed two years earlier:

> "Our last meeting to discuss the rest of the Job Descriptions was cancelled on the evening before for no apparent reason and has not been rearranged.
>
> "We are now in a situation where the Trust is in breach of a) the national Agenda for Change policy b) its own Disputes Policy and c) the Collective Binding Agreement signed in good faith by UNISON, Unite and the Trust at the end of the Amin and Clerical strike in 2013."

The fallout of the dispute has continued to this day. Medical Secretaries, Receptionists and others are still waiting for their Job Descriptions to be reviewed while numerous new senior management posts have been created across the trust.

Disastrous management

While the underlying pressure of the overhead costs of the PFI payments were undoubtedly a factor in this protracted dispute which disrupted the lives of hundreds of relatively low-paid support staff, it's impossible to overlook the supremely poor management skills of the highly paid HR and other directors, whose talents appeared to be in prolonging and deepening the conflict rather than seeking any resolution.

This was underlined in May 2013, when more details emerged of the "Workforce Challenge" proposals, which included listing the full time posts of UNISON's Branch Secretary Adrian O'Malley and the staff side secretary Maria Thompson as up for redundancy – under the flimsy pretext of opening up more "partnership working".

This issue was taken up in an excellent article by the *Daily Mirror's* Paul Routledge, who noted that:

> "This new package of measures would effectively scupper the ability of Unison members, numbering more than 3,000, to choose full-time union reps on the NHS payroll. The cost to the health service of this long-standing arrangement is probably less than £50,000 a year. It is money well spent on good industrial relations, easing life at work in the cash-strapped NHS."[152]

However Mid Yorkshire bosses had very different ideas, spelled out in a garbled document, which was roundly condemned by Paul Routledge:

> "I have seen a copy of the proposed partnership agreement. It is a monument to management speak, a parcel of drivel that would embarrass any half-capable GCSE English candidate. It makes you shudder just to read it. That's not the point.
>
> "Behind the human resources psychobabble is a clear intention to stuff the union. Less time for anyone to represent the members, and only then with the permission of the bosses.
>
> "Tell us what you're doing, and why, and we might allow you to do it.' I paraphrase, because to print the entire document would send you screaming into the sunset. Nobody should be made to read the effusions of HR boss Graham Briggs.
>
> "In the US, it would be deemed a cruel and unusual punishment, and therefore illegal."

This dispute was eventually resolved following Adrian bringing a claim of Discrimination on Trade Union grounds and whistleblowing to the Employment Tribunal. After a day being grilled by UNISON'S barrister, Graham Briggs in December 2013 signed a Memorandum of Understanding with the union for paid facility time for the elected branch stewards and the threat of redundancy was lifted.

---

[152] Routledge, P. (2013) Mealy-mouthed NHS bosses put union reps on critical list, Daily Mirror, 17 May, https://www.mirror.co.uk/news/uk-news/paul-routledge-nhs-bosses-putting-1893521

Fears for future under new Tory "reforms"

At the end of April 2012, with the controversial Health and Social Care Act having just been finally forced through Parliament, a detailed report on the Trust by the *Health Service Journal's* Dave West raised the obvious question of whether the cash handouts which had managed to keep the Trust afloat so far would continue once GPs (through the Clinical Commissioning Groups to be established under the new Act) took over responsibility for commissioning decisions. West noted:

> "The health economy is one of the most deprived in the country, with associated problems particularly long-term conditions leading to early acute illness. It means there is heavy demand on general acute services. These can often have a lower – if any – earnings margin for the trust, compared to elective procedures. At the same time the trust sees relatively less demand for the financially beneficial elective work. There is very little opportunity for the trust to ease its finances with private sector income." (*HSJ* 24 April 2012).

Other challenges included the development of new trauma centres in Leeds, Hull and Sheffield, which were expected to reduce the number of serious emergencies dealt with at MYHT – and make recruitment of A&E specialist doctors more difficult.

The confusion also deepened in April 2012 when extra beds opened in the casualty unit at Dewsbury District Hospital to help cope with demand following the night closure of the A&E Department at Pontefract.

In May 2012 another *Health Service Journal* reporter, Ben Clover, revealed that Mid Yorkshire Hospitals had been one of 19 trusts formally warned by the Department of Health's "Director Of Provider Delivery" Matthew Kershaw that it had fallen behind the schedule required by the "foundation trust pipeline" to prepare them for foundation status.

Writing to Stephen Eames, Kershaw had suggested that "the unsustainable providers regime could help identify a sustainable service strategy." According to the *HSJ* summary, Kershaw also pointed out that the finances of the trust's PFI project had been based on a plan to reduce the workforce by 20%, which had not been achieved[153].

Kershaw's letter came soon after the resignation of all four of MYHT's non-executive directors – creating a clean sweep of chair, Chief Executive and non-executives from the board since the beginning of the year.

In June of 2012 the confusion continued amid rapid changes. Rumours that specialist care services at Dewsbury were to be closed were being strenuously denied. Meanwhile the trust attempted to set a target to reduce accident and emergency admissions in Wakefield by 8%. A month later consultation was opened on plans to shift a number of specialist services out of Pinderfields, to Dewsbury and Pontefract, to help deal with capacity problems at Pinderfields.

Neuro rehabilitation services, a 12 bed unit, would move from

---

[153] It did not feel like it at the time, but Mid Yorkshire Hospitals had a lucky escape on this. Kershaw was soon to make headlines in his own right when he was appointed by as the 'Trust Special Administrator' as part of the 'unsustainable providers regime' which brought the break-up of the South London Hospitals Trust. SLHT had been bankrupted by the rising and increasingly unaffordable extra costs of two disastrous PFI contracts, for Queen Elizabeth Hospital, Woolwich, and Princess Royal University Hospital in Farnborough. Kershaw's proposals, which were subject to just four week's pretence of "consultation," were to break up SLHT and slash back its staff numbers, to write off its accumulated £207m debts, and subsidise the two PFI contracts to the tune of over £22m per year for the next 20 years. But he also decided to CLOSE the remainder of the third hospital in SLHT, and, worse, to CLOSE acute services and 60% of the buildings at the highly successful and solvent Lewisham Hospital, which was not part of SLHT at all. The plans all hinged upon the assertion that an "urgent care centre" could replace 77% of the work of Lewisham's busy A&E, and that community health services would somehow reduce the need for hospital care.

It was the cuts at Lewisham which triggered the biggest opposition to his plan, with a large and powerful local campaign which resulted in a successful legal challenge to the proposals, upheld on appeal. (Lister 2012, https://healthemergency.org.uk/pdf/LondonHealthEmergencyResponseto TSA-Dec2012.pdf)

Pinderfields to Dewsbury to deal with patients who had suffered strokes, brain injury and other conditions, and link up with Dewsbury's stroke rehabilitation services. Ophthalmology services would be transferred from Pinderfields to Pontefract. There would also be additional orthopaedic services at Dewsbury and Pontefract to expand elective capacity, after it was revealed that half of the trust's hip and knee replacement operations were being sent to independent sector hospitals, draining scarce resources out of the Trust – and out of the NHS.

In August 2012 it was revealed that – as a result of cash shortages – nurses at Dewsbury Hospital were having to clean wards two days a week. Standards of care for elderly patients at Dewsbury were strongly criticised in a report by inspectors, and trust bosses were given a formal warning by the Care Quality Commission, following a similar warning over the hospital's maternity unit six months earlier.

PFI overheads – and inadequate tariff payments

With the Trust headed for a £26 million deficit, there was speculation as to the actual figure being paid out as the unitary charge on the PFI hospitals. The Dewsbury local paper *The Press* reported that the 2012-13 year payment was £43 million: trust bosses claimed that the figure was £34.2 million, but a spokesperson refused to answer questions on how much Balfour Beatty was making from the deal, arguing that "all information relating to our PFI deals is commercially sensitive."

In October 2012 *nationalhealthexecutive.com* reported a study showing that the tariff payment for A&E had fallen so low that seven out of every ten Accident and Emergency departments were losing money, even though they were having to deal with increasing numbers of patients. Hospitals had increased their efficiency in diagnosing and treating patients in A&E, but trusts were receiving an average of just £79-£123 for each A&E patient while costs averaged between £69 and £129.

The study, by the Foundation Trust Network, argued that numbers of admissions could be reduced by providing increased nursing and physio services in A&E before discharging patients, and by increasing out of hours primary and community services – precisely the policies that have been repeatedly discussed, but never materialised in Mid Yorkshire.

Also in October plans were finally revealed for downgrading the A&E service at Dewsbury and also its maternity unit, which was to be "centralised" – at Pinderfields. The formal public consultation was due to start in January 2013.

In November the Commons Public Accounts Committee named Mid Yorkshire as one of ten hospital trusts in serious financial trouble. PAC chair Margaret Hodge argued that it was unclear how the Department of Health could continue to underwrite PFI payments to hospitals like Mid Yorkshire, and said:

> "We do not know whether a bankrupt trust would be allowed to fail, or how and when ministers will intervene. And it is not clear how the Department of Health would ensure essential services are protected if the trust fails." [154]

In December the *Health Service Journal* reported David Bennett, the chief executive of the health regulator Monitor saying that he felt it would be worth examining the possibility of a public sector buyout of the £330 million PFI hospital at Peterborough, a slightly larger PFI contract than Mid Yorkshire, which was then in deficit to the level of almost 25% of its turnover, and, like MYHT, entirely dependent on external additional funding to fend off insolvency[155].

In January 2013 the MYHT board heard that the year-end deficit was forecast to hit £24.7 million: this was technically an improvement against the original plan. The finance performance report resounded with pride at the fact that:

> "all statutory duties are being met ... with the exception of the duty to break even".

According to the March 2013Board Papers the Trust's financial plight and performance both appeared to have improved marginally to the end of the financial year. However MYHT was still heavily reliant on financial handouts, as the financial situation of the NHS

---

[154] https://www.yorkshirepost.co.uk/news/nhs-trusts-face-going-bust-over-new-deal-on-funding-1-5074263

[155] https://www.hsj.co.uk/topics/finance-and-efficiency/bennett-moots-pfi-buyout-for-peterborough/5052807.article

became tighter, with the heaviest pressure on front line trusts with high volumes of emergency work, like Mid Yorkshire.

Another MYHT "consultation": 200 more beds at risk

All hopes of balancing the books of MYHT now hinged on forcing through a massive programme of cuts under the Clinical Services Strategy. Yet again the Trust planned to cut their way out of problems, by axing 200 beds, hundreds of jobs and downgrading services at Dewsbury in the hopes of delivering £15m 'savings' by 2017.

The plans, set out for the public in a skimpy and superficial A5 document, were submitted to a token "consultation" in early March 2013, which in theory was due to run to the end of May. However it was already clear before it started that health chiefs had made up their minds, and intended to drive through their "Option 2" regardless of public views and opposition.

The £38m plan to reorganise services would have reduced Dewsbury's A&E to an urgent care centre, and downgraded Dewsbury hospital to deliver only elective and rehabilitation services – with all serious emergencies and complex cases having to travel to Wakefield. The bed cuts had been planned at the very same time as the new Pinderfields hospital had been cramming extra beds into its 'state of the art' 4-bed bays to ease the pressure on bed numbers – at the expense of patient care, safety and efficiency.

The Trust admitted however that all of the cuts together would not save enough to put the Mid Yorkshire Hospitals Trust back into financial balance even by 2017. Even if it all worked exactly as planned the Trust would still be running at more than £10m in the red each year. So the prospect was even more cuts to follow, and more cuts after that.

At the centre of the Mid Yorkshire crisis was still the soaring cost of the £311m PFI scheme. The basic costs had risen to more than £40m a year for the Unitary Payment, and were set to rise every year, index linked, for another 29 years. In total the bill for the new hospital had grown with payments now totalling over £1.5 billion – while the Trust also had to fork out millions more in capital charges and had lost considerable potential revenue income from car parking and other facilities that had been taken over by the PFI consortium, making the real cost of the scheme much higher.

Another contradiction was that while the new Pinderfields was built too small to deal with local health needs, only part of the capacity of the new £60m Pontefract Hospital was being used.

The rising cost of PFI payments year by year meant that plans had to revolve around maximum use of the hugely expensive new buildings: so none of the 200 beds scheduled to close were in Pinderfields.

The cost of a PFI hospital does not go down even when services are reduced: the only savings are from reduced numbers of staff. This has been why, in the quest for savings, Dewsbury Hospital, which does not have a PFI bill attached, has been systematically milked of services to generate savings.

Another inadequate "business case"

The Trust's 2013 "Outline Business Case" *Meeting the Challenge* was once again neither a full outline, nor a business case. There was nothing to show a proper breakdown of where beds would be closed, or how the changes correlated with local patterns of demand and health needs: no explanation of where the "extra" 50 beds and other bits and pieces of expanded services would be tacked on to the (consortium-owned) Pinderfields Hospital, and no correlation between the sums of money referred to and the specific changes, cutbacks and investments.

Meeting the Challenge and the supporting Data Sheet on Emergency/Urgent Care amounted to little more than an extended admission of the failure of all the previous proposals to shift care out of hospital and expand services in primary care and in the community. Once again there were no details of where the notional "community teams" would be based, how they would be organised, when and how they would be recruited and trained, or why these same proposals should have been expected to work this time when on every previous occasion the fine words had delivered none of the promised changes.

The failure to shift the pressure off A&E was illustrated by an Emergency Services Data Sheet which made clear that attendances at MYHT's A&Es increased by a massive 9% in 2012-13 – and the fact that many of these were seriously ill was underlined by an even larger increase in emergency admissions, up by 10%.

The total Trust caseload of over 220,000 A&E attendances each year was already enormous by almost any comparison; but so too was the proportion needing a hospital bed. No less than 33% of A&E attenders at Pinderfields had to be admitted to hospital, a high figure partly inflated as a result of the downgrading of Pontefract – from where now all the more serious cases diverted to Pinderfields.

These figures for emergency services were described as the highest or second highest in the North of England: however another way to look at it would be to argue that the development of alternative, community based services and primary care in Wakefield and Kirklees has been the weakest or second weakest in the North of England. It's clear however that those patients requiring admission from A&E had needs well beyond any likely expansion of community health services.

Time and again the number of emergency admissions was described in *Meeting the Challenge* as "unnecessary", "avoidable", or inappropriate – without explaining what other services might have been able to take this additional caseload, or how such services might be established. Glib summary tables suggested that a total of 202 beds could be replaced by "investment in services outside hospital" – without at any point saying what services, or where the necessary investment might have come from.

The £38m development funds that were available (p44) were all to be invested in hospital beds and services, almost all of them at Pinderfields. To cut A&E attendances and 17,000 emergency admissions a year, reduce outpatient appointments by 20%, deliver minor surgery in (undisclosed) alternative 'non-hospital' locations, and reduce lengths of stay in hospital would clearly cost a similar amount if not more – and require hundreds of staff, properly managed and organised with appropriate information systems and transport. Yet the "Business Case" offered no concrete proposal on what body might be in a position to foot the bill for this.

The two local Clinical Commissioning Groups, which since 2013 had formally taken charge of the local NHS budget, appeared content to express general support for the *Meeting the Challenge* proposals without any commitment to make the resources available. Yet it was clear that until viable alternative services had been put in place, established, and accepted by local people, there could be no real prospect of altering the current focus on services around emergency departments and hospital care.

The document indicated that neither the Trust nor local commissioners had learned anything from previous failed exercises. It was like groundhog day – yet another account of the same old promises. *Meeting the Challenge* did not even meet its own challenge and boldly set out a clear way forward. Instead:

- MYHT stated they wanted to reduce the use of hospitals, and treat more patients in their own homes or in the "community": but they outlined no practical plan to set up and resource suitable alternative services.
- They claimed their aim was to speed patients through hospital more quickly, but they gave no detail on how they hoped to achieve this.
- They wanted to reduce use of A&E services, but had not analysed the needs of those attending A&E, or established what alternatives might have ensured they were treated in other ways.

They announced the need to give more support to frail elderly patients in their own homes, and admitted that a major stumbling block to this was the patchy and often inadequate services delivered by GPs and primary care. Of course the Trust was not in control of primary care: the body that previously did this had just been abolished – and the new body that had taken over – supposedly led by GPs – also had revealed no plans to improve GP services.

To make matters worse, many of the documents that had been produced were drafted not by the Trust's own highly paid managers, but churned out by even more expensive management consultants. The only real winners in all this had been city accountants like Ernst and Young. Management consultants have consistently proven they know nothing and care less about the people and health care services of Wakefield, Pontefract and Dewsbury. In fact some of the documents over the years have seemed to have been written by visitors from another planet.

But local health chiefs have also been contemptuous of their own staff and local communities: that's why they have repeatedly deferred to such inadequate "experts", and time and again organised meetings with "stakeholders" that excluded front line health workers and their organisations, and include only token, hand-picked "representatives" from patients and community groups.

While local services faced another five miserable years of cuts, debts, instability, pointless reorganisation and confusion under the plan, Ernst & Young and PWC were still laughing all the way to the bank – along with a growing list of the Trust's senior managers who had wangled themselves massive pay-offs to leave, rather than face up to the magnitude of their failure.

When the Branch published a detailed pamphlet on the history of the PFI up to date in April 2013[156] the Mid Yorkshire Trust was still lurching along, dependent on cash handouts and strategic decisions taken elsewhere. The projections on which they signed the PFI contract in 2007, and almost all of their figures and proposals since the 1990s had been shown to be hopelessly unrealistic, and had helped to push the Trust into an increasingly desperate situation.

Staff under pressure

The 2014 NHS Staff Survey once again found the Trust performing worse than average on some key issues:

- Work pressure felt by staff.
- Staff suffering from work related stress.
- Staff recommendation of the Trust as a place to work or receive treatment.
- Staff motivation at work.

In the 20154-15 Annual Report the Trust even acknowledged that there was further work needed on the following areas:

- Staff communication.
- Involvement in decision making.
- Training.
- Appraisals.
- Relationships with senior managers.

One conspicuous area of failure identified in the Annual Report

---

[156] Lister, J. (2013) *Dead Weight*, available
https://healthemergency.org.uk/pdf/DeadWeight.pdf

was management of staff sickness, where it appeared that the management effort had if anything been counterproductive. The blurb sounded positive:

"There has been continued focus on managing sickness absence over the course of the year. This has involved improving the support for staff with particular focus on the most common reasons for absence, for example musculoskeletal (MSK) problems.

But the results were far from positive:

• Sickness absence has increased slightly since last year from 4.39% to 4.71%.

• Stress related illness has increased from 22% to 23%, whilst MSK and back problems have decreased from 22% in 2013/14, down to 21% in 2014/15 (Annual report 2014-15: p62).

Morale would not have been improved by the news in the same Annual Report, which revealed Mid Yorkshire's chief executive Stephen Eames had received an increase of £10,000 in his salary in 2014-15 – at a time when other staff pay was still frozen.

The salary of the highest paid director rose from £245-250,000 to £255-260,000, around ten times the median total remuneration (half way between the highest and lowest) – which remained static at £25,000-£30,000. The gap between the luxury at the top and the average income across the Trust therefore widened. *Union Eyes* commented:

> "NHS pay injustice is not Mr Eames's fault: but we would like him to be with us in pressing for a change of course, rather than standing firm against staff trying to restore their Band 3 and 4 salaries."

The Trust ended the 2014-15 financial year boasting that it had delivered a deficit of only £9.1m ("an improvement against our plan of £18m"). Although the Trust performance included in year "savings" of almost £24m, the improvement primarily reflected the unexpected receipt of "additional income in year from the Department of Health."

In December 2014 the Trust's payment of £231,000 to management consultants Ernst and Young brought the total paid to them – dating back to December 2011 – to an incredible £10,696,552. UNISON had objected to these payments ever since it was first discovered that Ernst & Young were working with the Trust during the Workforce Challenge consultation in 2012/13.

The Trust had been happy to go on paying out at the rate of over £3.5 million a year for private sector management advice even while it was proposing to make staff redundant, cutting the pay of hundreds of admin staff and imposing stringent Cost Improvement Programmes of up to 6% a year on wards and departments in its efforts to balance its books.

To make matters worse, at the end of 2014 the Trust announced that there would be another two more years of multi-million Cost Improvement Programmes to come. UNISON submitted questions under the Freedom of Information Act to the Trust in an attempt to find out what the Trust has got for its money, and received the following reply.

> "Detailed pricing information is withheld. It is the Trust's opinion that disclosure of this information is exempt under Section 43(2) of the FOIA in that disclosure would be likely to prejudice the commercial interests of the third party."

This was nonsense: the Trust is mandated to publish details of all spending over £25,000 every month on its website: that's where UNISON found out £10,696,552 had been spent on consultants up to then.

The Branch also asked the Trust for:

• A list of the service reviews, departmental reviews and consultations Ernst and Young had been employed by the Trust to carry out and or take part in.

• The remit Ernst and Young had been given by the Trust for each of the above

• The recommendations made to the Trust by Ernst and Young for each of the above

• The cost to the Trust for each of the above

• All documents that had been produced by Ernst and Young for the Trust Board and its sub committees.

• All documents relating to the Trust ensuring Value for Money and the delivery of results/targets from Ernst and Young.

• All documentation relating to the tendering of management consultancy work carried out for the Trust by Ernst and Young.

In reply the Trust acknowledged that it had the information requested, but:

> "To obtain this information would require using significant resources and I estimate that it will cost more than the appropriate limit to consider your request.
>
> "I believe that to undertake the work required and to be able to provide this information would fall under section 12 of the FOI Act (See Annex below) in that the cost of complying with the request would exceed the appropriate limit of £450.
>
> "The appropriate limit has been specified in regulations and for public bodies other than central Government (£600) it is set at £450.
>
> "This represents the estimated cost of one person spending 2½ working days (calculated at £25 per person, per hour, per day) in locating, retrieving and extracting the information."

In other words they could give no clear or coherent account of what advice they had received, and refused to tell the unions and the public how and what they had spent £10.7m of taxpayers' money on. *Union Eyes* commented:

> "This sorry episode sums up the role of the private sector in the NHS. Private companies appear to be immune from scrutiny and accountability, and are allowed to hide behind the protection of 'commercial confidentiality'.
>
> "In the case of Mid Yorkshire, they are also supported by a Trust Board which does not believe £10.6 million is "particularly excessive".
>
> "Our members in the HSDU who were subjected to a review by E&Y which recommended the removal of a paid break, or our Admin staff, who were downbanded to save a small fraction of the money E&Y have received, may have a different opinion on how Trust money should be better spent. [...]
>
> "When we are facing staff shortages on the wards, how many nurses would £3.5 million a year pay for?"

The UNISON branch put down a motion on this for the 2015 UNISON Health conference, calling for action against the use of management consultants in the NHS, and urging UNISON nationally to expose the scandalous waste of public money spent on management consultancy within the NHS, and campaign for a value for money audit of all projects delivered by management consultants, for all public contracts to be brought under the remit of the Freedom of Information Act and for the transparency and accountability of all contracts signed by NHS bodies.

Trust's secretarial error

Management consultancy was not the only way in which the Trust was seeking to squander public funds on private sector providers. The Admin & Clerical review in 2013 had seen Medical Secretary posts reduced and staff downbanded from Band 4 to Band 3.

But that same year, despite needing to save money, Mid Yorkshire Trust, spent £148,756.17 outsourcing typing backlogs to a private company called Dict8. Dictaphone recordings were sent out electronically to an external company for typing. Once it was returned, Medical Secretaries were then expected to copy and paste the letters onto the appropriate templates, listen to any gaps in dictation and correct as appropriate. Whether this would save any time at all was questionable.

Whilst copying and pasting may be quicker, often the quality of the typing was well below standard. UNISON raised this issue in November 2014 with Bob Chadwick, Director of Finance, who stated that he had been speaking to departments to ask them to review how much they were spending on Dict8, and that the company should only be used when there were backlogs.

However a Freedom of Information Request from UNISON showed that the Trust had continued to spend money on Dict8 and between April and October 2014, spending a further £50,625.82. Typing was once again outsourced over the Christmas period, so this cost was only going to increase.

In the two years preceding the reduction and downbanding of staff, 2010/11 and 2011/12, the spending on Dict8 had only amounted to £10,703.96. In 2012/13, the year of the admin review, spending on Dict8 rose sharply almost five-fold to £48,764 – proving that the reduced staffing levels were already having a significant impact.

Altogether spending on this outsourced work amounted to a grand total of £248,146.64: this would have paid for approximately 12 full time secretaries. As UNISON had argued, the new medical secretaries' structure had failed. It needed more staff –and less money spent on outsourcing.

Another illustration of the poor value of private contractors was given by the contract for the digital scanning of patient case notes which came up for renewal and was put out to tender by the Trust in 2014. Medical Records staff had been told that three options were to be considered:

- To outsource the project
- To bring the project in-house
- To have a 'hybrid' system using both an external scanning company and in-house scanning bureaux

By the beginning of 2014 the vast majority of paper case notes had been scanned and the number remaining had reduced to less than 50,000. Therefore Medical Records staff believed that with a slight increase in staff hours and adequate resources, a scanning service provided entirely in-house would not only be viable, but safer and more efficient.

They highlighted obvious pitfalls with outsourcing which had been experienced over the preceding six years while the service had been provided by the EDM scanning company, based in Wolverhampton.

For example, patient safety had been compromised on a number of occasions when notes required for acute admissions or short notice clinic appointments couldn't be retrieved – either because they were in transit between the Trust and Wolverhampton, or because they couldn't be traced once they got there. It had always been clear to Medical records and other hospital staff, if not senior Trust management, that notes kept on a hospital site would be far easier to retrieve at short notice.

NHS trained staff were also better placed to identify and resolve quality control issues. But this was not enough to sway the Trust, which held only two meetings with staff. So by the time of the second meeting in October the deadline for the submission of tenders had passed. The Trust decided to award the contract to EDM. The union was handed an 'excerpt' from the business case, in which it was stated that 'value for money' had been given the highest weighting and was therefore the main factor in deciding to outsource to EDM again.

Medical records staff found it difficult to comprehend the Trust's concept of 'value for money' which had resulted in nearly £4m being spent with EDM from April 2010 – for a project which staff had been told would deliver a much safer and efficient paperless system within 12 months, but which was still not complete seven years later.

Early in 2015, UNISON members in Medical records went into dispute with the Trust over plans to increase workloads for Pinderfields based staff, whilst failing to replace staff leaving the department. Their argument was simple: if the Trust could find £millions to squander on external companies, why couldn't it find the money to staff and resource its own hospital services properly?

Chapter 7

A missed opportunity – and a Tory majority

The 2015 General Election should have been a golden opportunity for the Labour Party to bang home the problems that were already being created by the 2012 Health and Social Care Act, and challenge the five years of austerity that had frozen NHS spending in real terms, as well as attacks on public services and welfare benefits.

However the failure of the Labour leadership to come to terms with the track record of the previous New Labour government experimenting with market-style 'reforms', widening privatisation and competition, together with a lack of any radical alternative policies, meant that the chance was lost. While the Liberal Democrats paid a heavy electoral price for their shameless coalition with the Tories that had enabled David Cameron's government to push through measures including the NHS reorganisation, Labour was unable to capitalise, and the Tories secured a small majority.

Almost immediately afterwards they banged home this victory with the announcement of savage new anti-union laws which they hoped would make it increasingly impossible to take or sustain strike action. More than half of a union's members would have to vote in any ballot which leads to a strike for the strike to be legal, and on top of that 40% of members would have to vote in favour of the strike - regardless of turnout - in key health, education, fire, transport, border security and energy sectors – including the Border Force and nuclear decommissioning.

This meant that union branches in the NHS would have to substantially up their game and improve their levels of activism and organisation if they were to be able to mount any resistance to further attacks on pay and conditions. Mid Yorkshire Hospitals Branch has been one of those that have taken this challenge most seriously and strengthened its organisation in response.

Bye Bye EY?

In the second half of 2015 chief executive Stephen Eames and Bob Chadwick, Director of Finance announced that Ernst and Young were no longer 'advising' the Trust. 'EY' as they were now known, had been employed by the Trust since December 2011, to advise on how to make savings and address trust overspending.

After four years of their involvement the Trust was still in financial difficulties – and the Trust still had no answers when asked to define the legacy of the EY and other management consultants within the Trust.

Every request UNISON had made for an explanation of what the money had been spent on and what value for money E&Y had delivered had been met by silence under the cover of "commercial confidentiality".

Paula Sherriff MP for Dewsbury also demanded – without success – an explanation of what this money was spent on and what benefits the Trust had received.

The end of the EY era began in June 2015, when the government announced they would require trusts to get prior approval before commissioning consultancy costing more than £50,000, or extending existing consultancy arrangements to push the cost above £50,000.

This was in reaction to public anger at the unbelievable total of £420 million that had been spent on consultancy services by NHS organisations in 2014/15: the trust regulators Monitor and the Trust Development Agency published guidance which admitted that

> "We know that the NHS often achieves poor value for money from this expenditure, either because the work is poorly scoped, procured and managed, or because the findings are not fully implemented. Given the current level of provider deficit we cannot continue to spend on this scale without getting good value for money."

If this restriction had not been put in place, it is likely that EY's Mid Yorkshire gravy train would have continued even longer.

According to Trust Board figures, Mid Yorkshire Hospitals Trust was once more facing a £14.8 million deficit for 2015-16, projecting a year-end deficit of £16.65 million, and failing to meet targets for A&E waiting times, ambulance handover times at A&E, and referral to treatment within 18 weeks.

18% of staff surveyed said they would not recommend friends or family to seek treatment in the trust's hospitals and just 58% would recommend it. Less than half of the Trust's staff would recommend it as a place of work – well below the NHS average.

Another change at the top

In the spring of 2016, five years after the opening of the new Pinderfields Hospital, Trust CEO Stephen Eames announced he was off to North Cumbria University Hospitals Trust – where the deficits were almost double the projected £23 million financial mess he was leaving behind. It seemed that even the regular generous pay increases which had brought his salary and expenses to more than £260,000 a year were not enough to keep Mr Eames at Mid Yorkshire.

He told the February Board meeting that the request for his input at NCUH had "come from a very high level in the NHS," and that he had been selected for his "experience and expertise". Mid Yorkshire staff were all supposed to feel proud: apparently his departure was "an accolade for the Trust". Many regarded it as a blessed relief.

As he set off for Carlisle, Eames left the third busiest Emergency Department in England seeing just 82% of patients within the target 4-hour period – miles short of the 95% target: hardly the results that might be expected from a chief high-flying executive of such calibre.

Union Eyes commented:

> "He will be missed: but maybe not for the reasons he would like to imagine."

As he went, Eames's plans to run down A&E services at Dewsbury Hospital, and centre all emergency services at Pinderfields were being accelerated. The Board meeting in February 2016 was told

> "The emergency department [at Pinderfields] will have a consultant on duty 24 hours a day, seven days a week."

And if the threatened closure of A&E at Huddersfield Royal infirmary 15 miles away went through, leaving no hospital in Kirklees, there was the danger they could be busier still. The Mid Yorkshire Trust had announced its plan to bring the hospital 'reconfiguration' – in other words the closure of acute services at Dewsbury - forward by eight months to September 2016. Eames told MYHT staff on 17th February that he expected 1st September to be the date used as "the basis for all our planning on delivering Meeting the Challenge."

UNISON had always maintained that the downgrade of Dewsbury Hospital was driven by the Trust's desperation to stabilise its finances rather than improve service delivery for patients, and questioned the logic of bringing forward this ill-conceived reconfiguration by six months – before all of the facilities required were even in place. The fact that large numbers of staff were left uncertain about their future with less than six months to go appeared to reinforce UNISON's case.

UNISON had been provided only with a 'Provisional Workforce Plan' to give an indication of the staffing requirements for Facilities departments on each hospital site after services are centralised at Pinderfields. Facilities management had warned that these figures were "subject to change dependent on PGH and DDH final configuration." Despite management claims that the Trust was prepared for the reconfiguration, the evidence made clear the opposite was the case. Ambulances were regularly being diverted to Dewsbury and elsewhere due to Pinderfields being full, and overflow wards were a permanent fixture.

Union Eyes asked the obvious question:

> "What state will Pinderfields be in when Dewsbury's Emergency unit is closed and over 60 more beds are taken out of the system?
>
> "Rather than being brought forward, the closure of Dewsbury's Emergency and acute services should be halted before it's too late and patient care within the Trust is put further at risk."

Unhappy workforce

The bitter fruits of years of poor management policies were revealed when the shocking findings of the 2015 NHS national staff survey were published, which found the trust with worse than average findings on 23 of the 32 measures, putting it in the bottom 20% of hospital trusts in England.

Trust management was obliged to respond at some length. However it was no unrepresentative result: almost half the 7,200 staff eligible to take part had done so. Especially concerning was the low staff opinion of the quality of care they give to patients, with Mid Yorkshire the worst trust in the country for staff saying they would recommend the services to a friend or family member needing care.

No doubt this was also related to the stubbornly poor trust performance on A&E waiting time targets, and delays in diagnostic tests and treating cancer patients. But it was clearly linked to the growing pressures on staff, and poor engagement and communication with senior management. This had left staff feeling less able to contribute towards improvement of services, less valued for their work, less convinced their job made any difference to patient care, and less satisfied with the quality of care they are able to deliver than the average. One of the telling comments noted by the Trust Board was that:

> "Senior management seem to overwork or bully middle management sufficiently that none of them stay for very long. We are there constantly re-inventing the wheel, with a constantly changing group of non-clinical managers and nobody takes any responsibility to help us achieve service objectives.
>
> "This leaves the clinical team feeling completely unsupported."

Other comments included:

> "As a trainee I have worked in [more than] 10 other Trusts. The atmosphere and patient safety here causes me the most concern of any of these."
>
> "I have worked for the NHS for nearly 30 years and the current state of affairs saddens me greatly."
>
> "Culture of bullying is widespread within the organisation. The Trust's core values are a joke."

Even on two of those questions which the Trust singled out as showing Mid Yorkshire scoring 'better than average' – the percentage of staff working extra hours, and staff feeling the trust provides equal opportunity in career progression, the trust's scores were far worse than the previous year, and below the average for similar trusts.

The numbers reporting work-related stress and work pressure were also worrying, since stress can lead to sickness and absence – both of which were already above NHS targets. It was worsened by the rising caseload (about to be worsened further by the run-down of Dewsbury Hospital) and by the real terms freeze on NHS budgets since 2010, and pressures on the trust to balance the books by reducing headcount numbers of staff and restricting spending on temporary staff to fill vacancies.

Although the trust had promised "soon" to spend an extra £1 million on recruiting extra nursing staff, it seemed that much of this would be wiped out by the cuts which they would be compelled to make if they were to secure any of the extra £1.8 billion NHS "transformation fund" in 2016-17.

The Trust itself said in its report to the March Board:

> "Happy, engaged staff provide better patient care and experience and work more productively."

UNISON agreed this should be the aim, but asked "Are the management able to make the change required?"

Overhead costs

One added reason for the pressures in Mid Yorkshire hospitals trust was of course the inflated overhead costs flowing from the PFI hospital. The trust was forking out an increasingly large sum of money each year to the private consortium that owned both Pinderfields and Pontefract Hospitals: however some of the money was now flowing into different pockets.

There had been a series of changes behind the scenes since the original PFI deal was struck back in 2007 with Consort Healthcare (Mid Yorkshire) Limited, the small company through which PFI funds were raised and the profits are funnelled back to shareholders. Consort Healthcare was made up of Balfour Beatty, which was the main building firm and provider of support services in the new hospitals, the Royal Bank of Scotland and HSBC.

By 2016 RBS had sold off its stake, and Balfour Beatty had disappeared from the scene. RBS had started pull away from the PFI project soon after Pinderfields hospital was completed, selling off 50% of its shares 2011 to HSBC Infrastructure Company Limited (HICL), incorporated in the tax haven of Guernsey. That sale raised £32.8m, and Consort subsequently reported that they had made £6.2m profit on the deal. Then in the autumn of 2014 the remaining 50% of RBS shares were sold off, again to HICL. This time the purchase price was much higher, at £61.5m – and the company claimed that the price was £13.5m more than expected, yielding a massive £42.2m profit.

So the profits from selling shares added up to a hefty £48.4m in 7 years – from an original investment of just £30m by Balfour Beatty and RBS. Consort Healthcare (and with it the Mid Yorkshire Hospital trust's buildings) was by this point now entirely owned by the offshore outfit, making it one of more than 100 HICL investments in health, education and transport, valued at more than £1.8 billion. The unitary payments on the PFI contract were disappearing into the tax free void as the trust struggled to pay the rising bill.

But the staff delivering support services in Pinderfields and Pontefract had been sold off too, when Balfour Beatty's facility management business was sold to Cofely UK Limited. This company was itself a subsidiary of Cofely GDF Suez, a French-based company which originated from the Suez Canal Company in the mid-1800s. From April 2015, as part of that company's changing PR profile, the Cofely brand was replaced by the new name Engie.

This company had won another 5 year contract with the Trust, so it seemed support staff in the Trust were set to carry on working for this multinational, with the profits flowing out of the country to shareholders elsewhere. In August 2015 Moody's, the international firm that rates the risk of loans and reliability of companies, upgraded the rating of Consort Healthcare Mid Yorkshire from 'Baa3' to 'A3' – after MYHT agreed not to press for financial penalties over the problems with water quality and ventilation in the new hospital buildings.

As the unitary charge rose ever further above the expected level, the profits seemed set to flow safely to shareholders for another two and a half decades – while NHS staff battled to keep services afloat in the teeth of the Tory government's spending freeze.

The PFI unitary charge payment to cover the lease ("availability charge") of the Pinderfields and Pontefract hospital buildings and support services ("support charge") had been expected to rise each year by 2.5% or inflation, whichever is the higher, from £33m in 2011-12.

But the actual payments had been racing ahead of the projected level, meaning that by 2015/16 the trust had already paid out already £52m more in unitary charge than had been expected.

Indeed after five years of payments the trust had paid almost £252m on hospitals that cost £311m to build: but the payments, still rising, had another 25 years to go! No wonder bankers were so keen to buy up a share of the action, with profits guaranteed.

Questions over reconfiguration

As the reconfiguration of acute services moved towards its final phase in MYHT, the question had to be answered: was it making anything any better? Millions had been spent and huge disruption had been caused by building extra beds on the already expensive Pinderfields Hospital site, to enable it to handle thousands of additional patients who would previously have used their local Dewsbury Hospital. Children's services, women's services, emergency surgery and gastroenterology had all now been transferred from Dewsbury to Pinderfields.

The completed reconfiguration would leave both Dewsbury and Pontefract without emergency services – and pack everyone over to Wakefield – with all the pressure on ambulance services and the transport problems that would create. People seeking to visit in-patients from Dewsbury also faced a longer and more awkward journey, especially if they were reliant on public transport, so it was unlikely that anyone in the neighbourhood of Pontefract or Dewsbury would see the reconfiguration as a success.

Indeed even while the final services were run down at Dewsbury, the busy Wakefield Walk-In Centre – the type of service CCGs had kept saying was the future – also seemed likely to close from April 2017, as the CCG completed a "review" of emergency services.

That change would again funnel even more patients onto the increasingly hectic and pressurised Pinderfields site, where beds and front-line services were already running at full stretch, and retention of nursing staff was already a problem. Both Wakefield and North Kirklees CCGs had expressed concern over bed capacity and "patient flow".

Had any money been saved?

Had the reconfiguration saved any money? Who could tell? The Trust had wound up with a deficit of around £20 million in 2015-16, but had gone on, without any obvious explanation, to sign up to an NHS England "control total" which required them to deliver a surplus of £4.2m, although in theory this would be helped by a possible £16.7m bail-out from the "Sustainability and Transformation Fund".

UNISON noted that the savings generated from the Cost Improvement Programme had achieved less than a third of their target half way through financial year: if this continued it would create a new £16m gap in the budget. The trust already had a two decade-long track record of looking on the bright side and scraping through with one-off fixes and loans – with the bad news always tending to emerge 'unexpectedly' in the second half of the financial year.

Union Eyes warned:

> "There are few "efficiencies" yet to make in this trust without impacting on patient care: we are so "Lean" we are almost anorexic."

With the Trust having only just parted company from Ernst & Young, UNISON had hoped that this might have signalled an end to the Trust throwing its cash at so called financial experts from the city. Sadly, like drunks who can't let go of the whisky bottle, the Trust swiftly joined forces with yet another big accountancy firm, Deloitte LLP – who received £381,628.80 in August (well above the £50,000 maximum limit prescribed by NHS England) for "external consultancy fees".

When challenged on this by the unions at an October meeting management said the payment was for 4 weeks work "helping the Trust with this year's Cost Improvement Programmes (CIPs)".

They were part way through planning Cost Improvement Programmes for 2017/18 … for which Deloitte and another company 'Four Eyes' would get another £700,000! Once again with staffing levels on the wards at critically low levels UNISON argued it was outrageous for the Trust to be paying out at least another £1 million for management consultants to do the work that managers themselves were already handsomely paid to do. The grotesque gravy train had to stop.

UNISON success

However the anger at the recklessness of management extravagance of consultancy fees was balanced by a celebration of a UNISON negotiating success. Staff working in Catering, Domestics, Linen Services, Security and Portering within the Pinderfields and Pontefract PFI hospitals were NHS employees; but they were managed by Engie (formerly Cofely and BBW) under a national agreement called Retention of Employment (RoE). This maintained the same NHS Terms and Conditions and pension as other staff working within the NHS.

In 2015 UNISON had approached both the Trust and Engie to say that the temporary staff the company had employed on their Terms and Conditions to work within the RoE departments should now be transferred onto RoE contracts as per the national agreement. UNISON noted that the Engie contract had lower rates of pay, fewer holidays, less sick pay and no NHS pension.

This arrangement was therefore clearly better for the company's profits but detrimental to the staff who were working for less money and on worse conditions than their colleagues. UNISON formally objected to Trust Director Kevin Oxley that Engie were in breach of Schedule 33 Retained staff Agreement of the Private Finance Initiative signed by Mid Yorks Trust and Consort (the PFI consortium) in 2009. UNISON argued that the RoE agreement should be in place a for the full 35 year duration of the PFI contract.

UNISON were then given a copy of a Variation Enquiry which showed that the Trust and Engie had been discussing allowing Engie to contravene the RoE agreement and take staff on at lower terms and conditions. The Branch lodged a collective dispute with the Trust and wrote to Engie and Consort insisting that they stand by the RoE agreement.

UNISON National Officer Sara Gorton contacted the Department of Health for their interpretation of the RoE agreement, and received a reply from the DoH confirming that the RoE agreement was in place for the duration of the PFI and could only be varied with the agreement of UNISON. She wrote to Kevin Oxley, Mid Yorks Director responsible for the PFI, and in August Oxley confirmed that

Engie would be asked for a list of staff for transition onto RoE contracts, although this was not fully resolved until the end of 2017.

Union Eyes summed up:

> "If savings are to be made from the PFI contract we suggest the Trust concentrates on reducing the £4 million plus they pay Consort every month instead of cutting the pay of their lowest paid staff."

Hunt's US flagship slammed on safety

In the autumn of 2016 came news that a US hospital which had been proclaimed by Health Secretary Jeremy Hunt as 'perhaps the safest hospital in the world', and which has been paid a hefty £12.5 million by the Department of Health for a 5-year contract to help improve patient safety in hospitals in England, had itself failed a safety inspection.

A *Daily Mirror* report picked up the findings of the Joint Commission that monitors safety in US hospitals, which in May issued a "preliminary denial of accreditation" to the lavishly funded hospital, whose chief executive earned a monster $3.5 million per year, compared with the much more modest reward for even top NHS managers. Virginia Mason hospital was found wanting on no less than 29 separate counts. Since resources were clearly not the problem, it seemed more than likely that the deeply flawed US system and the perverse incentives created by the culture of commercial medicine were to blame.

It's astonishing that Jeremy Hunt should have thought the lavishly-funded (and now evidently not always very good) Virginia Mason could be in any way compared with the NHS in the midst of the decade-long funding squeeze begun in 2010 by George Osborne.

On 2014 figures, Virginia Mason with just 336 beds and revenue of $1 billion, had just over a third as many beds, and one sixth the number of patients – but significantly more funding than Mid Yorkshire Hospitals. Yet trust bosses invited in the American hospital to prattle on about their "Kaizen" (continuous incremental improvement) system that had just let them down back in the USA.

There's no doubt any NHS manager desperately struggling against the odds to deal with soaring deficits and rising caseload would give their right arm for even half the resources lavished on this clearly less efficient US hospital.

UNISON argued that the American bosses should spend a bit more time sorting out their own services, rather than lecturing people doing a more difficult job than theirs.

Another top-down reorganisation

Since January 2016 England's NHS has been carved up, by order of NHS England, into 44 "footprint" areas, in which commissioners and providers were supposed to collaborate together.

That might appear to be good news, if it meant the complex, costly and divisive competitive market system entrenched by Andrew Lansley's Health and Social Care Act would be swept away, and a new, re-integrated NHS was empowered to work together again to improve services.

But that was never really the case. Instead the main task of the STP plans and "partnerships" was from the outset was to balance the books of each "local health economy" – taking drastic steps where necessary to wipe out £2.7 billion of deficits that had been built up by trusts.

Each area had to draw up a 5-year Sustainability and Transformation Plan (STP), to be vetted by NHS England: yet even while they did so all of the legislation compelling local CCGs to open up services to "any qualified provider" or put them out to tender remained in full force. The private sector was still competing for and snapping up contracts, especially for community health services.

The STPs amounted to an attempted silent coup led by NHS England chief executive Simon Stevens, aimed at creating new arrangements in which the discredited 2012 legislation could be blatantly ignored, and changes driven through which could reduce spending to bridge the massive and growing gap between effectively frozen funding and steadily rising demand.

While politicians' attention was generally distracted by the referendum vote on Brexit in June 2016 – and the subsequent sharp exit of David Cameron as Prime Minister to be replaced by Theresa May who claimed improbably to be "strong and stable" – NHS England saw an opportunity to begin to break free and effectively impose a new reorganisation without involving parliament. In many areas STPs were clearly seen by NHS England and by local health chiefs as a means to force through delayed or stymied decisions on the location of hospital services, and downsize or close some services and downgrade others, despite local opposition.

The 44 "footprint" areas approved by NHS England in the spring of 2016 were promised support and encouraged to overcome the "veto powers" of individual organisations to stand in the way of controversial changes.

However there were two huge problems: the government, and the growing public resistance to the proposed changes and to the new, secretive bodies that had been established with no consultation – and no intention of consulting.

Theresa May's government showed no more willingness than had Cameron's to change the law once more to facilitate the new arrangements, even though this would be necessary in order to give any legal authority to the new STP implementation boards.

To make matters worse austerity policies were still firmly in place even under a new chancellor: there was still little or no NHS capital available to build any new facilities or modernise old ones. Far from investing to improve services, trusts and CCGs were being forced to work together to find ways of delivering the same or even more services for less money.

The initial plan was for the 44 Draft Sustainability and Transformation Plans to be completed by early summer 2016, rubber-stamped by NHS England by the end of the summer, and implementation to begin in the autumn.

Nowhere was this schedule possible to achieve. It was not until the end of the year that the last of the plans – still in many cases little more than sketchy outlines rather than finished plans – reluctantly published by NHS England after intensifying pressure on them from campaigners was joined by local and then national news media critical of "secret plans".

West Yorkshire STP – the illusion of integration

The West Yorkshire STP was published October 2016 as an 84-page document. However it was not really a plan as it made clear:

> "The STP sets out the strategic context in West Yorkshire and Harrogate and high-level proposals for how we might

get there. Our focus now shifts … to developing meaningful coproduction for turning these high-level proposals into more detailed implementable plans. Our next important milestone is the two-year operational NHS planning process through which we will translate into delivery." (p78)

The STP proposed no formal consultation on the overall plan, although several individual consultations were proposed or under way either around specific geographic areas, or diseases (cancer p52; stroke p53), or acute reconfiguration at Calderdale & Huddersfield FT (pp59, 60).

Some decisions were to be made locally, leaving the STP an amalgam of plans for the 6 separate areas within the footprint, along with some discussion of work at the 'footprint' level. Within this, Wakefield refers to new governance arrangements and ACOs (p43):

"Our five GP Federations are working in partnership with us to execute the Five Year Forward View and are fully aligned to development of an Accountable Care System. We have developed strong governance and accountability through our Health and Wellbeing Board supported by our STP which has clear lines of accountability. …

"Develop Accountable Care Organisation by 2020/2021 bringing provision and integrated commissioning together to improve quality of delivery for community care.

• "Full implementation of the 'Meeting the Challenge' reconfiguration of services, to deliver 7 day services for all acute care by 2019."

Overall the STP talks (p73) of

"Establishing appropriate governance arrangements to allow us to work more closely and take decisions collectively across commissioners, providers, health and social care."

This involves three aspects (p74),

• West Yorkshire & Harrogate wide commissioning / contractor function dealing with acute and some specialist services,

• Place-based commissioner bringing together the functions of LAs, CCGs and NHS England (primary care) commissioning

• Local 'commissioning' function embedded within ACO models.

The first involves extension and formalisation of joint committee arrangements between the CCGs, with identification of services that need to be commissioned on a West Yorkshire-wide basis.

The second involves organisations collaborating on a defined geographic footprint with collective accountability (note this includes local authorities). The third involves ACOs working to a capitated budget deciding how resources are used to best meet population needs (p74).

Conspicuously none of these models and proposals actually breaks down the division between commissioners (purchasers) and providers, and there is no serious discussion about the steps that would be necessary to enable a wider system that would take collective responsibility for balancing a collective budget. Each trust has been left to its own devices to deal with the deficits.

Towards the end of 2016 it became increasingly obvious to NHS England that STPs had already lost any advantage of surprise, while their obsessive refusal to divulge any of their plans or reveal the new structures they were proposing, had alienated local and national news media, a growing section of the local population in each area – and in some places even some of the local government leaders and officers who were supposed to give the STPs a veneer of democracy and respectability.

STPs as a brand had already become toxic, while many of their "plans" were self-evidently hopeless. Most raised more questions than answers, lacking any clear implementation plans, workforce plans or financial projections as well as any public consent.

NHS England Simon Stevens began to talk down the STPs, describing them not as plans, but "proposals" and insisting that there had been no proposal to establish new structures to supplant the CCGs and Trusts. The focus began to shift towards Accountable Care Systems and Accountable Care Organisations, as touched upon in vague terms in NHS England's Five Year Forward View.

Trust torn between two STPs

Part way through 2016, the Mid Yorkshire Trust found itself caught up in not just one Sustainability & Transformation Plan, but two. Not only was the trust, along with Wakefield CCG, lumped in along with Leeds and Bradford with a sprawling "West Yorkshire

STP" that stretched further north than Harrogate, almost as far as York, and as far south and west as Greater Huddersfield, but the trust was also signed up to a Working Together "Vanguard" project involving six other acute hospital trusts in South Yorkshire and Derbyshire – the separate South Yorkshire and Bassetlaw STP.

The West Yorkshire STP covers 11 CCGs and 2.5 million people: the Working Together Partnership covers 15 hospital sites, 45,000 staff and 2.3 million people. And while the West Yorkshire STP was seeking to generate savings of £725 million by 2020, the SYB STP was chasing an even higher £773m target. The Working Together Partnership was vague on its objectives – but clear in its concluding "key benefit" of organisations "working together to make savings where they can".

With the Mid Yorkshire reconfiguration near completion, and the plans to downgrade Huddersfield Royal Infirmary apparently driving forward in Calderdale regardless of local protests, it was becoming hard to imagine much more centralisation of hospital services short of outright closures. But pressures for mergers of "back office" services (the vital work done by clerical, secretarial and admin staff, non-clinical support) remained strong, and there was great managerial faith in the savings to be made from improving IT services.

The Mid Yorkshire Trust may have been torn between rival projects for rationalisation, but UNISON needed to be ready to fight on two fronts at once.

'Test beds' for profits

The Working Together Partnership Vanguard was working on a 'Test Bed' collaboration (although the only beds involved are the patients' own beds at home). The 'Perfect Patient Pathway' project aimed to harness technology to bring substantial benefits for patients suffering from long term health conditions, such as diabetes, mental health problems, respiratory disease, hypertension and other chronic conditions.

The website boasted that it aimed to "create an 'ecosystem' for innovations in technology to be tested before being embedded as routine care on a wide scale". One objective was to use technological innovations to promote and support "whole-person care," although it

202

turns out that it also creates new opportunities for private sector providers and hi-tech firms to pick up lucrative NHS contracts, reaching patients who otherwise would not be able to afford the equipment.

The Vanguard's ambition was for the NHS to do less and less – or in contemporary jargon: "shift self-care from the margins to the mainstream". However not all problems could be solved by patients under their own steam, especially frail older patients who had been so badly let down with the massive cuts in social care and the absence of adequate provision of long-promised community health care.

For the most vulnerable patients 'home-based monitoring devices' and smartphone apps were not a sufficient substitute for health and social care. "Discrete remote monitoring systems" were also promised to "support independent living" – but without staff to do the monitoring, and respond when they detect problems the system could not work for those with the greatest needs.

Winter crisis and the aftermath

The first half of 2017 was dominated by the aftermath of a massive winter crisis in the NHS triggered by cold weather and predictable increases in demand for emergency services, worsened by the closures of beds, staff shortages and financial pressures flowing from seven years of austerity policies affecting NHS funding and social care – run by local government.

A huge demonstration through London on March 4 embodied the growing public anger at government policies on the NHS. Nonetheless Theresa May, misled by the opinion poll figures suggesting that Jeremy Corbyn's Labour leadership (under heavy and consistent attack from all sections of the mainstream news media) was electorally weak, was convinced the Tories could win a snap election and strengthen their majority in Parliament.

Of course we now know that with the benefit of a few weeks in which the media were under pressure to provide more "balanced" coverage, with lingering concerns keeping the NHS as one of the major factors in the minds of voters, and with a level of grassroots support for Jeremy Corbyn that surprised Labour's own new leadership, the June 2017 Election did not go to Mrs May's plan. It severely weakened the position for the Conservatives, with at least five Tory MPs losing their seats as a result of local concerns over potential cuts in hospital services, and others seeing their majorities cut back.

May was obliged to go cap (and £1 billion) in hand to the tiny Democratic Unionist Party for support to secure a majority in Parliament. This weak position made it impossible at least in the short term for her to implement the new laws which her Manifesto had promised would facilitate the reforms plans of NHS England (and therefore presumably give legal powers to STPs).

As the year went on, in most areas any mention of STPs began to fade into the background, leaving only much smaller scale proposals for specific services to work more closely together. There was correspondingly greater emphasis on developing "Accountable Care Systems" (ACSs) – with SYB among those designated as early implementers.

Within the Mid Yorkshire Trust, UNISON continued to follow through on some issues that had been outstanding for months or years – and continued to win results. On 1st November 2017 over 50 Domestics, Porters and Security Officers finally moved onto NHS contracts under the Retention of Employment agreement. Another 50+ Catering and Facility Assistants moved over on 1st January 2018. This welcome news followed over two years of campaigning by UNISON following the employment by Engie of new staff on their own, inferior, Terms and Conditions. UNISON now received confirmation from the Department of Health that the RoE agreement is valid for the duration of the 35 year PFI deal which came into being in 2009.

The 104 staff who transferred to the NHS gained additional annual leave, unsocial hours enhancement and access to the NHS pension scheme. The agreement also ensured all new recruits would be employed directly on to RoE contracts, preventing a two tier workforce occurring in the future. The reinstatement of RoE within the Trust was a major victory in UNISON's fight against privatisation.

A new threat to support staff: Yorkshire and Mid Yorks Hospitals in the forefront

However the pressures on the Trust meant that even as this victory was secured, a new fight was looming as Mid Yorkshire and other trusts looked for new ways to make savings and balance their books – where necessary at the expense of their own staff.

In November a 'Briefing' from the West Yorkshire Association of Acute Trusts (WYATT) was circulated within Mid Yorkshire Hospitals' Estates, Facilities and IM&T Directorate. The briefing referred to the possible creation of 'wholly owned subsidiaries' for some services including Estates and Facilities functions.

The six acute Trusts within WYATT are Airedale, Bradford, Calderdale & Huddersfield, Harrogate, Leeds and Mid Yorkshire. Four of the Trusts, Bradford, Calderdale & Huddersfield, Leeds and Mid Yorks are cooperating jointly by forming a 'Special Purposes Vehicle' (SPV), which is a separate business owned by the Trusts. This has already been registered at Companies House.

The briefing failed to mention that the SPV would be, as was described to UNISON, "outside the NHS". This means the SPV would have freedoms, including paying staff outside national Agenda for Change Terms and Conditions.

"Wholly Owned" – but privatised

The four Trusts were, in effect, considering whether to set up a private company into which NHS staff and departments could be transferred. This was recognised by the unions right away as potentially the privatisation of many NHS departments by the back door.

The briefing also claimed that one of the potential benefits of "working collaboratively in this way includes ... valuing and supporting our staff!"

Quite how staff would be valued and supported by dumping them in a private company was not explained. UNISON made clear from the outset that there is no benefit to any staff, other than the highly paid project managers, in being part of a SPV.

UNISON and the other Trade unions within the Trust formally objected to the briefing at the monthly JCNC/Partnership meeting held on Tuesday 7th November. They were told that unions would not cooperate with the formation of the company and would lodge a collective dispute if they went ahead with the Full Business Case.

A meeting of UNISON officers, the other Trade Unions and Trust Directors from across West Yorkshire took place in Leeds on November 14, and received a presentation on the alleged benefits of being in a wholly owned subsidiary: as they had suspected there were no benefits for any staff who would have to transfer into the company.

The benefits were for management – to set their own wage rates, take staff off national Agenda for Change Terms and Conditions, introduce a two tier workforce and remove access to the NHS pensions. The meeting was told that the four Trust Boards would be discussing the Full Business case at their meetings in December and January. Airedale and Harrogate Trust had decided to look at forming their own SPV project separately from the other four trusts.

The unions' response was to refuse to cooperate with the transfer of our members outside the NHS and to make it clear they would lodge official disputes across the four Trusts if the business cases were agreed.

On December 2 UNISON and Unite reps in the Mid Yorkshire Trust met the Trust Chief Executive, Chairman Jules Preston and Directors Mark Braden and Andrew Jones, and put the case against the SPV. They were told that the Trust had not yet received the Final Business case from WYATT, but were expecting it for discussion at the Trust Board on 14th December.

The unions requested a copy of the case and the right to comment before any decision was made.

The NAO exposes the costs of PFI

2018 began with two body-blows for the image and illusion of PFI. The National Audit Office published a hard-hitting report which concluded that billions had been spent on inflated payments for PFI contracts since the 1990s, without any evidence to show that PFI offered any public benefits[157].

---

[157] NAO (2018) PFI and PF2, available https://www.nao.org.uk/wp-content/uploads/2018/01/PFI-and-PF2.pdf

The NAO calculated that there were currently over 700 operational PFI and PF2 deals, with a capital value of around £60 billion, in various sectors (the largest number (127) of which were in the Department of Health).

Annual charges for these deals amounted to £10.3 billion in 2016-17, and the bills were rising, so that even if no new deals were entered into, the taxpayer was already facing a total cost of £199bn by the 2040s. This sounds enormous, but is surprisingly just over three times the capital value of the projects.

In fact this overall figure for all PFIs seriously under-states the inflated costs of NHS hospital projects, where £13 billion worth of contracts for buildings, maintenance and FM services are estimated to cost at least £82 billion over the lifetime of the contracts – more than six times the capital cost[158].

The NAO report was completed before, but published three days after the high-profile collapse of a major player in PFI, the construction and services corporation Carillion.

Carillion's collapse, with just £29m in cash assets, left the company with combined pension liabilities, creditor payments and unpaid contractors adding up to £7 billion. A parliamentary inquiry report in May 2018 noted the complicity in the collapse of three of the major consultancy and accountancy companies – KPMG, EY and Deloittes – while PWC have picked up generous fees for putting the company into administration.

From 2007 onwards Carillion had periodically raised cash by selling off its equity stakes in a series of PFI hospital schemes – Great Western Hospital, Swindon, Glasgow's Southern General, Lewisham Hospital, a number of mental health units, James Cook University Hospital in Middlesbrough, Oxford's John Radcliffe Hospital and Queen Alexandra Hospital in Portsmouth. The bulk of these assets were bought up by companies trading off shore and paying no UK tax.

The annual rate of return when these contracts were sold off

---

[158] Appleby J. (2017) Making sense of PFI, https://www.nuffieldtrust.org.uk/resource/making-sense-of-pfi#pfi-has-been-in-the-news-lately-but-is-it-a-big-thing-in-health

ranged from a very lucrative 16.2% up to a staggering 38.7% – giving an insight into the extent PFI has become a cash cow for tax-shy speculators.

For its final few years the company had been paying out dividends faster than it was generating cash from its contracts. From 2009-2016 it paid out £554m in dividends, while over the same period the amount owed by the company in loans increased. In 2009 Carillion had £242m of loans: by the time of its collapse in January 2018 that had risen almost five fold to £1.3 billion.

While the auditors and non-executive directors – generously rewarded for their inaction – did nothing to challenge this reckless behaviour, the final straw came in the form of a relatively small setback, when remedial work to fix eight cracked beams in the Royal Liverpool Hospital project (90% of which was already complete) pushed the company over the edge.

Carillion's directors were summed up by the co-chairs of the Parliamentary Inquiry set up by the Work and Pensions Committee and the Business, Energy and Industrial Strategy Committee, as "delusional characters" who had "maintained everything was hunky dory until it all went suddenly and unforeseeably wrong".[159]

Another toxic brand: "accountable care"

While one of the major PFI contractors was demonstrating the lack of any public accountability of its board and the failure of accountants and regulators to keep it on track, by early 2018 NHS England was again trying to cut its losses and distance itself from another discredited brand.

Once it became the focus for increased campaigning during the second half of 2017, the term "Accountable Care – which had been unwisely likened by NHS England boss Simon Stevens in the 2014 *Five Year Forward View* and subsequent NHS England statements to quite different bodies which had yielded mixed results in the USA –

---

[159] Morby A (2018) Cracked beams at Liverpool hospital sparked Carillion collapse http://www.constructionenquirer.com/2018/02/06/cracked-beams-at-liverpool-hospital-sparked-carillion-collapse/

had become as toxic in the public perception as STPs had done in 2016.

While they were forced to abandon the 'Accountable Care' label, NHS England bosses were determined to hang on to the concept, and so the English language had to be contorted once more to come up with another new combination of bland and apparently inoffensive words in an effort to persuade the public that NHS bosses were committed to improving and re-integrating the NHS rather than maintaining the fragmentation and division that was still entrenched through the 2012 Act.

In February 2018 it was formally announced by NHS England that "accountable care" as a phrase had been discarded: from now on the discussion was to be on "Integrated Care" systems and organisations – same sour wine, new fancy bottles.

Indeed it appears the greater the emphasis on "Integrated Care" and the more frequently the term is used the less evidence there is that it actually means any form of integration at all.

Instead "integrated care" is being touted as a term to divert from the fact that commissioners and providers alike, including NHS England (which has awarded another new contract to failure-ridden private outsourcers Capita) are still resorting to privatisation, and carving out new ventures – in community health services and now "wholly owned companies".

However the resistance from the trade unions to the wholesale privatisation of support services was growing, and at the beginning of February management at Bristol's Southmead Hospital were forced by a growing campaign to abandon their plans to transfer 850 staff out of the NHS into a new company[160].

In other parts of the country, including West Yorkshire, trust boards continued to test their luck by pushing ahead with plans for subcos despite the growing groundswell of opposition. In Mid Yorkshire Hospitals the UNISON branch was mounting a consistent campaign to inform members and prepare for the possibility of strike action if plans went ahead.

---

[160] https://www.bristolpost.co.uk/news/bristol-news/southmead-hospital-bosses-scrap-proposal-1157104

The Branch published a response to the trust's attempts to put a gloss on their plans with a Frequently Asked Questions document.[161]

While other trusts across the country have adopted the subco approach, in Mid Yorkshire there has been additional pressure on trust bosses because of the inflated costs of the PFI contract. The Outline Business Case for the MY Wholly Owned Subsidiary says this in so many words:

> "The Trust has a persistent underlying deficit of approximately £20m, largely due to the PFI costs for Pinderfields and Pontefract Hospitals. In the past six years, the Trust has not been able to make inroads into this position, but unlike some other trusts with PFI pressures the position has not deteriorated any further." (OBC page 19)

The Trust where the battle over the subcos has reached the highest level since the Bristol victory has been at Wrightington Wigan and Leigh, where the Trust attempted to face down successive periods of strike action and the resistance of unions representing nearly 900 staff facing the threat of transfer out of the NHS and into a company misleadingly entitled "WWL Solutions".

The Trust, like many others exploring similar plans, hoped to save money primarily by exploiting a tax loophole that allows them to avoid VAT: analysis of the Business Cases that have been made available shows that – despite the grandiose claims some Trusts make about raising extra income and improving services – between 80 and 90% of the financial benefits from forming a Wholly Owned Company come from tax advantages.

However a number of trusts have admitted they also plan to save money by employing new staff in these companies on non-NHS terms and conditions, creating a 2-tier workforce. Existing staff transferred would be dependent on TUPE protection of their pay and conditions – and lose access to the NHS Pension Scheme. There is always the danger that TUPE protection itself could be set aside after the transfer is complete, by a company that would be free to make its own policy.

The WWL strikes were strong, lively and united from the

---

[161]https://www.facebook.com/search/top/?q=unison%20mid%20yorkshire%20health%20branch%20reply%20to%20faq

beginning, and when the initial action failed to stop the trust's plans, further strikes were called. In all three periods of industrial action were supported by UNISON, Unite and GMB members, including porters, cleaners, catering staff, electricians and plumbers employed at Wrightington Hospital, Wigan's Royal Albert Edward Infirmary and Leigh Infirmary. Strikers received tremendous support from people who care about the future of the NHS right across the country, as well as senior national and local politicians and union leaders.

WWL Trust Chief executive Andrew Foster felt it appropriate to brand the strikers as "lazy scumbags", but this backfired. "I'm a Lazy scumbag" T-shirts were made – and strikers fought even harder. Foster had been appointed as the person in charge of workforce planning for the Combined Authority by Greater Manchester's Mayor Andy Burnham. But Burnham made increasingly strong statements against subcos, leaving Foster isolated and his future uncertain.

Nonetheless on June 27, just days before a 5-day strike began, the WWL Trust Board met, and decided to ignore the strikes and press ahead with the plan. A week later, after UNISON had given notice of a further seven-day strike beginning on July 17, the Trust was persuaded to step back from the confrontation.

An intervention from Wigan Council's leader and deputy led to a £2m financial offer to the Trust to compensate for the savings they expected – on condition the subco plan was permanently ditched. Trust and unions accepted. Exactly what has been agreed was unclear. Wigan council's chief executive is also the Accountable Officer of Wigan CCG, and an enthusiast for 'new models of care'. It's likely there will still be pressure on staff to deliver savings – though they will remain within the NHS.

This is an important victory, but it does not mean that the unions have won the war: the fight to keep staff 100% NHS is continuing as this book is completed. Most regions of England still have trusts planning subcos, with particular concerns in the South West and Yorkshire and Humberside where a significant number of trusts are proposing to transfer hundreds of staff outside the NHS.

In Mid Yorkshire hospitals, where 58% of UNISON estates and facilities staff had voted and 97% of votes were for strike action, the first strike against outsourcing, which had been called for 2 July, was suspended after the trust management agreed to investigate keeping the staff in the NHS pension scheme and employment. Management also agreed to suspend a committee looking at inferior terms and conditions and a potential two-tier workforce.

In a statement to members, Mid Yorkshire Health Unison branch said:

> "Our strike action is suspended but the dispute and strike ballot result remains in place until 12 December. We will update you regularly on the talks and if they break down strike action will be reinstated immediately."

When it appeared management might try to force the plan through anyway, the strike threat was reimposed, and a 3-day stoppage announced. This forced a binding agreement by management not to proceed[162].

Summer 2018 – the NHS 70th birthday

The NHS turned 70 years old on July 5 2018, with the cash pressures driving NHS England to draw up an expanding list of treatments that would no longer be routinely available. While a few of these are recognised as not universally effective, the majority will still be available but only if given specific agreement by local CCGs (in other words subject to tight rationing).

More than 120 trusts across the country were still wrestling with the still rising bill for PFI deals signed in happier times when NHS spending was rising above inflation each year. In Liverpool Royal and Birmingham's Midland Metropolitan Hospital PFI building work was still at a standstill six months after the collapse of Carillion.

Soon after the 70th anniversary celebrations were over, the abrupt resignation of Boris Johnson as Foreign Secretary brought a change of health secretary, replacing the long-serving and hugely controversial Jeremy Hunt with the largely unknown quantity of

---

[162] We have since heard (September 2018) that the regulator NHS Improvement has called upon trusts to halt any further steps towards creating subcos pending a review and new guidance. It's not clear if all trusts will comply. https://www.union-news.co.uk/win-unions-welcome-pause-in-subco-roll-out/

Matt Hancock, a man with no track record of speaking about health or social care, but generously sponsored as a co-thinker by an obscurely-funded right wing free market pressure group the Institute of Economic Affairs (IEA). Hancock's first statements were predictably cautious and defensive

Gifted an exclusive editorial slot in the *Health Service Journal* (which had tactfully downplayed his credentials as a favourite of the IEA), he was keen to play the game and profess his loyalty to the NHS:

> "Britain can be proud of many institutions we have built through history, but the one that makes me most proud is the NHS. Seventy years ago, as a nation we said healthcare should be free at the point of use, according to need not ability to pay. I cherish that notion profoundly now as the founding fathers did back then. ...
>
> ... "I am very much driven by the 70 year old founding principles of the NHS..."[163]

Hancock's editorial also skilfully pushed other buttons, setting out his stall as a newly-invented caring Health Secretary:

> "Two things are abundantly clear: firstly, how hard NHS staff work. And secondly, how people feel undervalued."

Obviously one of the reasons they feel undervalued right now because they and the NHS have been consistently under-valued since 2010, with a real terms freeze on funding, frozen or below inflation pay increases for eight years in a row, and a Health Secretary (Hunt) determined to tough out repeated strikes by junior doctors to impose a new contract on them, before proceeding to axe bursaries for training nurses and other health professionals. Health workers have once again had to learn the hard way that Tory-led governments don't value them or the services they deliver.

Now Hancock is trying to imply a new approach:

> "People choose to work in the NHS because they are driven by a desire to improve their fellow citizens' lives; to care for those they don't know. I want to ensure this mission and

---

[163] https://www.hsj.co.uk/comment/-hancock-ill-defend-undervalued-nhs-staff/7022914.article

public service that motivate people to go into the NHS as teenagers stays with them until the day they leave it.

"I understand that sense of service. It is rewarding. But it can't be taken for granted either. I am determined to ensure duty is rewarded by the sort of system people deserve. That means taking on issues like bullying and harassment, recruiting and retaining staff and improving options for flexible working."

It will be interesting to see how long this persona can be maintained. Already Hancock has declared his enthusiasm for new, often controversial and questionably effective technology, quoting flawed research and presuming evidence where so far there is little or none:

"I am determined to seize the opportunities of the modern age we live in. Technology has a proven ability to radically change the world for the better – be it in finance, in education and in transport. But nowhere does technology have greater potential to improve lives than in healthcare.

"I've seen it for myself. Artificial intelligence can help spot early stages of cancer, giving patients a better chance of survival. Algorithms will be able to organise and analyse medical records, so frontline staff can spend more of their valuable time dealing with patients not writing on paper."

With health unions and campaigners more alert and mobilised than they have been for many years, successful challenges being waged to controversial local plans, and a government in visible turmoil over Brexit as this book is completed in July 2018, we will conclude this chapter pointing out that the future is in the balance.

Labour, as the main opposition party, has moved as far as recognising the need for fresh legislation to end and further privatisation and sweep away the chaotic market mechanisms put in place by the 2012 Health and Social Care Act, and shadow chancellor John McDonnell has made general statements during his speech to the Labour party Conference in September committing to "bring existing PFI contracts back in-house".

While these are welcome developments, it's clear that even a change of government will not being any automatic correction of policies which have dislocated services and wasted billions. The fight will go on: and UNISON's Mid Yorkshire Health branch will be in the thick of it, fighting for principle and for the values of the NHS.

Chapter 8

PFI versus local accountability

Repeated efforts in the late 1990s to get local MPs to stand up and resist the drive towards a £100m PFI project to replace both Pinderfields and Pontefract hospitals with a single site new hospital failed, not least because the New Labour government from 1997 became zealots promoting the idea, making it much more difficult for individual back-benchers to follow any other line.

Wakefield's Labour MP David Hinchliffe, then chairing the Commons Health Committee, and publicly critical of PFI schemes elsewhere in the NHS, was unwilling to throw his support behind a local campaign.

When he subsequently stood down as an MP in 2003 at the early age of 54, it was quite obvious that he had been under sustained pressure from Blairite loyalist MPs on the Health Committee. In an interview with the BBC's Politics Show, he was blunt in his criticism:

> "When the prime minister talks about modernisation, some of the ideas we're bringing forward are from the dustbin of Margaret Thatcher."[164]

After he ceased to be an MP Hinchliffe has become even more explicit in his criticisms of PFI, including the schemes in Yorkshire, and his local hospital Trust.

Speaking to the Yorkshire Post in 2017, he argued that his criticisms of PFI in a select committee report had been watered down by 'loyalist' Labour MPs, while the cost of the Pinderfields scheme was "nothing short of scandalous".

> "I have sympathy for those NHS Trusts - such as Mid Yorkshire - which have the albatross of PFI around their necks but, in my view, there should have been much more vigorous efforts by them and local MPs to press nationally for a renegotiation of the debt repayment arrangements."[165]

---

[164] http://news.bbc.co.uk/1/hi/england/south_yorkshire/3144790.stm

[165] Parsons, R *(2017) PFI debts 'an albatross around the necks of Yorkshire*

216

Other local MPs were even less politically willing than Hinchliffe to challenge PFI, and more susceptible to political pressure. The main elected politicians basically didn't want to get involved let alone head up a campaign.

So other tactics needed to be devised. The UNISON Branch won the support of campaigning comedian Mark Thomas whose Channel Four series Mark Thomas's Comedy Product was then raising many vital issues to public awareness.

The local referendum

Early in 1999, with support from Mark Thomas and working through the local *Wakefield Express,* UNISON invoked a little-known clause of the Local Government Act 1972, to trigger a referendum on whether or not the trust should proceed with its proposals for a PFI scheme.

The front page headline story in the *Express* on February 5 1999 set out the argument:

"Have your say over hospital

"The public of Wakefield are today given the opportunity to have a huge say in the future of the city's hospitals through a referendum…

> "The referendum on the funding of the health service is presented in conjunction with Wakefield Council and follows union concern over steady privatisation.
>
> "Behind-the-scenes discussions are taking place for a shake-up in the district's health services with enormous consequences for both Pinderfields Hospital and Pontefract General Infirmary.
>
> "Now those making the decisions are being urged to listen to the people that any proposals will affect – YOU.
>
> […]
>
> "Unions in Wakefield are already worried by the suggestion put forward to shut down Pontefract General Infirmary, sell

---

hospital bosses', Yorkshire Post *August 14,*
https://www.yorkshirepost.co.uk/news/health/pfi-debts-an-albatross-around-the-necks-of-yorkshire-hospital-bosses-1-8701426

off the land and buildings, and build a new £100 million 'super hospital' elsewhere in the district using private cash. [...]

"But today's *Wakefield Express* gives everyone throughout the district the opportunity to have their say .... Responding to a call for a public poll on this vital issue, Wakefield Council have asked us to ballot our readership using the form inside. The result will be passed on to Wakefield Health Authority and the government."

Inside page coverage carried brief statements from UNISON and the council, with the page headlined "Comedy star backs our ballot" carrying quotes from Mark Thomas. It noted that although the council's initial reaction to the referendum proposal had been to turn it down on a legal technicality, they eventually decided it was the right thing to do.

Mark Thomas spelled out the danger of NHS hospitals and land being sold off for developers to turn into luxury flats while the NHS could wind up renting a new privately-funded hospital. He added:

"There is an attitude with things like PFI which says there is nothing we can do about it. But there is! This referendum law can be used for anything. The process has already started in Wakefield and we are urging everyone across the whole of the country to do the same."

The referendum, responses to be returned by February 22, asked for yes or no responses to three simple questions:

1) Do you support the full funding by the government of the current health services as provided by the Pinderfields and Pontefract hospital NHS Trust?

2) Do you support the full public capital funding by the government of any new hospital(s) development?

3) If public funding is not available would you support private finance in securing new investment in health services within the Wakefield district?

The response was an overwhelming endorsement of the campaign and the stance taken by UNISON. 97% of replies favoured public funding of services, with only 2% voting no. 72% favoured public capital funding for any new hospital, with a perhaps surprising 21%

voting no. But even more surprising was the massive 81% who voted on the third question to say they would rather not have a new hospital than accept private funding, with just 13% willing to see a hospital funded privately.

The findings from an unofficial test of opinion led to discussion of an official referendum to be run by the council, but this was hampered by the absence of any concrete proposal to be put to the vote. The *Wakefield Express* in its editorial comment on the outcome (headlined "Public's 'NO' to private funding") urged UNISON to continue and step up its campaigning to win "the battle for better health care and then against PFI".

Secretive process

In 2002 the trust was again merged, this time with a Dewsbury Trust that had already lost many of its local services. By 2004 another team of private management consultants, Secta, warned of an £11 million 'affordability gap' in the PFI scheme, and proposed it be scaled back and services 'reconfigured' to cut the costs – removing a whole floor from the new building.

By 2005, with the original scheme now described as "unaffordable", another "rescoping" review of the PFI scheme was calling for bed numbers to be reduced by 30% from the original planned total, leaving them 40% below the 2004 bed numbers: the new building would have "less outer wall area."

All of these discussions and developments took place behind closed doors: there was no public consultation, no transparency, and whatever information UNISON was able to pick up came mainly from leaks.

It was increasingly clear that whatever deal emerged from this process as the basis for a new PFI project, UNISON would have a fight on its hands to secure any disclosure of the details and there would be no serious consultation.

After nine years of furtive and secretive negotiations, half-baked "consultations" and inadequate information the Board opted in 2007 to take a reckless gamble and press ahead with a hugely expensive PFI scheme that had more holes in it than a Tetley teabag.

The Trust achieved financial close and signed its PFI deal on 28 June, and should have made public its full business case (FBC) document within one month of that date. Three years later, despite a constant running battle invoking the Freedom of Information Act and the Information Commissioner's Office, key elements of the deal were still hidden from public view.

UNISON had to battle long and hard to extract a copy of the Full Business Case for the new hospitals, despite the fact that a condition for Department of Health approval for the FBC the previous summer had been that it should be published in its final form within a month of completion.

However when the massive collection of documents was eventually grudgingly handed over it was studded with over 60 deletions of information which managers claimed was "commercial and confidential". Simply listing the omissions, with a few sketchy and formulaic arguments on why they had been omitted, required 13 pages of A4.

Among the subject areas the Trust and the PFI consortium believed were still too sensitive to allow the public to know the details were:

•   Figures on the rate of return to be generated by the consortium

•   Numerous details on the treatment of non-clinical support staff under the TUPE (transfer of undertakings) arrangements, through which they would be seconded to work under the management of the consortium, while remaining NHS employees

•   A whole appendix analysing the transfer of staff to the management of the consortium

•   Details of any additional borrowing to be carried out by the consortium

•   Details on the time that would be allowed for rectification of problems with the building – a significant component of the accountability and monitoring of the PFI contract

•   Letters from some of the long list of high-cost financial and legal advisors giving their view of the contract and its financial implications, and allegedly supporting the project.

Perhaps just as worrying as the omissions were some of the clauses and conditions that were accepted, and the unrealistic projections on bed numbers and caseload which had continued unchanged from earlier negotiations, and which UNISON consistently argued were hugely over-optimistic.

Fighting for access to the Full Business Case

When, one month after the agreement was signed, UNISON duly requested a copy of the FBC, the Trust stated that the copy would be forwarded – by August 3. UNISON lodged a complaint with the Information Commissioner's Office (ICO), raising concerns that the trust had withheld the public disclosure of the FBC.

The ICO requested the Trust to conduct an internal review and to detail its reasons for the delay and nondisclosure at the time. The Trust maintained that it was right not to publicly issue the FBC at that time. Eventually the Trust finally released to the public and to UNISON its Version 1 of the document in December 2007, nearly 6 months after the agreement was signed.

On receiving the redacted FBC UNISON immediately responded to the Trust and the ICO to raise the Branch's objections over the extent of the information which was still withheld. In effect, virtually every piece of information referring to finances was withheld on the grounds of "commercial confidentiality." All financial transactions connected to the deal were viewed as a trade secret.

UNISON continued with the application for full disclosure of the FBC, emphasising that the value for money case could not be tested or proven whilst all the financial details were withheld. On December 27 UNISON were sent a letter from the ICO explaining that the case would be allocated to "case resolution team". UNISON requested its application be prioritised, and the ICO replied on February 6, 2008 that they disagreed, and backed the Trust's position that they would 'periodically review' the pattern process and disclose further information as and when they felt appropriate.

On April 11 the ICO communicated that the Trust was now ready to release further "substantial" information that had previously been withheld. However this substantial information (i.e. FBC addendum 5.1) was not received until May 27. On July 2, 2008 UNISON complained to the ICO that the 'substantial information' disclosed had turned out to be a mere two documents, leaving a further 61 documents still undisclosed.

One of the documents belatedly received was the papers and

minutes of the Trust's Hospitals Development Project (HDP) meeting – which had been held back in November 2004. This detailed the trust's decision when picking its preferred consortium partner from the shortlisted bidders. Although this information could be viewed as being substantial, it was of little use or relevance a full four years after the event.

ICO closes the door

The branch continued with its application for the disclosure of the FBC in its entirety. The ICO advised that it would review the case on a quarterly basis. On September 3 UNISON expressed concern that five months had passed with no updates being forthcoming. A letter dated October 2 was received from Claire Walsh, the ICO senior complaints officer, informing the Branch that its case had been allocated to her for investigation.

The Trust's director of corporate affairs Dawn Stephenson argued that the FBC was to be reviewed on a six monthly basis, and version 5.3 of additional information disclosure would be made available in July 2009. On March 19, 2009, Claire Walsh, the ICO complaints officer, clarified that she felt that some of the Trust's withheld information had in fact had been correctly withheld under section 41 exemption criteria. However a letter dated April 2, 2009 highlighted that the ICO and UNISON agreed that a list of 12 outstanding omitted documents was still being demanded by UNISON.

More than a year later, on June 1, 2010, Peter Martin, the clerk to the tribunal's service intervened, arguing that UNISON had not provided adequate grounds for appeal and requested the Branch forward further details. UNISON responded as follows:

> "We fully expect that it will be the Information Commissioner's Office view that technically it is not in the public's interest to know how much private profit is made out of our healthcare services. However we wish to record our objections."

Peter Martin responded by informing us that the "principal judge" had asked for further written reasons why UNISON considered the decision notice to be wrong. The Branch replied on June 15:

> "To secretly convert massive public funds into private profit using commercial confidentiality to avoid openness and

transparency is both morally and financially bankrupt. Health services will be at risk in order to allow secretive private profiteering. It is my view that this cannot possibly be in the public's interest."

To UNISON's great surprise Peter Martin's response stated that the tribunal's principal judge had accepted these grounds of appeal. However this made little material difference as the doors of transparency were being firmly slammed shut.

However a subsequent letter of June 25 from Richard Bailey the ICO solicitor said there had been some confusion about the Branch complaint. It was claimed the case had been resolved 'informally', claiming there had been no tribunal Decision Notice in respect of the case, and that previous references were in relation to another similar case!

The Branch reiterated that it had accepted some of the arguments, and nondisclosure of some of the information, but were still challenging on 12 undisclosed items. Richard Bailey replied as follows:

"It is the Commissioner's recollection that we had resolved informally…" and "… I note that you didn't respond to the Commissioner's letter of April 27, 2009 and, as such, file closed."

The letter of April 27, 2009 – from Claire Walsh – stated:

"Thank you for your help in resolving this complaint informally, and as agreed I will now close it."

UNISON did not receive this letter at that time. If the Branch had done it would definitely have challenged any suggestion that its claim had been informally resolved.

A letter dated June 30, 2010 from Peter Martin the clerk of the tribunal stated:

"… Only the complainant or public authority can appeal against a Decision Notice, therefore the tribunal is proposing to strike out your appeal."

Consequently this is exactly what happened – in July 2010.

The Branch experience highlighted the relative ineffectiveness of the Freedom of Information Act when dealing with requests for detailed financial information on PFI. It's also clear that commercial

223

confidentiality clauses are not compatible with the transparency that should apply to all public services contracts. However in this case all of the trust's financial transactions with its PFI 'partners' were subject to the so-called Project Agreement, which basically makes them a closely guarded trade secret.

As a result, despite the grudging and belated publication of reams of documents, crucial "affordability" and value for money deliberations in relation to this PFI deal (and many others) are not transparent.

This has an impact on the unions and on staff, since disputes between employer and staff in respect of jobs, pay and conditions cannot be resolved under these arrangements. They leave trade unions effectively attempting to negotiate with both hands tied behind their backs.

Dogs that don't bite or even bark

Much of the campaigning has taken place in the aftermath of the abolition of Community Health Councils, the bodies that until 2003 had responsibility to speak up for patients and uphold standards of care. They had statutory powers to inspect local services and to block controversial changes and refer them upwards to the Secretary of State for a final decision. Some were much more independent-minded than others, but the most determined of them had often been a thorn in the side of bad management and complacent ministers – hence Alan Milburn's determination to scrap them in the same legislation that established foundation trusts.

Even before the CHCs were abolished local campaigning in Mid Yorkshire had to battle on in the absence of any serious support from local CHCs. After they were scrapped there was even less help from the various largely toothless bodies that were set up in their stead.

The most recent such bodies, set up in the Health and Social Care Act of 2012, are Health Watch, local bodies with a national equivalent which have proved themselves largely useless and ineffective in almost every area. The same legislation also required local councils to take the lead in establishing Health and Wellbeing Boards, but again despite the possibilities that these might appear to offer for holding local NHS management to account, they too have proved to be largely supine and irrelevant bodies with little engagement with local NHS services and little or no contact with campaigners and health unions.

The powers to force a pause in controversial changes and refer them to the Health Secretary still exist, however: they remain as a seldom-used power of local government Health Oversight and Scrutiny Committees, although here too they depend upon local politicians having the awareness and political backbone required to take a stand – a potential threat which has yet to trouble any of the local NHS bodies in Mid Yorkshire who have clearly understood that they are free to pretty much do as they like.

In 2007 an editorial in the Branch newspaper by secretary Mick Griffiths tore into the local health and scrutiny committee's failure to scrutinise or challenge:

> "How lame has been the performance of our local Scrutiny Committee, which last month held a session in which [Director of Turnaround] Toby Lewis from our Trust was called to give a briefing on progress.
>
> [...]
>
> "All the councillors could manage on our behalf was a couple of soft questions, none of which probed beneath the surface of his completely misleading report. Nobody asked him to explain how he claimed to be cutting £35m of spending without affecting patient care.
>
> "Instead they just thanked him for coming, with the Chair declaring that the Committee were encouraged by what they had heard.
>
> "But they only need to look up the Trust's link on the NHS website to see bold red boxes proclaiming that both its quality of services and its use of resources are branded WEAK by the Healthcare Commission.
>
> "With 'scrutiny' as feeble as this, no wonder nobody in Wakefield is getting the real picture of the Trust, its finances and declining services. And we can be sure that if – despite Mr Lewis's strenuous denial to the committee – there has been a further downsizing of the Hospital Development Plan, the Scrutiny Committee would be the very last to know.

A first step to fighting for an improvement in services and a halt to cuts is a determined effort to uncover the present situation. The Scrutiny Committee needs to get its finger out and get on with just that task if is not to be made a laughing stock by Trust and PCT bosses."

Political weakness

As a result of these weaknesses, the long history of the fight to uncover details of the PFI scheme, challenge some of its key assertions and hold trust management to account for the contracts they have signed with such long-term implications has had to be largely waged by the unions and local campaigners, including the local Trades Union Council.

Despite some honourable exceptions, most local politicians – MPs and councillors alike – have generally been less than helpful, and reluctant to rock the boat with the New Labour government after 1997. Many of them lacked any real commitment to challenge the trust's actions even after the change of government in 2010.

While local politicians have been of little use, campaigners in Mid Yorkshire have been fortunate however in having local newspapers and news media that have been willing on a number of occasions to publish hard news and critical comment on the NHS, including the views of UNISON and health unions.

It's vital that these avenues to reach a wider public remain open, while the fight goes on for politicians big enough and brave enough to stand up.

Part Three

Chapter 9

What's to be done about PFI? Some answers

As the problems and real costs of PFI have become increasingly apparent, more attention has been devoted to ways of minimising the damage or winding up onerously expensive PFI projects.

By August 2008, on the eve of the banking crash that changed so much in terms of public sector funding, PFI analyst Mark Hellowell – pointing to the sharp reduction in the numbers of projects approved from 2004, after years in which rising numbers of schemes had been signed off, was already asking "Is PFI on the critical list?"[166]

Hellowell drew particular attention to the impact on PFI of the imposition of the so-called "payment by results" system of a fixed tariff setting the level of payments per treatment in acute hospitals, which took no account of the inflated overhead capital costs faced by PFI hospitals. Capital costs for trusts with PFI hospitals were 4.3% higher than allowed for in the tariff. By 2005/6, he argued, half of NHS trusts with major PFI projects were in deficit, many seriously, compared with less than a quarter of trusts overall.

In addition, Hellowell argued, the new accounting system to be brought in from 2009/10 could make it impossible to keep PFI projects off the public sector balance sheet, and result in billions of additional liabilities being recorded – apparently increasing public sector borrowing.

However even while he argued that PFI had by then been "discredited within the NHS", Hellowell was mainly predicting that schemes would dry up rather than advocating existing schemes should be terminated.

As the impact of the banking crash became apparent, management consultants McKinsey were brought in by the Labour government in a badly-kept secret project to explore ways of generating £20 billion of "savings" from NHS budgets after the ten years of above inflation

---

[166] Hellowell, M. (2018) Is PFI on the critical list? *Public Finance* 28 August, available https://www.publicfinance.co.uk/2008/08/pfi-critical-list-mark-hellowell

spending increases came to an end in 2010.

McKinsey duly came up with a host of ideas, many of them irresponsible and some ridiculous, and most lacking even a modicum of supporting argument or evidence. They were brought together in 122 largely disconnected and unexplained Powerpoint slides that have since been termed the McKinsey "report."[167] One of these ideas was to explore possibilities of squeezing down costs of PFI projects.

McKinsey projected possible savings of 11-17% (£100-£200m) on the current £1.3bn spending on PFI unitary charge payments by refinancing the loan capital, given that interest rates had fallen from 5.5% in 2008 to 0.5% in 2009:

> "renegotiating the interest charges of 80% of the PFI schemes by 2–3 bp [basis points] could reduce financing cost by £0.1–0.2bn" (slides 13 & 46).

No such large-scale renegotiation took place. But PFI schemes on the previous basis were increasingly unaffordable, and by the summer of 2010 a substantial *BMJ* article explored different scenarios for minimising the costs.[168]

The Conservative and Liberal Democrat coalition government had announced an austerity programme for public sector spending, including plans to cut capital spending from £49bn in 2009 to £20.6bn in 2014-15. Even after the collapse of interest rates it was still cheaper for government to borrow than for the private sector.

The National Audit Office was urging the Department of Health to "use its 'leverage' to persuade PFI contractors to share efficiency savings with the NHS, although there was little indication that this would receive a favourable response from PFI consortia.

Mark Hellowell warned that the crisis in Britain meant that rather

---

[167] McKinsey & Co (2009) *Achieving World Class Productivity in the NHS 2009/10 – 2013/14: Detailing the Size of the Opportunity*, Department of Health, available:
https://healthemergency.org.uk/pdf/McKinsey%20report%20on%20efficiency%20in%20NHS.pdf
[168] Davis, P. (2010) Is this the end of the road for the PFI?, *BMJ* 24 July, *BMJ* 2010;341:c3828, available https://www.bmj.com/bmj/section-pdf/186625?path=/bmj/341/7765/Feature.full.pdf

than refinance PFI deals at lower interest rates, financiers and contractors were likely to seek more profitable opportunities to market PFI in other countries "with British companies now setting up missions in Mexico and Brazil".

University of East Anglia academic Dr Chris Edwards had argued for a buy-out of the costly Norfolk & Norwich Hospital PFI contract, which he initially calculated would cost £300m but save money overall – £217m by the end of the contract in 2037. However when he had been through the whole 400-page contract Dr Edwards concluded that the cost of a buy-out would be higher … and there would be no savings. (p176-177)

Tear up contracts

The same *BMJ* article also quoted former Labour government advisor Paul Corrigan, who had come to an even more radical conclusion:

> "He advocates simply tearing up PFI agreements. In a world where agreements are torn up every day, the NHS ought not to fear this as controversial, he says.
>
> "PFI is a big sum of money in the NHS, but against the debt restructuring of the last three years it's weeny. You might think this would be breaking the rules, but the number of rule books ripped up in banking over the last three years is astronomical." (p177)

This idea was brushed aside by a Treasury source, who also dismissed Corrigan's suggestion of Treasury involvement in renegotiating contracts:

> "Revisiting the costs of contracts would have to be on a case-by-case basis and I wouldn't expect we'd see huge reductions as a result."

A year later, as the deficit problems of trusts with some of the biggest PFI schemes became even more serious, the Treasury announced a plan to deliver £1.5 billion savings across all 495 operational PFI projects in England. It was claimed that one of the pilot studies that prompted this decision was at Queen's Hospital in Romford, but there has been little indication that whatever changes were agreed there has done much to resolve that trust's chronic financial problems.

According to the bold promises of the statement:

> "The Efficiency and Reform Group in Cabinet Office, supported by experts from the Treasury and Local Partnerships, will now lead a programme to secure the savings across the public sector.
>
> "The programme will bring together ongoing major government supplier renegotiations with project level savings initiatives being delivered by local contract management teams across the country.
>
> Updated guidance and advice on how savings can be made will be published on the Treasury website to support all PFI contract holders."[169]

Among the proposals was "making efficient use of space, for example from subletting or mothballing surplus building space." In fact the excess running costs of PFI, which have left some trusts unable to staff or utilise substantial areas of the costly new buildings has been a common problem, especially in London PFI hospitals, such as Queen Elizabeth Woolwich, Lewisham, Queen's Hospital in Romford[170], UCLH and the biggest and most costly PFI of all, Bart's Health, with one and a half whole floors standing empty[171]. In a number of these cases "surplus" space has been sub-let to private medical corporations, at least for a time.

By June 2013, departments were claiming to have secured £1.6 billion of signed savings from operational contracts, although just £63m of these were from Health and Education projects, almost all of the savings were "forecast future savings," to be realised over the remaining years of the contract, rather than immediately, and of the

---

[169] HM Treasury (2011) Treasury announces plans to find £1.5 billion savings across PFI contracts, Press Release 19 July, available https://www.gov.uk/government/news/treasury-announces-plans-to-find-15-billion-savings-across-pfi-contracts

[170] https://www.independent.co.uk/life-style/health-and-families/health-news/world-s-largest-private-healthcare-company-hca-plans-expansion-into-nhs-8659439.html

[171] Mendick, R. et al (2015) The PFI hospitals costing NHS £2bn every year, *Daily Telegraph*, https://www.telegraph.co.uk/news/nhs/11748960/The-PFI-hospitals-costing-NHS-2bn-every-year.html

684 operational contracts, 566, with a total remaining unitary charge of £151 billion, had not reported any savings.

Most of the 'savings' that were reported were theoretical forecast future savings, which they hoped to realise over the remaining years of the contract, rather than immediately. While the National Audit Office found that a majority of the projects it checked for the Treasury were plausible, it's clear that the totals of money saved were a very small proportion of the annual total of unitary charge payments – and that health PFIs had realised virtually none at all.[172]

Buy-outs

In 2014 headlines were grabbed by the news that the first NHS trust had managed to buy out a small PFI contract – by borrowing £114m via the lower lending rates available through the local council. The early termination of the Hexham Hospital PFI – which had cost £54m to build and was costing the trust approximately £8m a year with a further 18.5 years left to run, with a total cost of £249m over 32 years – was expected to save the Northumbria Healthcare Foundation Trust £67m to the end of the contract, just £3.6m a year.[173]

However few PFI hospitals had cost as little as Hexham, and fewer still of the most troublesome ones. The continuing government squeeze on local government budgets has made it even less likely that any other councils can be found to offer the cut price loan that enabled the Northumbria trust to make a relatively modest saving. Nor will many PFI contracts contain the unusual 'get out' clause that allowed the Hexham contract to be bought out early.

Far from being a model for how to end PFI contracts, Hexham was the exception that proved the rule – that in general buy-outs are too expensive to yield savings, and the capital required is not

[172] NAO (213) Savings from operational PFI contracts, HM Treasury, https://www.nao.org.uk/wp-content/uploads/2013/11/Savings-from-operational-PFI-contracts_final.pdf
[173] Mercer, H. and Whitfield, D. (2018) Nationalising Special Purpose Vehicles to end PFI: a discussion of the costs and benefits (p15), PSIRU, http://gala.gre.ac.uk/20016/1/20016%20MERCER_Nationalising_Special_P urpose_Vehicles_to_End_PFI%20_2018.pdf

available on the scale required for even a modest-sized general hospital. Even the Deloitte partner who had advised the trust, while claiming there was "a lot of interest" from up to 10 other trusts, told the *Financial Times* Northumbria had benefited from a "relatively unique" situation because of the council's relationship with the hospital.[174]

Scotland

One area of Britain where it did appear PFI had been successfully replaced by an alternative was Scotland, where the SNP's 2007 Manifesto had rejected PFI as a type of privatisation, and the SNP in government replaced it with their own NPD (non-profit distributing) scheme, which was supposed to end the 'exorbitant PFI' policy of New Labour eliminate 'excess profits' and protect the public interest.

However Mark Hellowell and Allyson Pollock were quick to point out that the scheme was not really so new or so different:

> "The NPD model, which was introduced to Scotland under the previous Labour-led administration, is a close relative of PFI. Under both models, a private sector 'special purpose vehicle' is established to take on a number of project tasks, in particular the design, construction, and operation of new or refurbished infrastructure.

The SPV is typically composed of a construction firm, a facilities management firm and a private equity group. Projects are mostly financed by private debt (loans from banks, or money sourced through the capital markets), and around 10 per cent private capital from the SPV member companies.

The key difference between PFI and NPD is that, whereas in the former, the SPV capital includes a small element of private equity, in the latter its members invest only loans. In consequence, while SPV shareholders receive returns on their capital in NPD, the level of these returns is to a large extent 'capped' at the point at which contracts are signed·"[175]

---

[174] Plimmer, G., Neville, S. (2014) NHS trust becomes first to buy out its PFI contract, *Financial Times* October 1, https://www.ft.com/content/cc4f10b2-4951-11e4-8d68-00144feab7de

[175] Hellowell, M., Pollock, A.M. (2009) Non-Profit Distribution: The Scottish

Hellowell and Pollock went on to show that at this early stage in the NPD approach there was little evidence that the scheme would eliminate "excessive profits" or continue to offer the Scottish government the political advantage they were claiming.

By 2015, a *Guardian* report highlighted delays and mounting costs of the SNP schemes:

> "Dozens of schemes that were to sign off funding terms from 1 September 2014 have been delayed as a consequence, leading to extra costs for councils and the NHS which the SFT has so far not quantified.

> "Although no clear costs for delays are yet available, a Guardian investigation suggests the first 24 projects in the SFT's Hub programme to build new schools and community centres, as well as its programme for large standalone schemes for roads and hospitals, are already slated to set back the taxpayer about £10bn in borrowing and running costs from now until 2048."[176]

And by 2017 sufficient details of the £212m Dumfries Hospital had emerged to reveal that the SNP's scheme was only marginally different from the PFI method that had proved so expensive in England. The private sector consortium that built the hospital was charging an interest rate of 5.1% on borrowings of £218m, and an even more eye-watering 11.3% on £24.2m of "subordinate debt" – when the Scottish government could have borrowed to fund the scheme with public funds at an interest rate of just 1.6%.[177]

Approach to Private Finance in Public Services, *Social Policy & Society* 8:3, 405–418,
https://pdfs.semanticscholar.org/1b34/c11aa1323040956d6609bccbdf24c264260e.pdf

[176] Carrell, S. (2015) Scottish government turning to more private money for public projects, The Guardian, July 27, available https://www.theguardian.com/uk-news/2015/jul/27/scottish-government-rely-private-money-public-projects-childrens-hospital-eu-rules-state-spending

[177] Arthur, S. (2017) 'The SNP abolished PFI, or did they?', Jubilee Scotland, January 27, https://www.jubileescotland.org.uk/the-snp-abolished-pfi-or-did-they/

More buy-out plans

In June 2017, NHS Improvement chief executive Jim Mackey, who had been involved as chief executive of the Northumbria trust at the time of the Hexham Hospital buy-out, wrote to trusts to announce that a working group had been established to explore the possibility of more buy outs at a time when interest rates were the "lowest since the Napoleonic war". NHSI planned to hold an event for providers with "early PFI deals".[178]

In November 2017 a new scandal once again refuted the claims that PFI contracts transferred the risk of failures to the private sector, with revelations that the Queen Elizabeth Hospital in Woolwich, now part of the Lewisham & Greenwich Hospitals Trust, was facing a £48m repair bill to make one of its hospitals safe. Loopholes in the drafting of its Private Finance Initiative contract had left the trust stuck with the bill for tackling "cost cutting at construction" and "failures in specification and design standards."

Applying for additional government funding to help cover the otherwise unaffordable costs, the Trust argued that:

"The infrastructure issues arise from unresolved legacy problems with the 60 year PFI agreement between the Meridian Hospital Company and the now dissolved Greenwich Health Authority, and derive from failures in specification and design standards, cost cutting at construction and contract terms that give the present trust limited redress against defects arising from the initial design and installation."[179]

By January 2018, as Carillion collapsed, Jim Mackey, whose previous efforts had yielded no results, was back in post at Northumbria trust and again making statements about seeking an

---

[178] Dunhill, L. (2017) Mackey reveals next steps to tackle 'ridiculous' PFI deals, *Health Service Journal* June 1, (£)
https://www.hsj.co.uk/news/mackey-reveals-next-steps-to-tackle-ridiculous-pfi-deals/7018409.article

[179] Clover, B. (2017) Trust faces £48m repair bill for PFI hospital, Health Service Journal, 29 November, (£) https://www.hsj.co.uk/lewisham-and-greenwich-nhs-trust/trust-faces-48m-repair-bill-for-pfi-hospital/7021166.article

alternative to PFI funding.[180]

By June 2018 came two important decisions in broken PFI schemes.

The long-running legal battle to end the failed £321m PFI contract for the Roseberry Park psychiatric hospital in Middlesbrough won a ruling the High Court that found in the trust's favour and awarded them costs. The 312-bed hospital, which cost £73m to build opened in 2011 but has had chronic problems with its roof, plumbing and fire safety system, which the consortium, Three Valleys Healthcare Limited (TVH) had failed to address. TVH, which had contested the case, promptly went into administration. Middlesbrough MP Andy McDonald said:

> "Much of the hospital will have to be rebuilt. The process of decanting patients to other facilities to deal with these defects has been immensely disruptive for patients and their families alike." [181]

Also in June it was revealed that even the Treasury, which had effectively forced so many hospital trusts down the road of PFI contracts for lack of public funding options, had decided that the PFI contract for the Midland Metropolitan Hospital should be ended.[182]

In taking this decision, the Treasury was following the lead of the five banks that had been funding the PFI scheme which came to an abrupt halt when Carillion collapsed.

Two months later Treasury hopes of re-tendering the project as a revamped PFI were dashed by a report from Deloitte, revealing that

---

[180] Dunhill, L. (2018) Trusts in talks to establish 'NHS alternative to PFI', January 11, Health Service Journal, (£) https://www.hsj.co.uk/finance-and-efficiency/trusts-in-talks-to-establish-nhs-alternative-to-pfi/7021429.article

[181] BBC News (2018) Trust wins Roseberry Park hospital PFI contract battle, BBC news 29 June 2018, https://www.bbc.co.uk/news/uk-england-tees-44661222

[182] Price, D. (2018) Treasury agreed to terminate PFI on Midland hospital, Construction News, 25 June, https://www.constructionnews.co.uk/companies/contractors/carillion/treasury-agreed-to-terminate-pfi-on-midland-hospital/10032309.article

that cost would be increased by over £100m if funded privately:

> "Analysis by Deloitte, commissioned by the Trust, concluded that the hospital would cost £319 million to complete with standard public sector procurement, and £424 million if completed under a new PPP contract. The increase is due to the increase in risk for a contractor under a PPP contract."[183]

A similar conclusion has since been reached on the near-complete but structurally flawed and stymied Liverpool Royal Hospital, which some have suggested might be cheaper to pull down and start again rather than attempt to repair it.[184]

Labour and trade union policies on PFI

Labour policy on PFI has moved dramatically forward since the New Labour period, with few diehards still attempting to argue the merits of such a widely discredited plan. However it's clear there are still divisions on how to proceed.

A useful new study assessing five potential partial or more ambitious solutions has just been published by the Centre for Health and the Public Interest as this text is finalised.[185]

The debate has grown not only as a result of the Carillion failure, but in the aftermath of a statement by Shadow Chancellor John McDonnell at the 2017 party conference in Brighton that Labour would bring PFIs "back in house," which appeared to draw a line under the failed PFI approach:

> "The scandal of the Private Finance Initiative has resulted in huge

---

[183] http://www.infrapppworld.com/news/megaproject-1307-uk-health-authority-scraps-retender-of-cancelled-us-450-million-hospital-ppp

[184] Moreby, A. (2018) Taxpayers to bail out Royal Liverpool hospital project Construction Enquirer
https://www.constructionenquirer.com/2018/09/25/taxpayers-to-bail-out-royal-liverpool-hospital-project/

[185] Kotecha, V. & Hellowell, M. (2018) Dealing with the legacy of PFI – options for policymakers, CHPI, October,
https://chpi.org.uk/papers/reports/dealing-with-the-legacy-of-pfi-options-for-policymakers/

long-term costs for taxpayers while providing enormous profits for some companies," he said.

"Over the next few decades, nearly £200 billion is scheduled to be paid out of public sector budgets in PFI deals. In the NHS alone, £831 million in pre-tax profits have been made over the past six years.

"Never again will this waste of taxpayer money be used to subsidise the profits of shareholders, often based in offshore tax havens."

McDonnell added:

"We have already pledged there will be no new PFI deals signed by us in government. But we will go further. It is what you have been calling for. We will bring existing PFI contracts back in-house".[186]

Many including the *Independent's* Richard Vaughan[187] understood McDonnell's plan to be one of buying out the PFI contracts, which was estimated by the Guardian's Larry Elliott to cost anything up to £50-£60 billion.[188]

However this statement was swiftly fudged by a subsequent Labour Party statement:

"Labour staged an undignified retreat today on John McDonnell's boast that he would seize back private finance contracts worth £300 billion.

Senior colleagues clarified that, contrary to the shadow chancellor's speech yesterday, only a "handful" of the PFI deals would be taken over.

And the entire policy appeared to be being buried in the long grass of a case-by-case review, which could take years to

---

[186] http://www.bbc.co.uk/news/uk-politics-41379849

[187] Vaughan, R. (2017) John McDonnell: Labour will buy back PFI debt, *Independent* September 25, https://inews.co.uk/news/politics/john-mcdonnell-labour-will-buy-back-pfi-debt/

[188] Elliott, L. (2017) Labour's PFI pledge would be expensive – but it isn't a blank cheque, *Guardian* September 25, https://www.theguardian.com/politics/2017/sep/25/labour---pfi---contracts---john---mcdonnell

complete."[189]

To add to the confusion, Labour backbencher Stella Creasey has been waging a separate campaign, pressing for a "windfall tax" on the PFI companies which began with a more general call for taxation on their very high levels of profits[190], but went on to focus specifically on the profits that have flowed from the drastic cuts in corporation tax since the 1990s, which has come down from up to 30% when most of the deals were signed to a current level of 19%, with further reductions promised by the Tory government.[191]

The same policy suggestion, endorsed by research from the Centre for Policy in the Public Interest showing that these tax cuts could bring savings to PFI consortia of up to £190m by 2020[192], has been backed by UNISON.[193]

Of course there is nothing wrong with taxing profits, and making major corporations pay their fair share: but as People vs PFI have argued, there is a danger that this partial policy, which would tax only the 10% portion of PFI contracts that is funded via equity investment, leaving the remaining 90% untouched, will take the place of a wider strategy to tackle the continuing costs of PFI:

"Profits made from the PFI lending banks from servicing the

---

[189] Murphy, J., Cecil, N (2017) Labour in retreat over John McDonnell's PFI boast, *Evening Standard*, 26 September
https://www.standard.co.uk/news/politics/labour-in-retreat-over-john-mcdonnells-pfi-boast-a3643896.html

[190] Creasy, S. (2017) PFI is bankrupting Britain. But there are ways to set ourselves free, *The Guardian*, August 30,
https://www.theguardian.com/commentisfree/2017/aug/30/pfi-britain-hospital-trust-debt-burden-tax

[191] Mason, R. (2017) Hospital PFI firms set for £190m windfall from tax cuts – study, the *Guardian*, December 27, available
https://www.theguardian.com/politics/2017/dec/27/hospital-pfi-firms-set-for-190m-windfall-from-tax-cuts-study

[192] https://chpi.org.uk/blog/the-pfi-companies-windfall-from-falling-corporation-tax-rates/

[193] UNISON (2018) Time for a windfall tax on the PFI profiteers, says UNISON, 19 February, https://www.unison.org.uk/news/press-release/2018/02/time-windfall-tax-pfi-profiteers-says-unison/

debt, at interest rates above 8% – amounting to well over 50% of the entire PFI project cost during a 30 year contract remain untouched by the windfall tax proposals."[194]

The most recent CHPI publication examines three other partial approaches to the PFI costs and consequences:

• Improving the contract and performance management of PFI schemes, the "least radical" option, which might offer savings of up to £15m a year.

• Centralising part of the PFI interest payment to alleviate the financial burden on local NHS trusts; this would potentially reduce trusts' deficits by 30%, but would pass the extra costs of "around £400m" on to the Department of Health and Social Care.

• Terminating or buying out the PFI contracts – an approach which CHPI concludes is "unlikely to be affordable to most NHS trusts and the Department of Health and Social Care"

CHPI also considers, but is critical of a fifth proposal, which has been advocated strongly by People vs PFI. That is the more far-reaching proposal of both ditching PFI as the model for financing any future infrastructure projects and nationalising the Special Purpose Vehicles (SPVs) – the relatively small companies at the core of existing PFI contracts.[195]

This policy would require both an Act of Parliament to expropriate the shares of those investors who own the SPVs, and payment of an estimated £2.6 billion to take them all over.

CHPI takes a cautious line on this and has opted not to lend unqualified support to any of the five options. It warns that with the nationalisation of SPVs:

"Any government which chooses to take forward this radical

[194] People vs PFI (2018) *A PFI Windfall Tax – Radical Solution? or a Sticky Plaster on a Gaping Wound?*, online, May 17
http://peoplevspfi.org.uk/2018/05/17/a-pfi-windfall-tax-radical-solution-or-a-sticky-plaster-on-a-gaping-wound/
[195] Whitfield, D. Mercer, H (2015) *Nationalise the Special Purpose Vehicles and end profiteering from public assets*, People vs PFI, December,
https://peoplevsbartspfi.files.wordpress.com/2016/02/pfi-nationalise-the-spvs-pple-vs-barts-pfi-version-1.pdf

and ambitious proposal is likely to require a large majority in Parliament to pass such an Act. ...

"It is also likely to face legal challenges from PFI investors, which could take the form of a challenge under international trade law or under Human Rights legislation.

... "We also identify the fact that there is no guarantee that the re-financing of the PFI debt would occur as a result of this proposal, and that in order to reduce the high cost of PFI debt a further Act of Parliament might be required to nationalise these loans".[196]

However the CHPI analysis concedes that this would generate very substantial returns in the longer term, saving £900m a year, while all of the facilities management contracts for hospitals and schools would be insourced back to the public sector bodies, offering their staff much better terms and conditions.

People vs PFI take a much more positive approach, stressing the potential savings to be made in the medium term. They argue that £25 billion could be saved in PFI interest payments just in Scotland of this approach was adopted, with much higher potential savings across the UK, compared to the barely significant £190m by 2020 that might raised from a one-off windfall tax.

This policy has been adopted and promoted by John McDonnell, who has made clear that the "review" of PFI projects is to establish which PFI projects could best be taken back under public ownership in this way, and what level of compensation should be paid.

His adviser on PFI, Greenwich University academic Helen Mercer, pointing to similar views from the ratings agency Moody's, argued that there was no absolute legal requirement for compensation to be paid at market value. McDonnell emphasised that as a result:

"Parliament will determine the value of every industry and sector

---

[196] Kotecha, V. & Hellowell, M. (2018) Dealing with the legacy of PFI – options for policymakers, CHPI, October, https://chpi.org.uk/papers/reports/dealing-with-the-legacy-of-pfi-options-for-policymakers/ p7-8.

that we nationalise and bring back into public ownership".[197]

Mercer, with another PFI specialist Dexter Whitfield, set out the arguments for the nationalisation of the SPVs in much more detail in their April 18 pamphlet[198]. They note that:

> "The SPV is the mechanism whereby public assets become the source to provide private profit to banks, infrastructure funds, construction firms and private service providers." (P6)

PFI deals, they argue were highly profitable for investors when they were first signed, but have become even more profitable since then:

> "While the rates of return for the investor consortium were anticipated to be between 12 and 16% when the contract was signed, research has consistently established that realised returns have been well in excess of this.

> "Vecchi et al, for instance, argue that the rate of return to equity, meaning the combined value of the share capital and shareholder loan, is on average 9% higher than that anticipated. … corporation tax rates have declined by over a third since many of the contracts were signed, giving windfall post---tax profits." (p9)

In similar fashion to the CHPI report they also explore various suggestions on how PFI should be tackled, dividing the solutions into two types; "those which seek to work around that fundamental antagonism [between the public interest and private interests in maintaining PFI] and those which propose meeting the challenge head on." (p14)

> "The former seek to amend contracts, 'claw' back' money through taxation, or to redistribute the debt around the public sector, the latter proposals involve aligning public and

---

[197] Pickard, J. (2018) Labour hints at no compensation for PFI investors *Financial Times* February 18, https://www.ft.com/content/a73c4056-130b-11e8-940e-08320fc2a277

[198] Mercer, H., Whitfield, D. (2018) Nationalising Special Purpose Vehicles to end PFI: a discussion of the costs and benefits, April, PSIRU, http://gala.gre.ac.uk/20016/1/20016%20MERCER_Nationalising_Special_P urpose_Vehicles_to_End_PFI%20_2018.pdf

private interest by ending the contract."

Mercer and Whitfield work first through the previous proposals to end the contracts, noting that

- buy-outs require a voluntary agreement of the SPV shareholders and compensation to be paid. The authors conclude: that while buy-outs can secure some savings and bring services and facilities back under public control, they leave the PFI model intact, can be very profitable for the shareholders, and have to be negotiated one by one. (pp14-17)

- Termination of PFI contracts "relies on a specific set of circumstances to enable termination to take place, such as break clauses in the main PFI contract, bankruptcy of the SPV, or extreme financial constraints on the public authority." (p18)

The "work-around" solutions are also unsatisfactory in various ways.

- Renegotiation of unitary charge payments has been hard to achieve, offers limited savings with high transaction costs and does not challenge PFI (p19)

- Centralisation of PFI debts has the merit of lifting the problem off individual NHS trusts or other public sector bodies, and placing them firmly back with government. But this could actually make the debts more secure: it does not solve the bigger question of the PFI contracts. (p20)

- The proposal of a windfall tax (discussed above in this chapter) also falls into the category of a "work-around" solution that leaves the core problem in place.

- Default on the payments due under the contract is an option that is based on previous stands taken by national governments repudiating onerous payments on "odious debt" incurred by a previous corrupt and dictatorial regime. Mercer and Whitfield point out that there is no real framework of law that allows this approach to be implemented on PFI debt, so that however attractive and morally correct it might appear, any government adopting this line would face significant problems:

> "Default on debts, or insisting on a haircut puts the public sector firmly before private interest, is open and transparent and can provide financial relief for services. The

undeveloped legal basis could result in uncertainty for the service concerned, high legal costs and could only relate to each specific PFI contract – no court case would have any general applicability." (p22)

Having effectively established the need for an alternative to the previous policies on offer, the authors focus on the "principles, policies and mechanisms" for nationalising SPVs through an act of Parliament (Section 4), and "Acquiring SPVs based on current net shareholder equity" (Section 5).

They spell out the advantages of this solution compared with others:

"First, unlike buyouts and terminations nationalisation allows the government to 'write the rules' for the end of PFIs. Buy-outs involve commercial negotiations between individual public bodies with limited resources and major financial entities with access to expensive legal and commercial advice. Nationalisation means that levels of compensation to shareholders, banks and bond-holders and the public are determined by act of Parliament.

"Secondly, unlike default, centralising the debt, windfall taxes and renegotiation, nationalisation of the SPVs and ownership of the contract challenges the PFI model.

"Thirdly, unlike renegotiation, unitary payments can immediately be reduced for the majority of PFI projects: they would no longer need to cover all the costs incurred by private ownership including shareholder dividends, directors' and auditors' fees and charges for management companies." (p23)

The concluding section shows how the cost of acquiring the SPVs would be between £2.3bn and £2.6bn, but differs from the CHPI estimate by arguing that the nationalisation could generate immediate annual savings of £1.4bn from SPV admin costs and up to another £765m of profits per year to private contractors: so the entire process would swiftly pay for itself and generate very significant savings.

After more than 25 years of PFI schemes in Britain and PPPs around the world, it's high time this relatively straightforward, neat, legal and affordable policy was explicitly adopted by the Labour

Party as the government in waiting and endorsed by the unions whose members have been exploited by PFI contractors and consortia.

Mid Yorkshire UNISON Branch Secretary Adrian O'Malley, welcoming the policy as a clear and concrete way of implementing branch calls for renationalisation of the PFIs, said:

> "John McDonnell's speech to the 2017 Labour Party conference was music to the ears of our members and campaigners against the great PFI rip off. The Renationalisation of all PFI assets, with the absolute minimum of compensation to the city spivs and offshore tax dodgers who dominate the PFI industry, is an absolute necessity if we are to rebuild our vital public services.
>
> "We must be as ruthless with the PFI consortia as the government and employers have been with our members' terms and conditions. Our PFI has resulted in job losses, pay cuts, hospital closures and cuts in services. This has been repeated across the NHS and public sector.
>
> "Back in 2012/13, when our Admin staff were striking against pay cuts and redundancies, our chief executive lectured us that there was "no magic money tree". A mantra repeated by Theresa May in the 2017 general election.
>
> "PFI has been a magic money forest to big business that badly needs chopping down. Our hospitals along with every PFI scheme must be returned to public ownership under democratic, accountable, public control. Our NHS and public services should not be used to line the pockets of the already wealthy.
>
> "It's time to end the unhealthy profits from PFI."

John Lister, October 2018

Postscript

PFI/PPPs – the great global rip-off

British governments have pretty much pioneered the concept of the private financing of new hospital and health care projects through the Private Finance Initiative (PFI) in the last 25 years. British-based consultancy firms such as PriceWaterhouseCoopers (PWC) and British-led consortia have been at the forefront of efforts to promote this approach – in many countries referred to as "Public Private Partnerships" (PPP or P3s) – on an international level.

The most recent overview produced by PWC and the University of California San Francisco (UCSF) "Global Health Group," led by former World Bank Health boss Richard Feachem, looks at PPPs world-wide, with a specific focus on infrastructure (mainly hospital building) projects[199]. It follows on a similar PWC report back in 2010, which despite the impact of the recent banking crash, expected an expanding market to take a growing share of what they project to be steadily rising health spending to 2020 and beyond, predicting a "trillion dollar market for PPPs in healthcare"[200].

PWC followed this by looking outwards from a number of projects in Australia, to point to on potential markets for PPP in South East Asia, noting the first PPP-financed hospital in the city of Kuantan in Malaysia, and arguing that the rapid economic growth rates in the region offered excellent potential to service hefty PPP loans[201, 202].

---

[199]Abuzaineh, N., Brashers, E., Foong, S., Feachem, R., Da Rita, P. (2018). *PPPs in healthcare: Models, lessons and trends for the future.* Healthcare public-private partnership series, No. 4. San Francisco: The Global Health Group, Institute for Global Health Sciences, University of California, San Francisco and PwC. Available:
https://globalhealthsciences.ucsf.edu/sites/globalhealthsciences.ucsf.edu/files/pub/ppp-report-series-business-model.pdf
[200] PricewaterhouseCoopers (PWC) (2010) *Build and beyond: the (r)evolution of health care*, December, http://www.pwc.com/us/en/health-industries/publications/build-and-beyond.jhtml
[201] PricewaterhouseCoopers (PWC) (2012) *Build and Beyond; Bridging the*

While some of this has proved to be accurate, it seems that the pace of expansion in many countries has slowed. Citing figures from the *Project Finance and Infrastructure Journal* (IJGlobal) the 2018 PWC/UCSF report notes that:

"there are roughly 600 healthcare infrastructure projects/assets globally, the vast majority of which are PPPs."

Most PPPs are in Europe

The latest picture indicates that over 60% of these 600 projects are in Europe and 15% in North America: two thirds of all projects are to be found in the UK and Canada alone:

"by comparison Sub-Saharan Africa and the Middle East and North Africa together constitute less than 5% of projects globally." (ibid. p10)

According to PWC and UCSF the other countries with more than one operational project were Australia, France, Germany, India, Ireland, Italy, Japan, Mexico, Portugal, Spain, United Arab Emirates and the United States.

Another disparate group of countries each had one operational PPP project: Austria, Chile, Egypt, Kenya, Lesotho, Malaysia, Pakistan, Philippines, Romania, South Korea and Turks and Caicos Islands.

The list appears inconsistent with an earlier (2015) PWC/UCSF report on PPPs in Latin America (which strangely excludes Brazil). It highlighted 19 schemes in Chile, Mexico and Peru[203]. One reason

gap. February,
http://www.pwc.com/gx/en/healthcare/publications/bridging-the-gap-asia-healthcare-ppp.jhtml
[202] PricewaterhouseCoopers (PWC) Australia (2012) *The growing role of PPPs in Australia's healthcare system*, February,
http://www.pwc.com.au/media-centre/12/growing-role-of-PPPs-in-healthcare-feb12/htm
[203] Llumpo, A., Montagu, D., Brashers, E., Foong, S., Abuzaineh, N., Feachem, R. (2015). *Lessons from Latin America: The early landscape of healthcare public-private partnerships*. Healthcare public-private partnership series, No. 2. San Francisco: The Global Health Group, Global Health Sciences, University of California, San Francisco and PwC. Available

why this is omitted from the 2018 report appears to be that a change of government in Chile in 2014 brought an abrupt halt to what looked like an expanding list of PPP projects, questioning whether all 19 projects were in fact likely to be completed:

"Chile had tendered five PPP hospitals and announced plans to tender an additional nine hospitals in 2014. However, the change in administration in 2014 closed the PPP pipeline for the next four years and the country withdrew the tenders for seven of the remaining nine hospitals." (p6)

However according to a 2018 report from IJGlobal, Latin America, with GDP growing on average by 4% a year, is "very alluring for private investment".[204] Mexico appeared to be leading the way with seven PPP projects for small and medium sized hospitals with a total value of $571m agreed in 2015. A total of 26 hospital PPPs were being procured across Latin America, including plans for five health PPPs costing $590m in Colombia, six in Argentina and six in Peru.

Turkey left out

The 2018 PwC/UCSF report also surprisingly omits what has emerged as the second largest PPP hospital building scheme in the world, by the Turkish government, who according to IJGlobal are progressing with a $12 billion plan to build 38 integrated health campuses (IHCs), additional hospitals and a total of 56,000 beds, and are already well advanced with 18 major projects.

The Turkish government had been egged on by the World Bank and its private sector wing the International Finance Corporation (IFC), and for the past 10 years or so has been engaged in a scheme to dramatically increase the numbers of beds available in the country through building 34 city hospitals, with a capacity of 40,000 beds.

Many of the plans are on a scale larger than any other PPP schemes; the largest of all is the $1.2 billion Bilkent Integrated

---

https://www.pwc.com/gx/en/healthcare/pdf/healthcare-public-private-partnerships-latin-america.pdf

[204] Radeva, S. (2018) *LatAm healthcare PPPs – just what the doctor ordered*, IJGlobal, available: https://ijglobal.com/articles/134477/latam-healthcare-ppps-just-what-the-doctor-ordered

Healthcare Campus, which is to provide a staggering 3,804 inpatient beds as well as a 400-bed rehabilitation unit. Some of the other examples identified by IJGlobal are:

Kayseri:	1,583 beds, costing $616m[205].
Eskişehir:	1,081 beds, at $300m, 25 years of payments beginning at $55m[206]
Isparta:	600 beds, costing $285m[207]
Izmir Bayrakli (IHC):	2,060 beds, costing $417m[208]
Kocaeli IHC:	1,180 beds, costing $611m^2
Konya Karatay IHC:	838 beds costing $356m[209]
Gaziantep:	1,875 beds, costing $600m[210]
Ikitelli IHC:	2,682 beds, build cost $1.4 bn [211]
Bursa:	1,355 beds, costing $463m[212]
Adana IHC:	1,550 beds, costing $533m
Mersin	1,253-beds, costing $334m[213]

The first of the PPP hospitals to open in Turkey was in Yozgat[214], a relatively small 475-bed hospital costing $161m to build, most of the money coming from Japanese banks. Some of the other schemes are already complete, others are still under construction.

Financing for the other Turkish projects has come from a wide range of banks and other bodies, including the European Bank for

---

[205] https://ijglobal.com/articles/91652/kayseri-hospital-financial-structure-in-place

[206] https://ijglobal.com/articles/94686/akfen-wins-eski-ehir-turkish-hospital-ppp

[207] https://ijglobal.com/articles/82414/pb-for-turkeys-isparta-hospital-ppp

[208] https://ijglobal.com/articles/95596/canadas-edc-joins-turkish-hospital-ppps

[209] https://ijglobal.com/articles/99537/pricing-emerges-for-konya-karatay-health-ppp

[210] https://ijglobal.com/articles/106329/new-equity-raised-for-turkeys-gaziantep-hospital

[211] https://ijglobal.com/articles/107173/further-details-emerge-on-turkeys-ikitelli-hospital-ppp

[212] https://ijglobal.com/articles/130327/turkeys-bursa-hospital-ppp-reaches-financial-close

[213] https://ijglobal.com/articles/94644/financial-close-for-mersin-hospital-ppp

[214] https://ijglobal.com/articles/104308/first-turkish-ppp-hospital-opens

Reconstruction and , the Islamic Development Bank, Export Development Canada, the IFC, banks in Korea, Brazil, Austria, China, and corporations including Siemens and Samsung as well as the Samsung pension fund.

The Turkish government announced that the financing of the Kayseri project was explicitly based on "successful examples of similar programs in some European countries, in particular the UK"[215] although the rosy picture they present of the British PPP/Private Finance Initiative scheme is hopelessly unrealistic.

The 2018 PwC report makes clear one similarity between many of these projects and the earlier PFI schemes in Britain – the Turkish PPPs also guarantee an income stream to providers for additional non-clinical services (and in some cases in Turkey even clinical services) over and above the profits to be made from the construction and maintenance of the building:

> "For projects designed following the Infrastructure-based or Integrated PPP models, once design and construction are complete, the private partner remains responsible for maintaining the facilities, and may also provide additional nonclinical and/or clinical services depending on the terms of the contract. Examples of typical nonclinical services include: housekeeping, cafeteria services, utilities management and grounds maintenance."

Indeed as might be expected in an increasingly repressive and authoritarian country in which press freedom is largely suppressed and large numbers of academics have lost their jobs for expressing any opposition or criticism, none of the enthusiastic press releases or even news coverage reflecting government, management or consortium views makes any critical estimate of the overall long term cost of any of the Turkish PPP schemes. This should be no surprise; there was little such criticism in the relatively free mainstream British media either, at the equivalent stage of PFI deals.

None of the Turkish reports appear to discuss the apparently very substantial variations in cost per bed between the various schemes, or the issue of matching the very expensive, 25-30 year investment in

---

[215] https://www.scribd.com/document/33737968/PPP-Health-Campus-Projects

251

hospital-based services with the likely levels of demand, or the future likelihood of newer, alternative models of care which in other countries are seeking to make much less use of hospitals.

Least of all is there any real discussion of the profits to be made by the various commercial "partners": the contracts in Turkey, as in the UK, appear to be heavily stacked in favour of the commercial interests, effectively shielding them from any real risk – whether from inflation, fluctuations in the value of the Turkish lira, or the potential financial collapse of the hospitals:

> "Lease payments are increased annually by the arithmetic average of the Turkish Producer Price Index and Turkish Consumer Price Index for the preceding year. This annual increase may be further adjusted to take into account the increase in the Central Bank's currency basket, if such increase is higher than the average of the Producer Price Index and Consumer Price Index.[216]

> "With respect to renewal health PPP projects rather than lease payments, the provision of non-healthcare services or facilities is granted to the project company and a service fee is paid for such.

> "The project company has to procure the financing required for the health PPP project. In order to increase the bankability of the health PPP projects, the legislation stipulates that the Ministry of Health guarantees the lease payments during the term of the agreement. In addition, it has been reported that the Ministry of Health may provide a 'patient' guarantee to the project company." [217]

Few details of the payments to be made, and no details of the operation of the first these gigantic schemes have been published, while any serious media criticism and political challenge has been crushed in Turkey, so no full evaluation can be made of the extent to

---

[216] This is likely to be an important proviso given the subsequent sharp fluctuations in the Turkish economy and the value of its currency in 2018.

[217] Rodrigues, M., Şahbaz, D., Inal, E. (2013) Healthcare PPPs in Turkey, IJGlobal, available https://ijglobal.com/articles/82012/healthcare-ppps-in-turkey

which they offer value for money or repeat the weaknesses we have discussed in the British PFI schemes.

Canada

The scale of the Turkish PPP projects pushes the country into second place for the number and scale of commitment to PPP, behind Britain. In third place comes Canada: a PWC presentation in 2009 showed that out of $38 billion worth of PPP projects world-wide, schemes outside Europe were estimated at just £5.8 billion in total, £5bn of which were in Canada and Australia[218].

The most eager proponents of "P3" hospital projects have been successive provincial governments in Ontario, Canada's most populous province, where the scheme was first put forward by the Conservative government in the late 1990s, despite the strong objections of public sector unions and the Ontario Health Coalition (OHC).

By 2005 the OHC's Natalie Mehra combined the evidence already accumulating in Canada with other examples from Britain and Australia to produce a "Horrid hundred" list of "Flawed, Failed and Abandoned" P3 schemes, listed in alphabetical order. The common themes running through all these examples are familiar for anyone who has studied PFI in Britain:

Cost Overruns

Delays

Design and Construction Flaws

Quality Problems

Legal Disputes

Failed Contracts, Bankruptcies

Service Cuts

Mehra sums up the final point in terms that speak to the knock on costs of British PFI hospital projects:

"The high costs of P3s have caused service cuts and a shrinking scope of services publicly covered. In several

---

[218] Wootton, I. (2009) Privatisation in the healthcare industry. AEMH conference, Brussels, may 7, PWC, http://www.aemh.org/pdf/PrivatisationinHealthcareIndustry_AEMH7/pdf

projects, the business cases for P3s have rested on unrealistic assumptions of productivity and exaggerated claims of value for money that have proven false. In several cases, the redirection of public funds into P3s has pushed further privatization and reduced access to services."[219]

By 2008 there was already copious official evidence of the extent to which P3 financing was inflating the cost of projects and ripping off the public purse.

Ontario's Auditor General's report on the William Osler Health Centre project in Brampton (WOHC) found that:

The project depended upon a "value for money" report from management consultants which seriously inflated the projected cost of a publicly funded alternative – by $634 million over the life of the project

The actual project almost doubled in cost from the initial projection of $357m to $614m – but this increased cost still resulted in a much smaller hospital with fewer beds.

$200m could have been saved over the 25-year contract if the funding had been raised by the province rather than pay the higher interest rates of the privately financed scheme.[220]

A hard hitting 20-page section of its 2008 annual report argued that the use of a public-private partnership contract ("P3") for the construction of the WOHC had resulted in additional cost to the taxpayer. It made what might seem to be a common sense recommendation that had clearly not been applied: that institutions should conduct a rigorous value-for-money analysis prior to utilizing the P3 approach to procurement. The extra costs were a result of government policy:[221]

---

[219] Mehra, N. (2005) *Failed, Flawed, Abandoned. 100 P3s, Canadian and International Experience*, Ontario Health Coalition,
http://www.ontariohealthcoalition.ca/index.php/flawed-failed-abandoned-100-p3s-canadian-and-international-evidence/

[220] CUPE (2009) Fact Sheet: P3s – *The Wrong Prescription for Health Care*, https://cupe.ca/sites/cupe/files/Fact_Sheet__P3s_The_Wrong_presciption_-0.pdf

[221] Emanuelli, P. (2008) Ontario Auditor Finds P3 Hospital Costs $200 Million Extra in Financing, http://procurementoffice.com/ontario-auditor-

"WOHC had invested much time and effort in planning and delivering the new hospital project. However, WOHC did not have the option of choosing which procurement approach to follow. Rather, it was the government of the day that decided to follow the public-private partnership (P3) approach. We noted that, before this decision was made, the costs and benefits of alternative procurement approaches, including traditional procurement, *were not adequately assessed.*"[222]

This elementary failure was not for lack of potential technical and other expert advice: indeed this had been a major expenditure in setting up this and other P3 schemes:

"WOHC and the Ministry engaged approximately 60 legal, technical, financial, and other consultants at a total cost of approximately $34 million. About $28 million of these costs related to the work associated with the new P3 approach, yet they were not included in the P3 cost." (p105)

Indeed it may well have been some of this "advice" that led to wilful distortions in the tokenistic comparisons between a publicly funded project and the favoured P3:

"WOHC added to the estimates for the government to design and build a new hospital an estimated $67 million, or 13% of the estimated total design and construction cost, in risks of cost overruns transferred to the private sector. We questioned the inclusion of such a large amount because a properly structured contract under a traditional procurement agreement could have mitigated many of the risks of cost overruns.

"The province's cost of borrowing at the time the agreement was executed was cheaper than the weighted average cost of capital charged by the private-sector consortium—yet the

---

finds-p3-hospital-costs-200-million-extra-in-financing/

[222] Auditor General of Ontario (2008) *Annual report of the Office of the Auditor General of Ontario*, Chapter 3, Section 3.03, http://www.auditor.on.ca/en/content/annualreports/arreports/en08/ar_e n08.pdf, p 104

impact of these savings was not included in the comparison costs between the traditional procurement and the P3 approach." (p 12)

It seems that few if any of the lessons forcefully spelled out at the end of 2008 made much impact upon hospital management eager to develop new building projects, or Infrastructure Ontario, forcing all such plans to follow the route towards a costly P3 deal to finance it.

In the same time frame other provinces of Canada were also experimenting with P3 funded hospitals. In British Columbia the Abbotsford Regional Hospital and Cancer Care Centre, planned to open in 2005 was delayed three years by complex contractual negotiations. Construction costs increased from $210 million to $355 million, and the annual operating lease for the private sector contractor doubled in cost from $20 million to $41 million[16]. The result was a hospital $328m more expensive to build than the public sector comparator. Worse still, the contract had resulted in most of the key risks – ongoing inflation, contract enforcement, technological evolution, risks of sub-standard services, changing labour costs and more – all remaining with the public sector.[223]

In the Canadian context it is Ontario that has most doggedly ignored the evidence of previous failures to pursue the development of P3 hospitals – and many other non-health P3s – under the direction of Infrastructure Ontario, an ideologically-driven organisation with no ability or willingness to learn or to evaluate past errors. Ontario P3 projects have time and again incurred the criticism of the province's auditor general.

By December 2014 the auditor general's annual report concluded that Ontario had incurred $8 billion (equivalent to $1,600 per household) in higher costs on 74 P3 projects that were either completed or under way, $6.5 billion of this as a result of higher financing costs after failing to properly compare the cost of public finance with private borrowing. Time and again Infrastructure

---

[223] CUPE (2009) Fact Sheet: P3s – *The Wrong Prescription for Health Care*, available
https://cupe.ca/sites/cupe/files/Fact_Sheet_P3s_The_Wrong_presciption_-0.pdf

Ontario, reflecting and amplifying the pressure of Canada's then neoliberal prime Minister Stephen Harper and the federal government, was found to have used the misleading claim of "risk transfer" and inflated notional values of risk in order to justify more expensive P3 contracts.

Public sector union CUPE, emphasising the wider implications of the Auditor General's report for all 83 P3 schemes then underway across most provinces of Canada[224], drew attention to what were clearly "systemic problems with Ontario's entire P3 program and methodology—problems that naturally apply across Canada".

A follow-up CUPE article emphasised the secrecy surrounding the P3 contracts before and after they were signed. This is a familiar feature of PFI schemes in Britain, as is the way P3 deals have been structured around relatively small Special Purpose Vehicles – companies designed to shield the main corporations involved from any direct liability, and allowing them to walk away at any time, having risked only the equity holdings they have in the project, normally just 10-15% of the initial cost.[225]

However CUPE warned – correctly – that even such a damning report from the Auditor would not be enough to stop the pressure for more P3s:

> "The response of the Ontario government to the AGO report was very defensive, and already the P3 industry is spinning its response to downplay any problems and to further promote P3s.
>
> "But there are things we can do to reverse this dangerous tendency towards privatization and private pilfering of public accounts.
>
> "For example, auditors general in other jurisdictions can be urged to review provincial P3 programs, agencies and

---

[224] Sanger, T (2015) Ontario audit throws cold water on P3 love affair, The Monitor, February 2, CUPE, available https://www.policyalternatives.ca/publications/monitor/ontario-audit-throws-cold-water-federal-provincial-love-affair-p3s

[225] CUPE (2015) Ontario audit throws cold water on P3 love affair, March 11, https://cupe.ca/ontario-audit-throws-cold-water-p3-love-affair

projects as extensively as the Ontario auditor general did last year.

"Governments and public bodies could declare moratoria on further P3s, pending thorough reform and public review of the funding and procurement model. ...

"Finally, we should loudly insist on full public transparency and disclosure of all un-redacted financial details, including value-for-money assessments, associated with existing and new P3 projects."[22]

Yet again these basic lessons were ignored, and in 2016 and again in 2017 Ontario's Auditor General Bonnie Lysyk's annual report was obliged to return to the costly failures on hospital and other P3 projects. In 2017, with few of the previous issues having been resolved the focus shifted to the issue of maintenance contracts included in P3 deals. Indeed previous failures were being replicated again and again:

"AFP ['Alternative Financing and Procurement' – aka P3/PFI] agreements have not been structured to cover all maintenance work that hospitals require – Management at hospitals we spoke to are involved in long-term, ongoing disputes with private-sector companies over interpretations of the maintenance portion of their AFP agreements.

"They have not been able to realize many of the benefits they expected under AFP agreements, including having the cost of all maintenance that they require covered by the payments established in these agreements. Hospitals informed us that they are paying higher-than-reasonable rates to the private-sector company for carrying out maintenance work considered outside of the AFP agreement.

"... Infrastructure Ontario does not have a formalized performance evaluation program of private-sector companies during the maintenance phase of the AFP contract, and new AFP contracts are awarded without consideration of past performance.

"This has resulted in companies with past poor performance receiving contracts.

"For example, one private-sector company that has been in

dispute with a hospital since 2013 over what work is included in the AFP agreement was awarded contracts—in 2016 for $1.3 billion and in 2017 for $685 million—to design, build, finance and maintain two more hospitals. The dispute is still ongoing."[226]

Four hospitals with P3 maintenance contracts had either asked for additional funding from the Ministry of Health and Long-Term Care, or experienced a funding shortfall due to the higher costs of P3 maintenance contracts.

The provincial government has provided $5.3 million in top-up funding to six hospitals, to partly offset the higher administrative costs needed to manage P3 maintenance contracts, leaving the hospitals to cut funding in other areas to make up these shortfalls.[227]

More parallels with British PFI schemes, including of course the involvement of Carillion and inflated costs of long term maintenance contracts, can be seen in another Canadian province, in the case of the problems with a P3-funded mental hospital project in Saskatchewan.

CUPE activist Sandra Seitz wrote in the *Regina Leader Post* in the aftermath of the Carillion collapse early in 2018, arguing that the Province should take the opportunity of the company's bankruptcy to scrap the contract and fund the hospital through the public sector:

"Carillion's Canadian subsidiary is a partner in the $407-million contract to finance, build and maintain the new Saskatchewan Hospital North Battleford. Carillion Private Finance Ltd., based in the U.K., provided 50 per cent of the equity to the P3 hospital.

"The response from our government, through SaskBuilds, was surprisingly nonchalant: "The hospital project is not affected but, if it is, we can find another partner." But it appears the project is affected: The day after Carillion

---

[226] Auditor General of Ontario (2017) Annual report of the Office of the Auditor General of Ontario, Section 3.11, p 574, available http://www.auditor.on.ca/en/content/annualreports/arreports/en17/v1_311en17.pdf

[227] https://cupe.ca/ontario-p3-program-draws-auditors-fire-again

collapsed, Moody's Investors Service changed the rating outlook on this project from "stable" to "negative."[228]

Pointing out that Carillion was the lead company in the consortium that built the P3 Brampton Civic Hospital, costing Ontario an extra $200 million more than a publicly-funded scheme, Seitz went on to argue that P3 projects run the risk that private companies could go bankrupt, but the hospitals built as P3s are more expensive to build and maintain.

"Already we are paying quadruple the original estimated cost for the mental health facility. In August 2011, when Premier Brad Wall first announced the Saskatchewan Hospital would be rebuilt, he said the price tag would be $100 million. Less than three years later when the government issued the RFQ for the facility, the construction cost had jumped to between $175 and $250 million. When the contract was signed in 2015, the costs had ballooned to $407 million.

"One of the reasons the price tag for this P3 is so inflated is because we are on the hook to pay $185 million to Carillion (or its replacement) and Graham to operate and maintain the facility over 30 years. That's $6.2 million per year — for one facility. It is hard to imagine why the operating and maintenance costs would be so high, considering the former health region used to spend $3.1 million annually for all its facilities.

"The government claims that 30-year maintenance contracts are critical to keep the building in tip-top shape over its lifecycle. Moody's assessment of the facility, however, is that "the range of services to be delivered (in the facility) is quite narrow … the asset is quite small and somewhat simple to operate," and it only needs 11 full-time positions to operate. Why would we pay over $6 million per year to

[228] Seitz, S. (2018) Opinion: Cancelling Saskatchewan Hospital P3 would save millions of dollars, *Regina Leader-Post*, January 25, available https://leaderpost.com/opinion/columnists/opinion-cancelling-saskatchewan-hospital-p3-would-save-millions-of-dollars

operate the new Saskatchewan Hospital if only 11 people are needed?"

But while Ontario has the most P3 schemes and scandals, the biggest P3 schemes and scandals have been in neighbouring Quebec, where a project to build two giant 'super-hospitals' for Montréal and modernise the Ste Justine Hospital, which began back in 2004, with a total projected cost of $2.9 billion, has tripled in cost and is now estimated to add up to well over $8 billion over a 30 year contract. Questions are being asked about the adequacy and effectiveness of the government agency established in 2005 to keep control of the costs, the 'Bureau de la modernisation des CHU [Centres Hospitalier de l'Université'].[229]

Quebec's auditor general years ago argued that the province could have saved money by publicly-funding the project, and some analysts in 2014 argued that they could still save money by cancelling the contracts, even after paying the penalty costs of doing so.[230]

In France the government opted in 2014 to pay the penalty costs of early termination of the country's largest PPP contract, for the €315m Centre Hospitalier Sud Francilien, estimating cumulative savings from doing so would amount to $982 million.[231]

The two larger hospitals in the scheme were always conceived as P3 schemes, although there were the usual misconceived claims that this might cap the costs by transferring the risk of cost over-runs to the private sector. In the event, even after the huge inflation in cost

---

[229] Derfel, A. (2017) Quebec Agency monitoring superhospitals costs taxpayers $27 million, Montréal Gazette, September 6, https://montrealgazette.com/news/local-news/quebec-agency-monitoring-superhospitals-costs-taxpayers-27-million

[230] Nguyen, M., Hébert, G. (2014) Should the Quebec government buy back the CHUM and MUHC P3s? IRIS Socioeconomic brief, October, available https://cdn.iris-recherche.qc.ca/uploads/publication/file_secondary/CHU-PPP-English-WEB.pdf

[231] Derfel, A. (2017) Quebec Agency monitoring superhospitals costs taxpayers $27 million, Montréal Gazette, September 6, https://montrealgazette.com/news/local-news/quebec-agency-monitoring-superhospitals-costs-taxpayers-27-million

of the project, the consortium in charge of financing and building the smaller hospital, McGill University Health Centre (MUHC), wound up suing the government for an additional $330 million for additional costs arising from later changes to the plans.

In 2005 the government aimed to complete the MUHC for a maximum of $1 billion. This rose to $2.5 billion. The larger CHUM [Centre Hospitalier de l'Université de Montréal] hospital came out at a staggering $3.1 billion, and its research institute another $555m. The publicly-funded upgrade of Ste Justine Hospital, initially costed at $350m also nearly tripled to $940m.

The whole scheme rose from $3.6 billion to $5.2bn, to $6.4bn and $7.1bn as the signing of contracts was delayed, plans were altered and inflation took its toll. The Bureau whose job it was to hold down the cost insists, unconvincingly, that "The costs haven't exploded" – although the whole project is still not yet complete and additional phases will run on until 2021.[26]

The lawsuit from engineering firm SNC Lavalin seeking an extra $330 million, later increased to $360m for the MUHC construction, was eventually settled out of court in February 2018 for the reduced sum of $108m. On the same day Quebec's government also stomped up an extra $125m to settle a claim by the consortium that built the CHUM. By contrast the additional payment to square away the publicly-funded Ste Justine Hospital was just $9m.[232]

Monthly lease payments on the CHUM alone are admitted to be at least $12 million, giving an annual fee of around $144m, and a lifetime cost on the 30-year contract of $4.3 billion for just the one 772-bed hospital. It is expected that a similar fee will be attached to the MUHC, giving a combined cost for the two P3 hospitals of well over $8 billion: estimates by IRIS (Institut de recherche et d'informations socio-économiques) suggest the total cost could be up to $8.6 billion. Once again the details of these contracts are closely guarded secrets – at the insistence of their private sector "partners," which include Innisfree, the British-based investment firm with a

[232] Derfel, A (2018) PPP promise doesn't meet reality, Montreal Gazette, 13 February, https://www.pressreader.com/canada/montreal-gazette/20180213/281500751715640

finger in so many PFI pies.[233]

Even with such huge returns guaranteed the consortia still exploit every opportunity to screw additional excess profits from their long-term contracts: according to the *Journal de Montréal* the MUHC was billed $409 to replace a soap dispenser in the new building.

Australia

There were fewer schemes in Australia, but no shortage of further lessons on the folly of PFI. The Victoria government contracted with consortia to develop three major P3 hospitals in the mid-1990s. Under the terms of the contract, the consortia had to accept public medicare patients without extra billing. The consortia agreed to provide services at 96% of the cost for public hospitals.

The Latrobe Hospital commenced operations in September 1998 on schedule and on budget, but after 6 months the operator approached the State government seeking additional recurrent funding. They had underestimated the hospital's staffing requirements, payroll tax and costs, and made a number of wrong assumptions, notably:

- That sales tax exemption applicable to publicly run hospitals would apply
- That the State would renegotiate the contract

The operator also failed to understand Victoria's funding model, and did not take into account how constantly declining per-bed funding of public hospitals was built into the State's "casemix-funding" model. To make matters worse, the operator bid at a discount to the normal public hospital acute care service payment mechanism, which may have made the bid seem more attractive, but also made adequate returns unlikely.

In June 2000 Victoria recognised operators' financial problems and in late 2000 the State agreed to assume all operational and financial risk. In 2002 ownership and responsibility for operations

---

[233] Nguyen, M., Hébert, G. (2014) Should the Quebec government buy back the CHUM and MUHC P3s? IRIS Socioeconomic brief, October, available https://cdn.iris-recherche.qc.ca/uploads/publication/file_secondary/CHU-PPP-English-WEB.pdf

was formally transferred to State, after the operator paid the State $2m to get out of the contract.[234]

In New South Wales the State Auditor found that the new Port Macquarie Base P3 Hospital would cost $143 million for capital alone- almost three times what it would have cost to procure in the public sector. PMBH cost taxpayers $6M more in recurrent funding compared to the average public hospitals: the PPP contract locked the government into long term commitment to guarantee a private consortium with an annual, risk-free return of 13.71% – There were also hidden costs in the calculation of the "availability charge" and the government was committed to compensate for all tax expenses. This compensation was itself taxable.

For all this extra cost, the performance was poor: PMBH "consistently under-performed its peers. In 1998 PMBH's waiting times for elective surgery was more than double the State average."

After 20 years, the government would have paid for the hospital more than twice over - yet they still wouldn't own it:

> "The government is, in effect, paying for the hospital twice and giving it away". (NSW Auditor – General 2000)[231]

In 2006, the NSW government announced it would buy back the contract for the provision of health services at the Hospital to address poor service levels.

By 2013, health policy analyst Stephen Duckett estimated that up to 50% of PPP hospital projects in Australia were failing. [235] A PwC report aimed at the Australian market downplays the scale of these failures, although it did admit that:

> "In each case, the private sector had underestimated the cost of meeting its service obligations and, in the case of the

---

[234] Government of Western Australia Department of Health (2013) *The Australian Experience: Public Private Partnerships (PPPs)*
http://www3.ha.org.hk/haconvention/hac2013/proceedings/downloads/S7.2.pdf
[235] Duckett, S. (2013) Public-private hospital partnerships are risky business, The Conversation, July 30,
https://theconversation.com/public-private-hospital-partnerships-are-risky-business-16421

hospitals, had underestimated demand risk."[236]

More recently major hospital PPP schemes in Australia include the Midland Public Hospital in Western Australia (£207m); Victoria's Royal Children's Hospital (£544m); stage 2 of the Royal North Shore Hospital redevelopment in New South Wales (£663m) and the enormous new Royal Adelaide Hospital in South Australia (£1.7 billion).[237]

At least two of these projects seem to be going seriously wrong according to reports in 2017:

> "When the media is being blocked from a Supreme Court visit to one of the nation's biggest hospital construction sites in what is dubbed a 'defect tour', that is a sign that not all is going as it should.

> "Yet that was what happened when the Court toured the site of the $2 billion new Royal Adelaide Hospital last November, which the government alleges has faults including incorrect room sizes, air-conditioning defects, sewer pipes in a data equipment room, a 200-millimetre ceiling space and a 2.8-metre high loading dock instead of one which was meant to be 3.5 metres."

To make matters worse, the consortium responsible for delivering the project was "locked in a bitter dispute with the government about the latter's rejection of a plan to fix defects associated with the project:"

> "In November, *The Advertiser* reported that investors in the new hospital would seek to recover up to $4 billion in damages from taxpayers if the government moved ahead with threats to tear up the consortium's contract."[238]

---

[236] PwC Australia (2017) *Reimagining Public Private Partnerships*, https://www.pwc.com.au/legal/assets/reimagining-ppps-oct17.pdf : p15

[237] Brennan, R. (2013) Infrastructure in Australia, Government of Australia Powerpoint, https://www.austrade.gov.au/ArticleDocuments/3701/Presentation%20by%20Rory%20Brennan%20-%20Infrastructure%20Australia.pdf.aspx

[238] Heaton, A. (2017) Does Australia Fail in the Delivery of Major Hospital Projects?, https://sourceable.net/cant-australia-deliver-major-hospital-projects/

The same report listed similar problems with the $1.2 billion Perth Children's Hospital Project in Western Australia, where persistent delays meant there was no clear completion date in 2017, despite a commitment have finished 18 months earlier. Multiple problems on the project included allegations of subcontractors not receiving progress payments, and delays after asbestos was found in some of the Chinese-made roof panels.

The report quotes scathing comments from one construction industry advisor, David Chandler which again point to general problems with PFIs and PPPs:

> "Chandler talks about a decline in what is considered to be acceptable involving "dumbed down clients" who are willing to pay "whatever premium is needed to transfer the risk to powerful and unaccountable contractors."

[…] According to Chandler, healthcare projects are being led by large, risk averse enterprises which try to ring-fence themselves from accountability wherever possible."[32]

This ring-fencing is dependent in every case on secretive contracts and a near-total lack of transparency on deals that can span 30 years or more.

PPPs in Europe

According to PwC and UCSF, 60% of an estimated 600 global healthcare infrastructure PPP projects are in Europe. The EU early in 2004 changed the rules of the Stability Pact underpinning the euro, in order to encourage the use of PFI for public works, by excluding such investment from the total of public debts (as long as the private sector can be shown to be carrying the investment risk.[239]

However even now the lion's share of European projects are in England, and all too often it is romanticised versions of the British PFI model that are being taken as the starting point for costly schemes in other EU countries. After the England tally come Spain, France, Italy, Portugal and Germany. A number of other countries

---

[239] Murray Brown, J., Timmins, N. Wise, P. (2004) Brussels acts to exclude private finance for public works from stability pact rules. *Financial Times*, 7 February

have a single PPP project or have yet to embark on one.[240] The European Investment Bank records loans to just nine PPP health projects, 3 of them in Spain, two each in Italy and Germany and one each in Portugal and Sweden.[241]

There is relatively little in the way of an information base from so few PPP projects outside the UK. An EU Expert Panel commissioned to evaluate PPPs in health care[242] drew pretty similar conclusions to those of the National Audit Office on PFIs in England. The Expert Panel criticised the fact that

"Public disclosure of data and analyses behind PPP investments is very poor, inconsistent and not standardised. Therefore many of the conclusions of the report are based more on assumptions than actual data,"

The Panel concludes:

"The main conclusion is that there is not enough information to evaluate PPP procurement or public health services compared with conventional regimes (value for money not conclusive).

[...] A potential consequence of the above is that it is not possible to give any evidence-based recommendations to Member States about the role of PPP in health policy." [236]

---

[240] Abuzaineh, N., Brashers, E., Foong, S., Feachem, R., Da Rita, P. (2018). PPPs in healthcare: Models, lessons and trends for the future. Healthcare public private partnership series, No. 4. San Francisco: The Global Health Group, Institute for Global Health Sciences, University of California, San Francisco and PwC.
https://globalhealthsciences.ucsf.edu/sites/globalhealthsciences.ucsf.edu/files/pub/ppp-report-series-business-model.pdf

[241] Epec (2018) *PPPs financed by the European Investment Bank from 1990 to 2017*, February,
http://www.eib.org/attachments/epec/epec_ppps_financed_by_eib_since_1990_en.pdf

[242] EC Expert Panel (2014) Expert Panel on Effective Ways of Investing in Health (EXPH) Health and Economic Analysis for an Evaluation of the Public Private Partnerships in Health Care Delivery across Europe,
https://ec.europa.eu/health/expert_panel/sites/expertpanel/files/003_assessmentstudyppp_en.pdf

The main report considered by the Panel[243] notes particular weaknesses in an unsatisfactory range of PPP projects, including Portugal (where there were three different evaluations, and eventually a political decision was taken to return the PPP Hospital Amadora Sintra to the public sector) Romania (where the report describes the functioning of PPP dialysis centres "successful," although there was "no formal audit or evaluation") and Sweden, (where the €1.45 billion New Solna Karolinska Hospital project failed to achieve its objectives, and the government (county council) could have borrowed money more cheaply). The conclusion, in bold, is that:

> **"In this study (and in the literature) the Expert Panel has not found scientific evidence that PPPs are cost-effective compared with traditional forms of public financed and managed provision of health care."**(p39).

A similar view is taken by the European Court of auditors, having reviewed 12 PPP projects in the fields of transport and Information and Communication Technology. They make the point that while PPP allows public authorities to procure large-scale infrastructure through a single procedure, it also increases "the risk of insufficient competition and thus putting contracting authorities in a weaker negotiating position." The contracts take much longer to negotiate. And the transfer of risk was far from satisfactory:

> "The risk allocation between public and private partners was often inappropriate, incoherent and ineffective, while high remuneration rates (up to 14 %) on the private partner's risk capital did not always reflect the risks borne. In addition, most of the six audited ICT projects were not easily compatible with long contract durations since they were subject to rapid technology changes."[244]

---

[243]European Union (2013) *Health and Economics Analysis for an Evaluation of the Public Private Partnerships in Health Care Delivery across EU,* https://ec.europa.eu/health/expert_panel/sites/expertpanel/files/ppp_fin alreport_en.pdf

[244] European Court of Auditors (2018) *Public Private Partnerships in the EU: Widespread shortcomings and limited benefits* https://www.eca.europa.eu/Lists/ECADocuments/SR18_09/SR_PPP_EN.pdf

The Auditors recommend:
>"(a) not to promote a more intensive and widespread use of PPPs until the issues identified are addressed and the following recommendations successfully implemented;
>(b) to mitigate the financial impact of delays and re-negotiations on the cost of PPPs borne by the public partner;
>(c) to base the selection of the PPP option on sound comparative analyses on the best procurement option." (p11)

Spain

The Expert Panel also looked at the 'Alzira model' of PPP in Valencia, the Spanish alternative to British-style PFI, which is still being strongly promoted by PWC and UCSF, along with many other fans of PPP who have been won over by some selective reporting.

The Alzira hospital was built in 1999 at a cost of €61m as a Public Private Investment Partnership (PPIP), with a contract to provide a full range of hospital services to the local population for a fixed capitation fee, and initially promising to deliver services at up to 44% below equivalent costs in Spanish and Valencia hospitals[245]. This contract proved literally too good for the purchasers to be true, and was abruptly ended, to be replaced by another on more generous terms to the hospital after a lump sum of capital had changed hands.

The new contract included primary care services as well – but was still well below Spanish benchmark costs. The key to this has been 20-25% lower running costs than public sector hospitals, only partly achieved by use of new technology, but more significantly by the reduction of healthcare quality (staffing levels significantly – up to 25% – lower than public sector hospitals) reduced wage costs (73% of the staff are on the hospital's own, lower, scale of pay and benefits, working longer hours, while the remainder are still covered by their previous public sector contracts), and by effectively selecting less complex and costly caseload, by restricting the range of services the hospital offers, leaving patients needing more

---

[245] Acerete, B., Stafford, A., & Stapleton, P., 2011. Spanish healthcare public private partnerships: The 'Alzira model', *Critical Perspectives On Accounting*, Elsevier, vol. 22(6), pages 533-549.
https://ideas.repec.org/a/eee/crpeac/v22y2011i6p533-549.html

sophisticated treatment to use public hospitals instead[246].

However maintaining the cut-price tariff to keep the contract meant that the contractor Ribera Salud, (now 50% owned by US health corporation Centene) began losing money.

The PSPV, one of the three parties that won control of Valencia's regional government from the neoliberal right in May 2015, had made an election promise to de-privatise the system: but this has now been ruled out as too expensive, because compensation payments to private companies running hospitals would be too high.

As a result they could only afford terminate one of the contracts, the first one, for Hospital Ribera-Alzira (Valencia), which expired in April 2018. The PSPV reluctantly admitted Torrevieja hospital will remain in private hands until 2021, because returning it to the public sector would cost €28.5 million. The other three Alzira-style hospitals would be up to twice as expensive to take back, and Valencia has not had the money to spare.

However this later development, underlining the fact that the entire Alzira experiment was a political project of the right wing regional government, and remained controversial, has been largely ignored by the eulogistic reports on the PPP hospitals by UCSF/PwC and others[247].

The EU's Expert Panel however was far from convinced. They note general weaknesses with the implementation of health PPPs in Spain.

They cite the Spanish National Association of Public Health and Health Administration which warned in 2012 that private management strategies, especially PPPs did not deliver advantages that justify their implementation: "PPP Infrastructure contracts have

---

[246] Bes, M. (2009) Spanish health district tests a new public–private mix, *Bulletin of the World Health Organization*, Volume 87: 2009 Number 12, December, 885-964 http://www.who.int/bulletin/volumes/87/12/09-031209/en/

[247] Sosa Delgado-Pastor, V., Brashers, E., Foong, S., Montagu, D., Feachem, R. (2016). Innovation roll out: Valencia's experience with public-private integrated partnerships – Executive Summary. Healthcare public-private partnerships series, No. 3. San Francisco: The Global Health Group, Global Health Sciences, University of California, San Francisco and PwC

led to important problems related with the increased financial costs".

Valencia's Regional Court of Auditors' found (2013) that "potential savings using traditional public provision compared with "PPP 10 year contract" would have amounted to €16.7 million annually (40% less than the PPP contract)." Spain's National Competition Agency (2013) also expressed concerns over "many inadequacies in the processing of tenders and contracts of PPP from 1997 to 2010".[248]

The Expert Panel, working through a detailed report, note that on both occasions when the Alzira hospital PPP was put out to tender, in 1997 and 2003, there was only one bid – and therefore no competition. There were no figures to show the extent to which neighbouring hospitals were adequately reimbursed by the PPP hospital for the costs of treating the patients from the Alzira catchment with more serious conditions than Alzira could manage.

Even prior to the electoral defeat of the right wing Valencia government, the president of the Comunidad Valenciana Region had declared that they would not privatise any more services through PPP. Elsewhere in Spain the Castilla-La Mancha government abandoned their plans for a PPP hospital project, and under pressure from mass protests and strikes the Madrid Region government also decided in January 2014 to scrap its plans for 6 PFI hospitals. (Expert Panel 2014, p21)

Critics also point out that none of the recommended structures for managing PFI-style policy are applicable in Spain (where there is no specific Public/Private Partnership unit, model standardised contracts, public sector comparator, or any method of project evaluation.) [249,39]

Even after listing what appear to be positive aspects of the Alzira

[248] EC Expert Panel (2014) Expert Panel on Effective Ways of Investing in Health (EXPH) Health and Economic Analysis for an Evaluation of the Public Private Partnerships in Health Care Delivery across Europe, https://ec.europa.eu/health/expert_panel/sites/expertpanel/files/003_ass essmentstudyppp_en.pdf: p20

[249] Stafford, A. (2018) The Alzira Model, slides from presentation to Socialist Health Association, https://www.sochealth.co.uk/2018/01/02/the-alzira-model/

project, Spanish critics note the lack of public access to data, and argue that as a result:

> "In the specific case of our study, the results are not conclusive enough to clearly acclaim the PPP model, due to our finding strengths and weaknesses in both the public and PPP models. To date, papers aimed at enhancing knowledge of PPPs in the health care sector have not reached forceful conclusions."[250]

Sweden

Another variant model in Europe has been the privatised 240-bed St Goran's Hospital in Sweden, run by Capio, on a 6-year contract with Stockholm County Council which requires the hospital to treat only publicly-funded patients, and divert private paying patients to another Capio clinic.

The hospital, which had been a pilot project in local autonomy, was controversially sold to Capio in 1999 and transformed into Sweden's first private for-profit hospital: but it now functions as a privately owned, publicly funded enterprise, and a curious, unique hybrid version of a PPP.[251]

PPPs – even less appropriate in the developing countries

Outside of the wealthier OECD countries there have, predictably been even fewer PPP schemes signed off and completed. The World Bank approved 78 projects for health related facilities between 2004 and 2016[252], of which by far the best known (and notorious for its

---

[250] Caballer-Tarazona, M., and Vivas-Consuelo, D. (2016) A cost and performance comparison of Public Private Partnership and public hospitals in Spain, *Health Economics Review*. 2016; 6: 17. doi: 10.1186/s13561-016-0095-5

[251] Nikolic I.A., Maikish, H. (2006) Public-Private Partnerships and collaboration in the health sector: an overview with case studies from recent European experience. World Bank HNP Discussion paper http://siteresources.worldbank.org/INTECAREGTOPHEANUT/Resources/HNPDiscussionSeriesPPPPaper.pdf

[252] IEG (2018) *Public-Private Partnerships in Health. World Bank Group Engagement in Health PPPs*, https://openknowledge.worldbank.org/bitstream/handle/10986/25383/10

shortcomings) was in Lesotho.

This was the first major hospital built in Africa through a 'Public–Private Investment Partnership.' The showpiece $120 million Queen Mamohato Memorial Hospital, a referral hospital in Lesotho's capital city, Maseru, run by South African private hospital corporation Netcare, opened its doors on 1st October 2011.

The project – which was signed off at the urging of the World Bank's pro-privatisation International Finance Corporation (IFC) who argued it heralded a new era for private-sector involvement in health care in Africa[253,254] – has remained at the centre of controversy.

Critics had from early on been raising concerns that spending so much on the hospital – which had been promoted as delivering improved services for no extra spending – would actually widen health inequalities and draw vital health-care resources away from patients with severe health needs in other parts of Lesotho.

As the new hospital opened, a *Guardian* report on the dire state of health services, especially for Lesotho's rural poor, indicated the shortage of affordable health care in much of the country and the much higher costs of private treatment. It argued that the new hospital was harder to access for many who had been able to get treatment as outpatients at the previous, dilapidated QEII Hospital it replaced[255].

By April 2014 there was fresh evidence of the scale of the

9572-WP-PUBLIC.pdf?sequence=1&isAllowed=y

[253] IFC (2009) *Success Stories – Lesotho: National Referral Hospital*. June, International Finance Corporation, Washington DC, http://www.ifc.org/ifcext/psa.nsf/AttachmentsByTitle/PPPseries_Lesotho/$FILE/SuccessStories_LesothoWEB.pdf

[254] IFC(2009) *Breaking new ground: Lesotho Hospital Public Private Partnership – a model for integrated health services delivery*. Smartlessons, IFC, Washington DC http://www.ifc.org/ifcext/pas.nsf/AttachmentsByTitle/Smartlesson_LesothoHospital/$FILE/LesothoHospital_Smartlesson.pdf

[255] *Guardian* Development Network (2011) Lesotho's ailing public health system. http://www.guardian.co.uk/global-development/2011/oct/o7/lesotho-ailing-public-health-system

problem. A critical report from Oxfam revealed that Lesotho's shiny new hospital was soaking up more than half of the country's entire health budget, costing at least 3 times what the old hospital would have cost – while the consortium shareholders were coining it in, expecting a 25% return on equity and a total cash income of 7.6 times the original investment. It reported Lesotho's Ministry of Health PPP coordination unit complaining that the payments on the PPP had increased by 80% since the original contract was signed five years earlier [256].

The report stung the newly-appointed World Bank Group President Jim Kim into promising that the Bank would make itself the "go-to" people to understand how health sector public private partnerships have worked around the world. He said he would be personally looking into the Lesotho case.[257]

But as the financial nightmare has continued in Lesotho, Jim Kim's promise has proved to be as empty as the initial promises on how the project would work out.

The new 425-bed hospital (390 beds for the public sector and 35 that run separately as a private patient unit) was a long-overdue replacement for the 100-year-old Queen Elizabeth II Hospital, which had been built back in colonial days by the British government and, with 450 beds averaging 83 per cent occupancy, was also far and away the country's biggest and most intensively utilised hospital.[258]

The PPIP contract, signed in 2009, involved building the new hospital on a greenfield site on the edge of the city and the provision of clinical services for the 18-year lifetime of the contract, including the refurbishment, re-equipping and operation of three filter clinics and the training of health professionals.

---

[256] Marriott, A. (2014) *A Dangerous Diversion*, Oxfam
https://www.oxfam.org/sites/www.oxfam.org/files/bn-dangerous-diversion-lesotho-health-ppp-070414-en.pdf
[257] Marriott, A. (2015) *Why is the World Bank Group dragging its feet over its disastrous PPP policy on funding healthcare?* November 20,
https://oxfamblogs.org/fp2p/why-is-the-world-bank-group-dragging-its-feet-over-its-disastrous-policy-on-funding-healthcare/
[258] Lister, J. (2013) *Global Health Versus Private Profit*, Libri, Faringdon.

The contract was to 'treat all patients who present at the hospital, regardless of the type of condition' – up to a maximum of 20,000 in-patient admissions and 310,000 outpatient attendances annually, 'with very few clinical exceptions'[259] although these exceptions include all patients needing transplants, elective cardio-vascular surgery, chemotherapy and radiotherapy. Any patients treated above the specified maximum number would be charged at $786 per in-patient and $4.72 per outpatient.[1]

In exchange, the Lesotho government agreed to pay an annual fixed service payment, which was to rise only by inflation each year. The lop-sided contract can be traced back to the weakness and inexperience of the Lesotho government and the failure of the IFC to give appropriate advice. A consultancy report establishing a 'Baseline study' for the PPP contract warned of such a problem in 2009, pointing out that:

> "At present, sufficient expertise in hospital operations, financial oversight and analysis and systems analysis to manage the PPP contract in the interests of the Government and people of Lesotho does not exist…"[260]

The same report argued that the new hospital could not be adequately operated for less than 30 per cent of Lesotho's whole health budget. As the cost crept up towards 40 per cent, there would be an increasingly adverse and severe impact on district health services. The report urged the Ministry to set an upper limit (40 per cent or less) to the amount of its recurrent budget to be devoted to the new hospital. This was not done, but the project carried on regardless.

---

[259] According to the IFC magazine *Handshake* (No. 3, p.28). Note that unless numbers of patients are reduced, 83 per cent occupancy of 450 beds would imply 95 per cent or higher occupancy of 390 beds.

[260] Lesotho–Boston Health Alliance (2009) *Queen Elizabeth II and the New PPP Hospital: baseline Study, Vol 1, Draft Financial Report*, 12 March, p72. CABRI Dialogue: Ensuring Value for Money in Infrastructure projects (p6 footnote) December, http://cabri-sbo.org/images/documents/6thAnnualSeminar/session_4_group_a_lesotho_mathundsane_mohapi_english.pdf

Capital costs

Supporters of the scheme claimed that it would be 'cost neutral' both to the government and to patients, whose fees for access have not been increased from the previous level. However, this is not a full picture of the situation. A very significant increase in spending and government investment had *already taken place*. The run-up to the PPP hospital project in Maseru was marked by a significant increase in spending on health, both by government and from other sources.

The Health Ministry had to raise a large share ($51 million) of the capital investment for the hospital. This is compared with the Lesotho Ministry of Health and Social Welfare's total budget of just $100 million in 2007–8, which had been dramatically increased (by 169% from the previous year). In 2005–6, the Ministry's combined recurrent and capital budget had been just $47 million.

Between 2006 and 2009, the cost of the PPIP scheme increased by more than 33 per cent above the original projection, which had estimated an annual 'unitary charge' of $24.1 million for the hospital plus services. Meanwhile the Lesotho government lost income after a new treaty which reduced the flow of revenue from the South African Customs Union.

Revenue costs

The new hospital and its three primary-care feeder clinics were supposed to cost the Government of Lesotho (GoL) $32.6 million a year as a unitary charge for the core contract, index-linked to inflation, for 15.5 years, to March 2027[261]. However, according to the Health Minister the annual budget for the QEII hospital and the filter clinics had been less than $17 million in 2007-8 – so the new deal represented a near 100 per cent increase in costs and gave the lie to claims that the project was 'cost neutral'.

---

[261] Smith, M. (2009) *Case Study: Financing a new referral hospital Lesotho* CABRI Dialogue: Ensuring value for money in infrastructure projects. https://www.cabri-sbo.org/uploads/files/Documents/case_study_2010_cabri_cabri_seminar_cabri_6th_annual_seminar_english_13._session_4_group_a_lesotho_math_undsane_mohapi_english.pdf

By 2012/13 the cost had risen again, to $45m a year – 41% of the nation's total health budget. Two years later the PPP hospital and filter clinics were costing $67m a year – more than double the projected figure and 51% of the health budget.[262]

While the whole contract has remained shrouded in secrecy (like so many PPP deals), one key report showed how the consortium stood to make profits from a number of sources:

- A guaranteed profit on the capital investment
- A 10 per cent guaranteed return on its operating budget
- Full payment for any additional patients treated above the contract maximum
- And payment for those sent to South Africa for specialist treatment.[5263]

In theory one of the benefits of the new hospital was that it would reduce the need for costly referrals of patients to South Africa for specialist treatment. However since these referrals offered a profitable sideline for Netcare this always seemed unlikely. In the event the numbers of referrals *increased* by 61% between 2007 and 2012.[259] In 2006-7, the Lesotho government spent FY $24.8 million on 3,281 external referrals, of which 55 per cent were oncology cases. A *Timeslive* survey in 2011 showed Netcare charged 2,000 Rand ($255) or more per night for bed only, in addition to consultant fees. If bills like this are potentially to be picked up by the Lesotho Ministry of Health, it gives no incentive for Netcare to reduce referrals.

By comparison with some health PFI and PPP deals, it appears that Netcare's likely direct profit is relatively modest. However, the

---

[262] Marriott, A. (2014) *A Dangerous Diversion*, Oxfam
https://www.oxfam.org/sites/www.oxfam.org/files/bn-dangerous-diversion-lesotho-health-ppp-070414-en.pdf
[263] Smith, M. (2009) *Case Study: Financing a new referral hospital Lesotho* CABRI Dialogue: Ensuring value for money in infrastructure projects.
https://www.cabri-sbo.org/uploads/files/Documents/case_study_2010_cabri_cabri_seminar_cabri_6th_annual_seminar_english_13._session_4_group_a_lesotho_math_undsane_mohapi_english.pdf

$62 million capital investment by the Government of Lesotho and the ongoing unitary charge mean that public funds are not only paying for the beds used by citizens of Maseru and further afield – but also subsidising Netcare's 35-bed private hospital on the site, which has full access to the operating theatres, staff and other facilities in the main hospital, but only treats the minority who are wealthy enough to pay the full fees for their treatment.

So while the future looks rosy for Netcare, the GoL is committed by the contract to spend upwards of 50 per cent of its health budget on a hospital whose main catchment area is Maseru, which has 350,000 inhabitants, just 16 per cent of the Lesotho population of over 2 million. The numbers to be treated at the hospital are capped at a relatively low level by the PPIP contract despite official figures showing a hospitalisation rate of 3.2 per cent of the population per year in 2011 – equivalent to 64,000 admissions. This has brought an unaffordable excess bill for the Lesotho government.

For Netcare as a private, profit-seeking company it makes perfectly good sense to take advantage of this situation to secure a foothold in Lesotho and establish facilities which will contribute to their growing profits. However it is less clear that the project is consistent with the IFC's professed (if largely hollow) commitment to wider values of equity.

A more useful contribution from the World Bank would have been to lend the money to build the new hospital at low interest directly to the Ministry of Health and to help ministers and civil servants negotiate a tight agreement to ensure prompt delivery on budget. This would have given the hospital management additional scope to negotiate as necessary with potential providers to deliver services without the long-term rigid constrictions of a PPIP which may soon turn out to be unaffordable.

In an effort to fend off the criticisms of the project from Oxfam, from other critics in Lesotho and around the world, and from the Lesotho government and Health Ministry, a team of academics from Boston University and a token one from Maseru were commissioned by the IFC to produce a 2013 study of the results achieved by the new hospital.[264]

The report skated nimbly and without serious comment past the 40% increase in the death rates for patients on medical wards and a 27% increase in death rates for women surgical patients, the complaints over waiting times and costs of transport to the new hospital site, the increased cost to the government of treating each patient, the secretive contracts, the evidence of fat profits being made by Netcare, the unaffordable numbers of patients referred at high cost to South African hospitals and many other issues.

Instead the authors produced a series of figures showing improved performance, quality of care and outcomes for patients – all of which are of course welcome improvements. But even this report was obliged to concede that – despite the initial promise to be cost neutral – the new hospital is significantly more expensive:

> "The PPP hospital requires greater MOH resources to operate than QEII, in part due to the inclusion of the cost of capital repayment (DBSA loan), the need to include value added tax (VAT) in the unitary payment (although VAT will ultimately be returned to the government, so it is net-zero cost), and additional services offered (e.g. an additional filter clinic (Gateway), Intensive Care Unit, and Neonatal Intensive Care Unit). ... The MOH is getting much better quality of care and patient outcomes through the PPP, albeit at a greater cost." (p6)

Oxfam has continued, without success, to press for the World Bank, together with the government of Lesotho to produce, as Jim Kim promised, a fully independent and transparent expert financial audit and broader review of the Lesotho health PPP project.

During the final stages of completion of this book an even more up to date critique of the Lesotho PPP by Oxfam has been published

---

[264] T. Vian, N. McIntosh, A. Grabowski, B. Brooks, B. Jack and E. Limakatso (2013) Endline study for Queen Mamohato Hospital Public Private Partnership (PPP)' Final Report , September, Centre for Global Health and Development, Boston University, Department of Family Medicine, Boston University and Lesotho Boston Health Alliance, Maseru
http://devpolicy.org/pdf/Endline-Study-PPPLesotho-Final-Report-2013.pdf

as part of a fresh effort by the European Network on Debt and Development (Eurodad) to draw out the lessons of these schemes, especially in poorer countries where resources are even more stretched and the impact of extra costs can be measured in people denied access to any form of health care. Oxfam's Anna Marriott tries to force the Bank and its subsidiaries to focus on the hard facts rather than the spin:

> "Due to the complexity of the contract and a high number of disputed fees which are still part of an arbitration process, the actual cost of the PPP to the government remains contested and uncertain. Most recently, a 2017 Lesotho public health expenditure review by UNICEF and the WB reinforces concerns about the financial sustainability of the PPP.

The review data shows that actual expenditure on the PPP – what government paid rather than what they were invoiced – amounted to 35 per cent of recurrent health expenditure over the four years leading up to 2017, or 30.6 per cent net of Value Added Tax (VAT).

It is important to note that total health expenditure has increased dramatically since the PPP baseline year, indicating a concerning rise in the actual cost of the PPP to the government. The review's figures suggest that in 2016 Tsepong's 'invoiced' fees amount to two times the "affordability threshold" set by the Government and the WB at the outset of the PPP."[265]

Since the Lesotho deal was signed, subsequent attempts by the IFC to get a PPP-funded new hospital project off the ground in Benin have been abandoned, and it seems that so far there have been no more projects as irresponsible as the Lesotho adventure.

However the World Bank's *Forward Look* towards 2030 remains obsessed with the focus on supporting private investment "enabled by the IFC and MIGA [the Multilateral Investment Guarantee Agency] across the full range of clients, including the poorest

---

[265] Romero, M.J., Ravenscroft, J. (2018) History RePPPeated: How Public private Partnerships are Failing, Eurodad/Heinrich Böll Stiftung, October, https://eurodad.org/files/pdf/1546956-history-repppeated-1538666055.pdf

countries". Despite the continued rhetorical commitment to addressing the needs of the poor, it's clear that the most attractive target for the World Bank's attention seems to be the "rising middle class" in Middle Income Countries:

"Private investment needs in MICs are immense, to finance the demand from the growing middle class for housing, infrastructure, health, education, higher protein diets and safe food, and jobs." [266]

As PSIRU director Jane Lethbridge points out:

"The International Finance Corporation (IFC, the Bank's private sector lending arm) has made investments in private sector healthcare companies in amongst others, India, China, Turkey, Kenya and Colombia, which all have expanding corporate healthcare sector."[267]

She points to the obvious similarities between the problems of PPPs in developing countries and those we have seen in Britain, Canada, Australia and Europe:

"There is little evidence of increased health service efficiency from PPPs and there is a lack of transparency in PPP contract negotiations, which obscures the profits being made and limits public accountability of projects.

[...] The IFC has also recently helped to negotiate PPPs in three poor Indian states. In one deal, two private healthcare providers were awarded a $2 million contract and a $360,000 concession over 10 years. The *Telegraph*, an Indian newspaper, reported in 2015 that low income groups were facing difficulties in accessing services of these companies which were supposedly free."

---

[266] World Bank (2017) Forward Look a Vision For The World Bank Group In 2030 – Progress And Challenges, available http://siteresources.worldbank.org/DEVCOMMINT/Documentation/23745169/DC2017-0002.pdf

[267] Lethbridge, J. (2017) World Bank undermines right to universal healthcare, Bretton Woods Project, http://www.brettonwoodsproject.org/2017/04/world-bank-undermines-right-universal-healthcare/

World Bank's inadequate critique

The World Bank's own Independent Evaluation Group report on PPPs in health carefully avoids any specifics, is based on a desk-based study of the Bank's own reports, and is written in most evasive fashion to minimise embarrassment[268].

Even so some of its findings are shocking, confirming that the Bank's subdivisions – most notably the IFC – have been pushing PPPs as a stock solution to problems in some of the poorest countries with little awareness of the consequences:

> "Although there is a substantial body of research on the outcomes from PPPs in high-income countries, we know very little about applying the concept of PPPs in low- and middle-income countries and even less about outcomes." (p1)

Despite the immense resources available to the Bank, their "evaluation" was superficial in the extreme, suggesting a reluctance to probe any deeper for fear of revealing even more weaknesses and failures in IFC-promoted schemes:

> "This review relied entirely on existing evaluative evidence, primarily project evaluation data. Accordingly, IEG analyzed the results achieved at project closure for IFC Advisory Services and World Bank lending projects, and at the point of operational maturity for IFC investments. For World Bank projects, Implementation Completion and Results (ICRs) and their IEG reviews are the primary source of information on results. For IFC AS and Investment Services, this review will rely on Project Completion Reports and on one Expanded Project Supervision Report." (p5)

The IEG report reveals once again the Bank's eagerness to pronounce schemes a "success" long before any of the planned hospitals or facilities have even opened – as happened in Lesotho:

> "Success for AS [IFC Advisory Service] projects is defined

---

[268] IEG (2018) *Public-Private Partnerships in Health. World Bank Group Engagement in Health PPPs,*
https://openknowledge.worldbank.org/bitstream/handle/10986/25383/10
9572-WP-PUBLIC.pdf?sequence=1&isAllowed=y

as a PPP project reaching commercial closure. The case is similar for ICRs [Implementation Completion Reports], where outcomes are reported at the project closure stage, after a World Bank loan has been disbursed.

"Success is defined by the project development objective, often associated with the PPP reaching closure as well. However, little is known about the implementation of PPPs beyond contract closure, and even less is known about their effects on the twin goals [eradicating extreme poverty and boosting shared prosperity]." (p6)

In analysing "drivers of success and failure," the IEG states what non-Bank observers might see as a truism, noting the pressure on governments exerted by the IFC to push them down the road of PPP projects:

"An important aspect of success is the willingness or the capacity of governments to undertake PPPs." (p18)

Three examples show that this cannot be assumed. Some governments are strong-willed enough to resist the IFC's pressure, while some even appear willing to take public opinion into account:

"In the first example, the government decided not to proceed with the PPP models presented by the IFC AS. The Project Completion Report for the project indicates that "the problem lay in the inability of the decision maker to fully grasp and implement the core PPP Principle, which is the financial interaction between the private operation and the state budget...."

"In the second example, the government stopped the project even before reading the PSP plan because there was insufficient support in the country for the proposed reform.

"In the last example, the bidding process was cancelled not by the ministry of health, but by the ministry of finance. A meeting set up with the minister of health to try to resolve the problem was cancelled by the government. IFC tried, but was never able to confirm interest in pursuing the project from the new ministries of health and finance, and after having the project on hold for five semesters, IFC decided to terminate it, following a change in government." (pp18-19)

The IEG report reveals that in just one of twelve IFC Strategic Options Reports did the IFC discuss the possibility of a publicly-funded option. It offers a mild rebuke for this failure:

> "The extent to which it should be IFC's responsibility to include the public service option as part of its assessment is open to debate; nonetheless, it should become Bank Group practice to ensure that the public option is at least considered and systematically assessed (or that it has been assessed with support of other agencies). The efficiency and desirability from a social perspective of the PPP cannot be established without a comparison with the alternatives, the main one being the public option." (p20)

To make matters worse the IFC did not even offer appropriate advice on the potential costs and funding issues, even of a number of the schemes that had gone ahead. The IEG found "little evidence that fiscal implications are assessed in a systematic fashion." (p20)

Nor was there much evidence of genuine concern to ensure that the projects promoted as "pro-poor" turned out in practice to be accessible to poor people, or assessed for meeting their needs.

> "although the design of the majority of Bank Group interventions has a pro-poor focus, M&E [Monitoring and Evaluation] indicators are lacking to track results and to assess whether the poor were able to access the health services."

Only four of the 16 IFC advisory service interventions that were supposed to have a pro-poor focus had specifically pro-poor indicators that could be tracked at project completion.

> "… For the World Bank, while most of the nine closed projects had indicators related to the poor or underserved population at the design stage, the majority of indicators lacked adequate baselines or targets or were inadequate to be assessed." (p23)

The IEG also points out that the process of evaluating projects so early in the process makes it likely that issues that arise soon after the new facilities open will be missed. In other words the World Bank Group has little evidence to show whether or not the loans it has advanced or the schemes it has promoted have delivered benefits or caused problems for the people who were supposed to benefit:

"Most of these results show the inadequacy of the current M&E system for health PPPs – they also pose a possible reputational risk for the Bank Group."

Only four studies were available on the effects of PPP beyond financial close and the signing of the contracts. Findings in these reports indicate that in most cases more research would be needed, and that the monitoring and evaluation system used on health PPPs is insufficient.

"Frequently, PPPs encounter issues only after a few years of operation, requiring renegotiations or adjustments to the underlying contracts. The literature indicates a high incidence rate of renegotiations of PPP contracts. According to a 2014 study by the Organization for Economic-Cooperation and Development (OECD), 68 percent of infrastructure concessions in Latin America[269] were renegotiated; typically, such renegotiations occurred within two years of the contract award." (p25)

This method of proceeding ensures that nothing is learned from failures and that failed and inadequate models can be used again and again unless governments are savvy enough to stand firm and reject them.

While the Bank's independent team tactfully evade and understate the problem, Eurodad has continued to make the key points more forcefully, developing a critique of all PPPs, not just those in health projects. A blog in March 2018 noted that:

"The value of PPPs in the developing world has grown rapidly since 2004 - over an eight-year period, investments through PPPs increased by a factor of six, from US$25 billion to US$164 billion. Since then, the trend has been more volatile [...] But increased efforts by multilateral development banks to leverage private financing in both emerging and low-income economies indicate a more determined push towards reducing the risks for

---

[269] These projects were mainly PPPs in transport, water and sanitation, but the IEG points out that "social sector PPPs such as health are picking up" (Footnote p25)

private sector investors."[270]

Once again the familiar features of PFI schemes in England, and seen in PPP schemes around the world are cited as reasons for concern:

> "There is growing evidence that a more cautious stance towards PPPs may be warranted. The cost of PPPs may be one of their crucial weaknesses. Indeed, PPPs have certain characteristics which make them potentially more expensive than traditional public procurement. These characteristics include the cost of capital, profit expectations by the private partners and transaction costs associated with the negotiation of complex PPP contracts." [266]

While the UK's National Audit Office had found the interest rate for PFI deals is double that of all government borrowing, Eurodad has noted the even higher costs for governments in developing countries:

> "In many cases, governments have to guarantee above-average income streams in order to attract private investors. The list of guarantees offered to firms to make PPPs look 'bankable' may be substantial. They can include loan repayments, guaranteed rates of return, minimum income streams, guaranteed currency exchange rates and guaranteed compensation, should new legislation affect an investment's profitability."

> Other familiar problems with secrecy and incentives to avoid any rigorous analysis of projects are cited, and the blog presses for a change of policy:

> "CSOs [civil society organisations] are calling on the World Bank to stop favouring PPPs over other alternatives, ensure that governments undertake a careful cost-benefit analysis, and on this basis select the financing mechanism best suited for each project. International organisations advising governments must also be more straightforward about the full fiscal implications over the long term and the risk

---

[270] Romero, M.J. (2018) The fiscal costs of PPPs in the spotlight, http://investmentpolicyhub.unctad.org/Blog/Index/60

comparison of each option."

The conclusion is clear: while a few PPP/PFI projects might be less costly and problematic than others, the model is deeply flawed in its application in every country in the world, and even those pushing most enthusiastically for it are reluctant to face the practicalities and consequences of the projects they have urged forward.

Rather than embark on a new round of efforts to tweak PFI/PPP so that it works, the key questions in many countries and in England are to prevent any more flawed contracts being signed, and how to get out of costly failed projects with minimum extra cost and disruption to front line services.

Experience over the past 26 years is that governments are unlikely to come spontaneously to a sensible answer on PPPs, P3s or PFI: the key role in highlighting the real costs and consequences of a model that has consistently failed to deliver its promised benefits has to be played by campaigners using all of the available evidence, and academics and analysts with the courage to speak out and speak truth to power.

Some of the campaigning material and some of the links to campaigns with expertise in this area can be found archived on the London Health Emergency website www.healthemergency.org.uk while more up to date information on British and international PPPs, and some useful links to international campaigns can be found at www.healthcampaignstogether.com, the current website of Health Campaigns Together, the coalition of health campaigns and trade unions in England that since 2015 has taken the lead role in building a more powerful fight against all forms of privatisation and cutbacks in health care provision.